Read This First

The information in this book is as up to date and accurate as we can make it. But it's important to realize that the law changes frequently, as do fees, forms and procedures. If you handle your own legal matters, it's up to you to be sure that all information you use—including the information in this book—is accurate. Here are some suggestions to help you:

First, make sure you've got the most recent edition of this book. To learn whether a later edition is available, check the edition number on the book's spine and then go to Nolo's online Law Store at www.nolo.com or call Nolo's Customer Service Department at 800-728-3555.

Next, even if you have a current edition, you need to be sure it's fully up to date. The law can change overnight. At www.nolo.com, we post notices of major legal and practical changes that affect the latest edition of a book. To check for updates, find your book in the Law Store on Nolo's website (you can use the "A to Z Product List" and click the book's title). If you see an "Updates" link on the left side of the page, click it. If you don't see a link, that means we haven't posted any updates. (But check back regularly.)

Finally, we believe accurate and current legal information should help you solve many of your own legal problems on a cost-efficient basis. But this text is not a substitute for personalized advice from a knowledgeable lawyer. If you want the help of a trained professional, consult an attorney licensed to practice in your state.

Sixth edition

Credit Repair

by Attorneys Robin Leonard and Deanne Loonin

edited by Attorney Peg Healy

NOLO

SIXTH EDITION

Second Printing	JULY 2003
Editor	PEG HEALY
Illustrations	MARI STEIN
Cover Design	MARY E. ALBANESE
Book Design	TERRI HEARSH
Production	SARAH HINMAN
CD-ROM preparation	ANDRÉ ZIVOKOVICH
Index	NANCY MULVANY
Proofreading	ROBERT WELLS
Printing	CONSOLIDATED PRINTERS, INC.

Leonard, Robin.
    Credit repair / by Robin Leonard.-- 6th ed.
       p. cm.
    Includes bibliographical references and index.
    ISBN 0-87337-842-3
    1. Consumer credit--United States--Handbooks, manuals, etc. 2. Finance,
Personal--United States--Handbooks, manuals, etc. 3. Consumer credit--Law and
legislation--United States. I. Loonin, Deanne. II. Title.

HG3756.U54 L46 2002
332.7'43--dc21

                        2002071914
                        CIP

Quantity sales: For information on bulk purchases or corporate premium sales, please contact the Special Sales department. For academic sales or textbook adoptions, ask for Academic Sales. 800-955-4775, Nolo, 950 Parker St., Berkeley, CA, 94710.

Acknowledgments

Thank you to Shae Irving, who brought great ideas and energy to this project. For the fourth edition, thank you to James Judd for the material on identity theft.
—R.L.

Thanks to my friend and editor Kathleen Michon and to Ella Hirst for research assistance. A guarded thank you to my former housemate in Chico (wherever you are) for helping me learn the hard way about identity theft. And a true heartfelt thank you to my partner Elizabeth.
—D.L.

About the Authors

Robin Leonard graduated from Cornell Law School in 1985. She is the co-author of Nolo's *Money Troubles: Legal Strategies to Cope With Your Debts, Bankruptcy: Is It the Right Solution to Your Debt Problems?, Chapter 13 Bankruptcy: Repay Your Debts, Take Control of Your Student Loan Debt, How to File for Chapter 7 Bankruptcy, A Legal Guide for Lesbian and Gay Couples* and *Nolo's Pocket Guide to Family Law*.

Deanne Loonin is a staff attorney with the National Consumer Law Center (NCLC) in Boston. She also works with Nolo on debt and credit issues. Prior to joining Nolo and NCLC, she directed Bet Tzedek Legal Service's senior consumer fraud unit in Los Angeles. Deanne is a co-author of *Take Control of Your Student Loan Debt* (Nolo) and *Surviving Debt: A Guide for Consumers* (NCLC).

Table of Contents

3 Handling Existing Debts

4 Cleaning Up Your Credit File

5 How Creditors and Employers Use Your Credit Report

6 Building and Maintaining Good Credit

Appendices

 Resources

 Federal Credit Reporting and Credit Repair Laws

Forms and Letters

 How to use the Forms CD-ROM

Index

Introduction

Introduction to Credit Repair

Whether you've fallen behind on your bills, been sued or even declared bankruptcy, this book can help you take simple and effective steps to repair your credit. As you read, keep in mind these four important points:

You're not alone. The economic downturn has affected many people. Disposable incomes are down and savings are evaporating. Millions of honest, hard-working people—the same ones who received credit offers almost daily in better economic times—are having problems paying their bills. And over one and a half million people filed for bankruptcy in 2002.

You have legal rights. By knowing and asserting your rights, you can do a lot to get bill collectors off your back and give yourself a fresh financial start. Debtors who assert themselves often get more time to pay, have late fees dropped, settle debts for less than the full amount and get negative marks removed from credit files.

You can do it yourself. The information and forms in this book are good in all 50 states and the District of Columbia. You can follow the instructions on your own, without paying high fees to a lawyer or credit repair clinic. (See Chapter 6, Section G, for information on why to avoid using a credit repair clinic.)

Nobody's credit is too "bad" to repair. If you've been through devastating financial times, you may think you'll never get credit again. That's simply not true. As long as your financial troubles are behind you, you'll probably qualify for limited types of credit relatively quickly. Within about two years, you should be able to repair your credit so that you can obtain a major credit card or loan. Most creditors are willing to extend credit to people who have turned their financial situations around, even if their credit records are less than stellar.

This book contains in-depth information on all aspects of credit repair. Easy-to-use forms in Appendix 3 and on the enclosed CD-ROM help you with the sometimes daunting tasks of assessing your debt situation, planning a budget, contacting your creditors or bill collectors, and dealing with credit bureaus—all necessary steps in repairing your credit. (Instructions on how to use the forms on the CD-ROM are in Appendix 4.)

A. Credit Repair Fast Facts

Here are some quick answers to many common questions people have about repairing their credit. All of these topics are explored in more detail later in the book.

What's the first step in repairing credit?

To turn your financial problems around, you must understand your flow of income and expenses. Some people call this making a budget. Others find the term budget too restrictive and use the term "spending plan." Whatever you call it, spend at least two months writing down every cash or cash equivalent, such as check or debit, expenditure. At each month's end, compare your total expenses with your income. If you're overspending, you have to cut back or find more income. As best you can, plan how you'll spend your money each month. If you have trouble putting together your own budget, consider getting help from a nonprofit credit or debt counseling agency that provides budgeting help for free or at a low cost. (The steps for creating a budget are detailed in Chapter 2; credit and debt counseling agencies are discussed in Appendix 1.)

Okay, I've made my budget. What do I do next?

Now it's time to clean up your credit report. Credit reports are compiled by credit bureaus—private, for-profit companies that gather information about your credit history and sell it to banks, mortgage lenders, credit unions, credit card companies, department stores, insurance companies, landlords and some employers.

Credit bureaus get most of their data from creditors and collection agencies. They also search court records for lawsuits, judgments and bankruptcy filings. And they go through county records to find recorded liens (legal claims) against property.

Non-credit data made part of a credit report usually includes names you previously used, past and present addresses, Social Security number, employment history, and current and previous spouses' names. Your credit history includes the names of your creditors, type and number of each account, when each account was opened, your payment history, your credit limit or the original amount of a loan, and your current balance. The report will show if an account has been turned over to a collection agency or is in dispute. The report also lists creditors that have requested information about you in the past year or two. (See Chapter 4, Section A, for more information on the contents of a credit report.)

How can I get a copy of my credit report?

There are three major credit bureaus—Equifax, Experian and Trans Union. The federal Fair Credit Reporting Act (FCRA) entitles you to a copy of your credit report, and you can get one for free if:

- you've been denied credit because of information in your credit report and you request a copy within 60 days of being denied credit
- you are unemployed and intend to apply for a job within the 60 days following your request for your credit file
- you receive public assistance, or
- you believe your credit report contains errors due to fraud.

Certain states also require that credit bureaus provide consumers with one free copy each year.

If you don't qualify for a free copy, you will have to pay a small fee to obtain your report. (See Chapter 4, Section B, for information on obtaining a credit report.)

What should I do if I find mistakes in my report?

As you read through your report, make a list of everything out-of-date, such as:

- Lawsuits, paid tax liens, accounts sent out for collection, criminal records (but not criminal convictions), late payments and any other adverse information older than seven years.
- Bankruptcies older than ten years.

Next, look for incorrect or misleading information, such as:

- incorrect or incomplete name, address, phone number, Social Security number or employment information
- bankruptcies not identified by their specific chapter number
- accounts not yours or lawsuits in which you were not involved
- incorrect account histories—such as late payments when you paid on time
- closed accounts listed as open—it may look as if you have too much open credit
- accounts listed more than once, and
- any account you closed that doesn't say "closed by consumer."

If you see a problem after reviewing your report, complete the "request for reinvestigation" form the credit bureau sent you or send a letter listing each incorrect item and explain exactly what is wrong. Once the credit bureau receives your request, it must investigate the items you dispute and contact you within 30 days. If you don't hear back within 30 days, send a follow-up letter. If you let them know that you're trying to obtain a mortgage or car loan, they can do a "rush" investigation. (See Chapter 4, Sections C and D, for more information on reviewing and correcting your credit report.)

Will the credit bureau automatically remove the incorrect information from my report?

The credit bureau will review your letter or "request for reinvestigation" form. If you are right, or if the creditor who provided the information can no longer verify it, the credit bureau must remove the information from your report. Often credit bureaus will remove an item on request without an investigation if rechecking the item is more bother than it's worth.

If the credit bureau insists that the information is correct, call the bureau to discuss the problem.

If you don't get anywhere with the credit bureau, contact the creditor directly and ask that the information be removed. Write to the customer service department, vice president of marketing and president or CEO. If the information was reported by a collection agency, send the agency a copy of your letter, too.

If a credit bureau is including the wrong information in your report, or you want to explain a particular entry, you have the right to put a brief explanatory statement in your report. (See Chapter 4, Sections D and E, for additional information on correcting your credit report.)

What else can I do to repair my credit?

After you've cleaned up your credit report, the key to rebuilding credit is to get positive information into your record. For example:

- If your credit report is missing accounts you pay on time, send the credit bureaus a recent account statement and copies of canceled checks showing your payment history. Ask

that these be added to your report. The credit bureau doesn't have to add anything, but often it will.

- Creditors like to see evidence of stability, so if any of the following information is not in your report, send it to the bureaus and ask that it be added: your current employment; your previous employment, especially if you've been at your current job fewer than two years; your current residence; your telephone number, especially if it's unlisted; your date of birth; and your checking account number. Again, the credit bureau doesn't have to add these, but often it will.

(See Chapter 4, Sections F and G, for more information on adding positive data to your credit report.)

I've been told that I need to use credit to repair my credit. Is this true?

Yes. The main type of positive information creditors like to see in credit reports is credit payment history. If you have a credit card, use it every month. Make small purchases and pay them off to avoid interest charges. If you don't have a credit card, apply for one. If your application is rejected, try to find a cosigner or apply for a secured card—where you deposit some money into a savings account and then get a credit card with a line of credit around the amount you deposited. But don't try to get new credit or use a credit card you already have while you're still steeped in financial trouble. The last thing you want to do is continue down the road you're trying to get off of. (See Chapter 6, Section C, for more information about using credit.)

How long will it take to repair my credit?

If you follow the steps outlined in this book, it will usually take about two years to repair your credit so that you won't be turned down for a major credit card or loan. After around four years, you may be able to qualify for a mortgage.

B. When to Get Help Beyond This Book

This book can help you assess your financial situation and repair your credit. In some circumstances, however, you may need to take immediate action—or more drastic action—which may be beyond the scope of this book. Nolo publishes several detailed books on debtors' rights and bankruptcy, which may provide the answers you need. In some situations, it may make sense to see a lawyer right away. Use the chart on the following page to fully assess your situation.

C. Icons to Help You Along

Throughout this book, you'll encounter the following icons:

 The fast track icon alerts you that you may not need to read some material.

 This icon cautions you about potential problems.

 Suggested references for additional information follow this icon.

When to Get Help Beyond This Book

Seek additional help if...	Explanation	Where to get help
You're behind on your house payments.	Your lender has the option of foreclosing—declaring the entire balance due, selling the house at an auction and kicking you out.	General information on foreclosures is in Chapter 1. In California, see *Stop Foreclosure Now in California*, by Lloyd Segal (Nolo). You can get more specific help from your lender or a lawyer.
You owe child support or alimony.	If you can't afford to pay your child support or alimony, you need a court order reducing your obligation. Don't hesitate; child support and alimony are virtually never modified retroactively.	Contact your local child support enforcement agency (visit www.acf.dhhs.gov/programs/cse/ to find your local office). Although these agencies focus on getting support orders enforced, many will also assist with reviewing existing orders. Or visit DivorceNet (www.divorcenet.com) for links to state self-help services. Many states have online legal forms to request child support modification. Or, see a lawyer.
You're behind on a student loan.	Congress has enacted several laws to change the way student loans are collected and repaid, and has limited the defenses former students can raise when sued on outstanding loans.	See *Take Control of Your Student Loan Debt*, by Robin Leonard and Deanne Loonin (Nolo).
You owe income taxes.	The IRS has the right to seize virtually all of your assets of value and close to 100% of your wages without first suing you. Fortunately, you have several options in dealing with the IRS. You may be able to negotiate an installment agreement for repayment or drastically reduce what you have to pay.	See *Stand Up to the IRS*, by Frederick W. Daily (Nolo). Or see a tax attorney.
You face eviction.	In some states, an eviction can take place in just three days. Rather than risk being homeless, take steps to get immediate help.	In California, see *California Tenants' Rights*, by Myron Moscovitz and Ralph Warner (Nolo). Or contact a local tenants' rights group or a tenant's rights lawyer. Outside of California, you can get an overview of eviction and eviction defense issues in *Every Tenant's Legal Guide*, by Janet Portman and Marcia Stewart (Nolo).
You've been sued.	If you just received court papers, you need to file a response with the court within a tight time limit. If the creditor already has a judgment, it can try to attach your wages, take money from bank accounts and place a lien on your real estate (and in some states, personal property). You may be able to prevent certain collection tactics, particularly if you don't own much.	See *Money Troubles: Legal Strategies to Cope With Your Debts*, by Robin Leonard (Nolo). Or see a lawyer.
You are considering filing for bankruptcy.	Many people overwhelmed by their debts conclude that bankruptcy is the best option. There are several types, called "Chapters" of bankruptcy. In Chapter 7, you ask that your debts be wiped out. In Chapter 13, you set up a repayment plan whereby your creditors receive some—or all—of what you owe. Chapter 12 is like Chapter 13 but it's for family farmers. Chapter 11 is for individuals with enormous debts or for businesses that want to reorganize.	Forms and instructions for filing a Chapter 7 bankruptcy are in *How to File for Chapter 7 Bankruptcy*, by Stephen Elias, Albin Renauer, Robin Leonard and Kathleen Michon. Forms and instructions for filing a Chapter 13 bankruptcy are in *Chapter 13 Bankruptcy: Repay Your Debts*, by Robin Leonard. For information on figuring out if either Chapter 7 or Chapter 13 bankruptcy is right for you, see *Bankruptcy: Is It the Right Solution to Your Debt Problems?*, by Robin Leonard. (All are published by Nolo.)

Assessing Your Debt Situation

➡ If your debt problems are behind you and you're only concerned with cleaning up your credit report, skip ahead to Chapter 4, Cleaning Up Your Credit File. Also read Chapter 2, Avoiding Overspending.

Before you jump into rebuilding your credit, take care of any financial emergencies. Then you should tally up your debt burden and assess your options for handling what you owe.

A. Take Care of Financial Emergencies

A financial emergency is any situation that may leave you homeless or without some very important property or service. A pending eviction, a letter threatening foreclosure, an IRS seizure of your house, a utility cut-off and possibly a car repossession are financial emergencies. A nasty letter or threatening phone call from a bill collector, while unpleasant, is not an emergency. If you are being hassled by a collection agency, see Chapter 3, Section D.

If you face an emergency, act on it at once. Begin by contacting the creditor. You may be able to work out a temporary solution that will keep you off the street or on your wheels. If that doesn't work, you may need to get in touch with a lawyer to help you negotiate with your creditors. One option is to file for bankruptcy, assuming your overall debt burden justifies it. Currently, bankruptcy filing immediately stops all your creditors in their tracks and can buy you some valuable time. This may change, at least for eviction proceedings, if the bankruptcy legislation contemplated by Congress becomes law. (See Sections C.5 and C.6, below, for more information on bankruptcy and the pending bankruptcy legislation.)

B. Face Your Debt Problems

Some people with debt problems believe that the less they know, the less it hurts. They think, "I'm having trouble paying a lot of my bills. I can't stand the thought of knowing just how much I can't pay." But you must come to terms with your total debt burden. You cannot take steps to rebuild your credit without knowing exactly where your money goes—or is supposed to go.

Figuring out what you owe may result in a pleasant surprise. Most debt counselors find that people tend to overestimate—not underestimate—their debt burden. This may bring little comfort to those of you who find out that you owe more than you thought, but there is always a benefit: knowing what you really owe will help you make wise choices about how you spend your money.

Use *Form F-1: Outstanding Debts* (in Appendix 3 or on the CD-ROM) to tally up your total debt burden. Look at the most recent bills you've received. If you've thrown out your bills without opening them, you can probably find out the balance by calling the customer service department of the creditor. If you've long been avoiding your creditors and fear they'll hassle you when you call, ask for balance information only. If the customer service representative turns into a bill collector, explain that you are exploring your options and need to know how much you owe before you proceed. Let the representative know that you will contact the company as soon as possible, but for now you need only to know how much you owe. If the representative still hassles you, hang up and use your best guess as to how much you owe that creditor.

Total up both your past due installment bills, such as credit cards and loans, and any regular monthly obligations that are overdue, such as your utility bill.

C. Understand Your Options for Dealing With Your Debts

You normally have about a half dozen options for dealing with your debts—probably more than you imagined. Read this entire section before taking action.

1. Do Nothing

Surprisingly, the best approach for some people deeply in debt is to take no action at all. If you have very little income and property, and don't expect this to change, you may be what's known as "judgment proof." This means that anyone who sues you and obtains a court judgment won't be able to collect simply because you don't have anything they can legally take. You can't be thrown in jail for not paying your debts. And state and federal laws prohibit a creditor—even the IRS—from taking away such essentials as basic clothing, ordinary household furnishings, personal effects, food, most Social Security benefits, disability benefits, unemployment or public assistance.

So, if you don't anticipate having a steady income or property a creditor could grab, sit back. Your creditors may decide not to sue you because they know they can't collect. Many will simply write off your debt and treat it as a deductible business loss on their income tax returns. In several years, the debt will become legally uncollectible under state law. (See Chapter 3 for information on how to stop communications from collection agencies.)

Keeping exempt property. A complete list of property you get to keep even if your creditors sue you or you file for bankruptcy, called exempt property, is found in *Money Troubles: Legal Strategies to Cope With Your Debts*, by Robin Leonard (Nolo).

2. Find Money to Pay Your Debts

If you can come up with a chunk of cash to pay off some of your debts, your financial woes may lessen. But even if you feel desperate, don't jump at every opportunity to get cash fast. If you make a bad choice, you'll get yourself into deeper debt. This section discusses some of the options you should consider to raise money and options you should avoid, if possible. It's not a complete list. Unfortunately, new scams and bad deals crop up every day. So, proceed cautiously, whatever you are considering.

a. Sell a Major Asset

One of the best ways you can raise cash and keep associated costs to a minimum is to sell a major asset, such as a house or car. This is a particularly good idea if you can no longer afford your house or car payments. You will almost always do better selling the property yourself rather than waiting to get cash back from a foreclosure or repossession. With the proceeds of the sale, you'll have to pay off anything still owed on the asset and any secured creditor to whom you pledged the asset as collateral. Then you'll have to pay off any liens placed on the property by your creditors. You can use what's left to help pay your other debts. But before you take this step, be sure you have affordable alternative housing or transportation available. If not, you'll be in worse shape than before—without a roof over your head or a car to get to work.

b. Cut Your Expenses

Another excellent way to raise cash is to cut your expenses. It will also help you in negotiating with your creditors, who will want to know why you can't pay your bills and what steps you've taken to live more frugally. Here are some suggestions:

- Shrink food costs by clipping coupons, buying on sale, purchasing generic brands, buying in bulk and shopping at discount outlets.
- Improve your gas mileage by tuning up your car, checking the air in the tires and driving less—carpool, work at home (telecommute), ride your bicycle, take the bus or train, and combine trips.
- Conserve gas, water and electricity.
- Discontinue cable (or at least the premium channels) and subscriptions to magazines and papers. Most cable companies offer a low rate basic service that they don't advertise. Be sure to ask.
- Instead of buying books and CDs, borrow them from the public library. Read magazines and newspapers there, too.
- Make long distance calls only when necessary and at off-peak hours. Also, compare programs offered by the various long distance carriers to make sure you are getting the best deal.
- Carry your lunch to work; eat dinner at home, not at restaurants.
- Buy secondhand clothing, furniture and appliances.
- Spend less on gifts and vacations.

c. Withdraw or Borrow Money From a Tax-Deferred Account

If you have an IRA, 401(k) or other tax-deferred retirement account, you can get cash to pay off debts by withdrawing money from it before retirement — but in most cases you'll pay a penalty and taxes. Or, with a 401(k) plan, you may be able to borrow money from it (instead of withdrawing it). There are serious disadvantages to both options—you should only consider doing either to pay off debts if you have other substantial retirement funds or you are truly desperate. And even then, this should be a last resort. Always look to raise money from nonretirement resources first.

Different plans have different requirements for borrowing and withdrawing money. Withdrawing money early from a tax-deferred account is expensive. Generally, any money that you take out of your 401(k) plan before you reach age 59½ is treated as an early distribution. The one exception to the early distribution penalties and income taxes applies to Roth IRAs.

Instead of withdrawing money, you can usually borrow up to half of your vested account balance, but not more than $50,000. Then, you pay the money back, with interest, over five years. If you can't pay the money back within five years (or immediately, if you leave your job), your "loan" will be treated like an early withdrawal and you'll pay both an early distribution tax and income tax.

If you're seriously considering using the money in your retirement plan or IRA to pay off your debts, get a copy of *IRAs, 401(k)s and Other Retirement Plans: Taking Your Money Out*, by Twila Slesnick and John C. Suttle (Nolo).

d. Obtain a Home Equity Loan or Credit Line

Many banks, savings and loans, credit unions and other lenders offer home equity loans, also called second mortgages, and home equity lines of credit. Lenders who make these loans establish how much you can borrow by starting with a percentage of the market value of your house—usually between 50% and 80%. Then, they deduct what you still owe on it.

Obtaining a home equity loan has both advantages and disadvantages. If all of your debts are unsecured and your house is exempt from collection, it's almost never a good idea to put your home into jeopardy by getting a second mortgage or home equity line of credit. If you're behind on your house payment, you'll be better off negotiating a mortgage workout with your lender. (For more on mortgage workouts, see *Money Troubles: Legal Strategies to*

Cope With Your Debts, by Robin Leonard (Nolo).) If you are not able to negotiate a mortgage workout or, for other reasons, decide that you do want a home equity loan, be sure you understand all the terms before you sign on the dotted line. It is extremely important that you find out how much the loan will cost you each month and determine whether you can afford it. If you can't afford it, you'll likely lose your home.

Advantages of Home Equity Loans and Credit Lines

- You can borrow a fixed amount of money and repay it in equal monthly installments for a set period (home equity loan). Or you can borrow as you need the money, drawing against the amount granted when you opened the account; you'll pay off this type of loan as you would a credit card bill (home equity line of credit).
- The interest you pay may be fully deductible on your income tax return.

Disadvantages of Home Equity Loans

- Some home equity loans are sold by predatory lenders at very high rates. Predatory lenders target people in financial trouble or with past credit problems. Often, they sell loans that borrowers have trouble paying off down the line. (For more on predatory lenders and mortgages for people with poor credit, see *Money Troubles: Legal Strategies to Cope With Your Debts*, by Robin Leonard (Nolo).)
- You are obligating yourself to make another monthly or periodic payment. If you are unable to pay, you may have to sell your house, or even worse, face the possibility of foreclosure (the lender forcing a sale of your house to pay off what you owe). *Before you take out a home equity loan, be sure you can afford the monthly payment.*

- While interest may be deductible, it can be high.
- You may have to pay an assortment of upfront fees for an appraisal, credit report, title insurance and points. These fees can be as much as $1,000 or more. In addition, for giving you an equity line of credit, many lenders charge a yearly fee of $25 to $50.

e. Use the Equity in Your Home If You Are Elderly

A variety of plans help older homeowners make use of the accumulated value (equity) in their homes without requiring them to move, give up title to the property or make payments on a loan. The most common types of plans are reverse mortgages.

Reverse mortgages are loans against the equity in the home that provide cash advances to a homeowner and require no repayment until the end of the loan term or when the home is sold. The borrower can receive the cash in several ways—a lump sum, regular monthly payments, a line of credit or a combination.

There are pros and cons to reverse mortgages. In general, a reverse mortgage works best for older people with a lot of equity in their homes. In most cases, the reverse mortgage lender will look at your age, the amount of equity you have in your home and current interest rates to determine the amount it will lend you. All reverse mortgages cost money— closing costs (title insurance, escrow fees and appraisal fees), loan origination fees, accrued interest and, in most cases, an additional charge to offset the lender's risk that you won't repay. (A reverse mortgage is usually paid back by selling the house after the owner's death.) Almost every state allows lenders to offer reverse mortgages.

The most widely available reverse mortgage plans are the FHA's Home Equity Conversion Mortgage Program and Fannie Mae's Home Keeper Mortgage Program.

f.   Borrow From Family or Friends

In times of financial crises, some people are lucky enough to have friends or relatives who can and will help out. Before asking your college roommate, Uncle Paul or someone similar, consider the following:

- Can the lender really afford to help you? If the person is on a fixed income and needs the money to get by, you should probably look elsewhere for a loan.
- Do you want to owe this person money? If the loan comes with emotional strings attached, be sure you can handle the situation before taking the money.
- Will the loan help you out or will it just delay the inevitable (most likely, filing for bankruptcy)? Don't borrow money to make payments on debts you will eventually discharge in bankruptcy.

- Will you have to repay the loan now or will the lender let you wait until you're back on your feet? If you have to make payments now, you're just adding another monthly payment to your already unmanageable pile of debts.
- If the loan is from your parents, can you treat it as part of your eventual inheritance? If so, you won't ever have to repay it. If your siblings get angry that you're getting some of mom and dad's money, be sure they understand that your inheritance will be reduced accordingly.

g.   Options to Avoid

- **Borrowing From a Finance Company**

A few finance companies lend money to consumers. These companies make secured consolidation loans, requiring that you pledge your house, car or other personal property as collateral. The loans are just like second mortgages or secured personal loans; you'll usually be charged interest between 10% and 15% and if you default on the loan, the finance company can foreclose on your home or take your property.

Finance companies and similar lenders also make unsecured consolidation loans—that is, they may lend you some money without requiring that you pledge any property as a guarantee that you'll pay. But the interest rate on these loans can be astronomical, often reaching 25% or more. Lenders also charge all kinds of fees—many not disclosed—bringing the effective interest rate closer to 50%.

If you want to take out a consolidation loan, you are better off borrowing from a bank or credit union than a finance company. Many finance companies engage in illegal or borderline collection practices if you default, and are not as willing as banks and credit unions to negotiate if you have trouble paying. Furthermore, loans from finance companies may be viewed negatively by potential creditors who see them in your credit file. They often imply prior debt problems.

- **Tax Refund Anticipation Loans**

   Although getting a tax refund fast is often a good way to get quick cash, you should probably avoid a tax refund anticipation loan. A tax refund anticipation loan is a loan, offered by a private company, for the period of time between the day you file your tax return and the day you get your refund from the IRS. The amount of the loan is equal to the amount of your anticipated refund *minus* the loan fee (which is often quite high), *minus* the fee for electronic filing and *minus* the tax preparation fee. For example, if you expect a tax refund of $500, the company might charge you $75. You will get only $425 of your $500 refund.

   It is usually better to be patient and wait for your refund, rather than pay the high fee for a tax refund anticipation loan. In most cases, you can file your return electronically or by fax and get the money quickly. For more information on how to get a refund sooner and for answers to other tax questions, contact the IRS at 800-829-1040 (voice), 800-829-4059 (TDD) or visit its website at www.irs.treas.gov.

- **Payday Loans**

   The payday loan industry is growing fast. In many states, these loans are illegal. In others, lenders may offer a similar type of loan, but call it something else. Either way, think twice before you get one of these loans.

   A payday loan works like this: You give the lender a check and get back an amount of money less than the face value of the check. Some lenders offer an alternative automatic debit arrangement. For example, if you give the lender a check for $300, it may give you $250 in cash and keep the remaining $50 as its fee. The lender holds on to the check for a few weeks (often until your payday). At this time, you must pay the lender the face value of the check ($300), allow the lender to cash the check and keep the money or take out another loan and pay another fee. This is a very expensive way to borrow money. To find out more about the payday loan laws in your state, visit the National Consumer Law Center's website at www.consumerlaw.org.

- **Pawnshops**

   Visiting a pawnshop should be one of the last ways you consider raising cash. At a pawnshop, you leave your property such as jewelry, television, or musical instrument. In return, the pawnbroker lends you approximately 50% to 60% of the item's resale value; the average amount of a pawnshop loan is $50 or so.

   You are given a few months to repay the loan, and are charged interest, often at an exorbitant rate. If you default on your loan to a pawnshop, the property left at the shop becomes the property of the pawnbroker.

- **Debt Consolidation Companies**

   Debt consolidating, debt pooling, budget planning, debt adjusting or debt prorating companies produce poor results. They siphon off your limited resources in debt consolidation charges, pay only a few creditors and jeopardize much of your property. Some charge outrageously high interest. Others charge ridiculously high fees.

   Debt consolidating is either regulated or prohibited in most states. These laws usually don't apply to nonprofit organizations, lawyers and merchant-owned associations claiming to help debtors.

3. Negotiate With Your Creditors

If you can get some money, consider negotiating with your creditors. Negotiation can buy you time to get your finances in order. You can also negotiate to get your creditors to agree to accept considerably less than you owe as a complete settlement of your debts.

Suggestions and forms for negotiating with your creditors are in Chapter 3.

⚠ Beware of the IRS if you settle a debt.
A tax law could cost you money if you settle a debt with a creditor or if a creditor writes off money you owe—that is, ceases collection efforts, declares the debt uncollectible and reports it as a tax loss to the IRS. (26 U.S.C. § 108.) Debts subject to this law include money owed after a house foreclosure, after a property repossession or on a credit card bill you don't pay. A creditor must set a uniform policy to write off all debts after a set period of time, such as one, two or three years after default.

Any bank, credit union, savings and loan or other financial institution that forgives or writes off $600 or more of the principal of a debt ("principal" is the amount not attributable to fees or interest) must send you and the IRS a Form 1099-C at the end of the tax year. These forms are for the report of income, which means that when you file your tax return for the tax year in which your debt was forgiven or written off, the IRS will make sure that you report the amount on the Form 1099-C as income.

There are several exceptions stated in the Internal Revenue Code. For example, even if the financial institution issues a Form 1099-C, you do not have to report the income on your tax return if:

- the cancellation or write off of the debt is intended as a gift (this would be unusual)
- you discharge the debt in bankruptcy, or
- you were insolvent before the creditor agreed to waive or write off the debt.

Insolvency means that your debts exceed the value of your assets. Therefore, to figure out whether or not you are insolvent, you will have to total up your assets and your debts, including the debt that was forgiven or written off.

If you conclude that you are insolvent, complete IRS Form 982 and attach it to your tax return. You can download the form off the IRS's website at http://www.irs.treas.gov. Completing it is simple.

4. Get Outside Help to Design a Repayment Plan

Many people aren't well-equipped to negotiate with their creditors. Inside, they may feel that they are obliged to make full payment. Or, their creditors may be so hard-nosed that the process is too unpleasant to stomach. And some people just haven't honed their negotiation skills.

If you don't want to negotiate with your creditors, there are people and organizations available to help you. Creditors are often more than happy to work with respected organizations that work with debtors who are serious about repaying their debts. Reputable nonprofit credit and debt counseling agencies (see Appendix 1), the United Way or a church or synagogue are all excellent prospects. These organizations will help you figure out how much you owe, how much you can afford to pay each month and what your various options are—including bankruptcy. A credit or debt counseling agency will also talk to your creditors for you. Check your phone book's Yellow Pages under Counseling.

⚠ Use caution with lawyers and credit repair clinics. A lawyer can help, but lawyers charge high fees which rarely are justified, especially when you're heavily in debt. Whatever you do, don't use a credit repair clinic. (See Chapter 6, Section G.)

5. File for Chapter 7 Bankruptcy

Chapter 7 bankruptcy is the bankruptcy plan most people have heard about. It allows you to wipe out most consumer debts—credit cards, medical bills and the like. In exchange, however, you might have to surrender some of your property, such as a second car, valuable electronic equipment or a vacation home. To file, you fill out several forms that describe your property, your current income and expenses, your debts and any recent purchases and gifts. Then you file the forms with the federal bankruptcy court in your area.

Filing for bankruptcy puts into effect the "automatic stay." The automatic stay immediately stops your creditors from trying to collect what you owe them. So, at least temporarily, creditors cannot legally take (garnish) your wages, empty your bank account, go after your car, house or other property or cut off your utility service.

Until your bankruptcy case ends, your past financial problems are in the hands of the bankruptcy court. Nothing can be sold or paid without the court's consent. You keep control, however, of virtually all property and income you acquire after you file for bankruptcy.

At the end of the bankruptcy process, most of your debts are discharged—wiped out—by the court. You no longer legally owe the debts you owed when you filed for bankruptcy. If you incur debts after filing, however, you are still obligated to pay them. And you can't file for Chapter 7 bankruptcy again for another six years from the date of your filing.

Of course, bankruptcy isn't for everyone. One reason is that many types of debts can't be erased in Chapter 7 bankruptcy, including:

- child support or alimony obligations
- student loans, unless repaying would cause you undue hardship
- court-ordered restitution—payments you're ordered to make after a criminal conviction
- most federal, state and local income taxes less than three years past due, and any money borrowed or charged to pay those tax debts
- debts arising from intoxicated driving
- debts from a marital settlement agreement or divorce decree unless the bankruptcy judge rules it would be impossible for you to pay or that the benefit you'd get by the discharge outweighs any harm to your ex-spouse, and
- debts that a bankruptcy judge rules were incurred as a result of a wrongful act on your part—examples include debts incurred from fraud (such as lying on a credit application or writing a bad check), based on intentional injury (such as assault, battery, false imprisonment, libel and slander), larceny (theft), breach of trust or embezzlement.

For the past six years, the United States Congress has batted around legislation that would drastically change bankruptcy law. The bill is backed by the credit card industry and is unfriendly to debtors. In 2002, Congress came perilously close to passing this law but could not quite get it to President Bush (who had said he would sign it). Virtually the same bill was reintroduced in Congress in 2003 (HR 975) and may be law by the time you read this. To learn about the status of this legislation and the details of its provisions, check Legal Updates on Nolo's website (www.nolo.com). The websites of the American Bankruptcy Institute (www.abiworld.org) and the Commercial Law League of America (www.clla.org) also have up-to-date information on the legislation. If the bill does become law, it will most likely take effect 180 days after the President signs it.

For more information on Chapter 7 bankruptcy, see *How to File for Chapter 7 Bankruptcy*, by Stephen Elias, Albin Renauer, Robin Leonard and Kathleen Michon, or *Bankruptcy: Is It the Right Solution to Your Debt Problems?* by Robin Leonard, both published by Nolo.

6. Pay Over Time With Chapter 13 Bankruptcy

If you have steady income and think you could squeeze out regular monthly payments, Chapter 13 bankruptcy may be a good option. Chapter 13 allows you to keep your property and use your disposable income (net income less reasonable expenses) to pay all or a portion of your debts over three to five years. You can use wages, benefits,

investment income, business earnings or any other income to make your payments.

Most people file for Chapter 13 bankruptcy to make up missed mortgage or car payments and get back on track with their original loan, or to pay off a tax debt or student loan. These are not the only reasons people file for Chapter 13 bankruptcy, however.

If you cannot complete a Chapter 13 repayment plan—for example, you lose your job six months into the plan and can't make the payments—the bankruptcy court has the authority to change your plan. If the problem looks temporary, you may be given a grace period, an extended repayment period or a reduction of the total owed. If it's clear that you can't possibly complete the plan because of circumstances beyond your control, the bankruptcy court might even let you discharge (cancel) your debts on the basis of hardship.

If the bankruptcy court won't let you modify your plan or give you a hardship discharge, you have the right to:

- convert to a Chapter 7 bankruptcy, or
- dismiss your Chapter 13 case. A dismissal would leave you in the same position as you were in before you filed, except that you'll owe less because of the payments you made. Your creditors will add to the debt the interest that was abated from the time you filed your Chapter 13 petition until it was dismissed.

For more information on Chapter 13 bankruptcy, see *Chapter 13 Bankruptcy: Repay Your Debts*, by Robin Leonard, or *Bankruptcy: Is It the Right Solution to Your Debt Problems?* by Robin Leonard, both published by Nolo.

CHAPTER

2

Avoiding Overspending

➡ **If you skip this section, come back later.**
If you'd rather clean up your credit report or pay off your debts before doing a budget, skip ahead, but be sure to return to this chapter later. You must make a budget as a part of repairing your credit.

A n essential step in repairing your credit is to understand where your money goes. With that information in hand, you can make intelligent choices about how to spend your money. If you'd rather not create a budget yourself, you can contact a nonprofit credit or debt counseling organization. Information on credit and debt counseling agencies is located in Appendix 1.

📖 **Budgeting help.** Several excellent computer programs, such as Quicken, can help you keep track of your expenses, particularly those paid by check or credit card. Many of these programs have budget features as well. Be sure you have an opportunity to record your cash outlays, however, before relying on these budgeting features. This is because many commercial budgeting programs have you analyze your expenses paid primarily by check, and overlook the most obvious source of payment—cash.

A. Keep Track of Your Daily Expenditures

Your goal in this chapter is to create a monthly budget—to compare your average monthly expenses to your total monthly income. This section introduces *Form F-2: Daily Expenditures* (copies are below, in Appendix 3 and on the CD-ROM) on which you have space to record everything you spend over the course of a week, paying special attention to cash outlays. Here's how to use the form:

1. Make eight copies of the form so you can record your expenditures for two months. (To create your monthly budget, record expenses

for two months. By doing this, you avoid creating a budget based on a week or a month of unusually high or low expenses.) If you are married or live with someone with whom you share expenses, make 16 copies so you each can record your expenditures.

2. Select a Sunday to begin recording your expenses.
3. Record that Sunday's date in the blank at the top of one copy of the form.
4. Carry that week's form with you at all times.
5. Record every expense you pay for by cash or cash equivalent. "Cash equivalent" means check, ATM or debit card or automatic bank withdrawal. Be sure to include bank fees. Also, don't forget savings and investments, such as deposits into savings accounts, certificates of deposit or money market accounts, or purchases of investments such as stocks or bonds.

   Do not record credit card charges, as your goal is to get a picture of where your cash goes. When you make a payment on a credit card bill, however, list the items paid for. If you don't pay the entire bill, list the older charges that total a little less than the amount paid—attribute the rest of your payment to interest.

EXAMPLE: On Sunday night, you pay your bills for the week and make a $450 payment toward your $1,000 credit card bill. The $1,000 includes a $500 balance from the previous month, a $350 airline ticket, a few restaurant meals and accrued interest. On your Daily Expenditure Form for Sunday, you list $450 in the second column. In the first column, you identify corresponding expenses—and attribute some of it to interest. In this example, you have to look at your credit card statement from the previous month.

6. At the end of the week, put away the form and take out another copy. Go back to Step 3.
7. At the end of the eight weeks, list on any form under the category "Other Expenditures"

Daily Expenditures for Week of _____

Sunday's Expenditures	Cost	Monday's Expenditures	Cost	Tuesday's Expenditures	Cost	Wednesday's Expenditures	Cost
Daily Total:		Daily Total:		Daily Total:		Daily Total:	

Thursday's Expenditures	Cost	Friday's Expenditures	Cost	Saturday's Expenditures	Cost	Other Expenditures	Cost
Daily Total:		Daily Total:		Daily Total:		Weekly Total:	

seasonal, annual, semi-annual or quarterly expenses you incur but did not pay during your two-month recording period. The most common are property taxes, car registration, magazine subscriptions, tax preparation fees and insurance payments. But there are others. For example, if you do your recording in the winter months, don't forget summer expenses such as camp fees for your children or pool maintenance. Similarly, in the summer or spring you probably won't account for your annual holiday gift expenses. Be creative and thorough.

B. Total Up Your Income

Your expenditures account for only half of the picture. You also need to add up your monthly income. Use *Form F-3: Monthly Income From All Sources* (copies are below, in Appendix 3 and on the CD-ROM).

If you are married or live with someone with whom you share expenses, include income information for both partners.

Column 1: Source of income. In Part A, list the jobs for which you receive a salary or wages. In Part B, list all self-employment for which you receive income, including farm income and sales commissions. In Part C, list any other sources of income. Here are some examples of other kinds of income.

- **Bonus pay.** List all regular bonuses you receive, such as an annual $500 end-of-year bonus.
- **Dividends and interest.** List all sources of dividends or interest—for example, bank accounts, security deposits or stocks.
- **Alimony or child support.** Enter the type of support you receive for yourself (alimony, spousal support or maintenance) or on behalf of your children (child support).
- **Pension or retirement income.** List the source of any pension, annuity, IRA, Keogh or other retirement payments you receive.
- **Other public assistance.** Enter the types of any public benefits, such as SSI, public assistance, disability payments, veterans' benefits, unemployment compensation, worker's compensation or any other government benefit which you receive.
- **Other.** Identify any other sources of income, such as a tax refund you received within the past year or expect to receive within the next year, or payments you receive from friends or relatives. If, within the past 12 months, you received any one-time lump sum payment (such as the proceeds from an insurance policy or from the sale of a valuable asset), don't list it as income.

Column 2: Amount of each payment. For each source of income you listed in Parts A and B of Column 1, enter the amount you receive each pay period. If you don't receive the same amount each period, average the last 12. Then enter your deductions for each pay period. Again, if these amounts vary, enter an average of the last 12 months. For the income you listed in Part A, you probably need to get out a pay stub to see how much is deducted from your paycheck. Subtract the

Monthly Income From All Sources

1 Source of Income		2 Amount of each payment	3 Period covered by each payment	4 Amount per month
A. Wages or Salary				
Job 1:	Gross pay, including overtime:	$ _____	_____	
_____	Subtract:			
	Federal taxes	_____		
	State taxes	_____		
	Social Security (FICA)	_____		
	Union dues	_____		
	Insurance payments	_____		
	Child support wage withholding	_____		
	Other mandatory deductions (specify):			
	_____	_____		
	Subtotal	$ _____	_____	_____
Job 2:	Gross pay, including overtime:	$ _____	_____	
_____	Subtract:			
	Federal taxes	_____		
	State taxes	_____		
	Social Security (FICA)	_____		
	Union dues	_____		
	Insurance payments	_____		
	Child support wage withholding	_____		
	Other mandatory deductions (specify):			
	_____	_____		
	Subtotal	$ _____	_____	_____
Job 3:	Gross pay, including overtime:	$ _____	_____	
_____	Subtract:			
	Federal taxes	_____		
	State taxes	_____		
	Social Security (FICA)	_____		
	Union dues	_____		
	Insurance payments	_____		
	Child support wage withholding	_____		
	Other mandatory deductions (specify):			
	_____	_____		
	Subtotal	$ _____	_____	_____

Monthly Income From All Sources (cont'd)

1 Source of Income	2 Amount of each payment	3 Period covered by each payment	4 Amount per month
B. Self-Employment Income			
Job 1:	Gross pay, including overtime: $ _____	_____	
_____	Subtract:		
	Federal taxes _____		
	State taxes _____		
	Self-employment taxes _____		
	Other mandatory deductions (specify):		
	_____ _____		
Subtotal	$ _____	_____	_____
Job 2:	Gross pay, including overtime: $ _____	_____	
_____	Subtract:		
	Federal taxes _____		
	State taxes _____		
	Self-employment taxes _____		
	Other mandatory deductions (specify): _____		
	_____ _____		
Subtotal	$ _____	_____	_____
C. Other Sources			
Bonuses _____	_____	_____	_____
Dividends and interest _____	_____	_____	_____
Rent, lease or license income _____	_____	_____	_____
Royalties _____	_____	_____	_____
Note or trust income _____	_____	_____	_____
Alimony or child support you receive _____	_____	_____	_____
Pension or retirement income _____	_____	_____	_____
Social Security _____	_____	_____	_____
Other public assistance _____	_____	_____	_____
Other (specify): _____	_____	_____	_____
_____	_____	_____	_____
_____	_____	_____	_____
_____	_____	_____	_____
_____	_____	_____	_____
Total monthly income			$ _____

deductions and enter your net income in the Sub-total blank in Column 2.

In Part C, enter the amount of each payment for each source of income.

Column 3: Period covered by each payment. For each source of income, enter the period covered by each payment—such as weekly, twice monthly (24 times a year), every other week (26 times a year), monthly, quarterly (common for royalties), or annually (common for farm income).

Column 4: Amount per month. Multiply or divide the subtotals (or amounts in Part C) in Column 2 to determine the monthly amount. For example, if you are paid twice a month, multiply the Column 2 amount by two. If you are paid every other week, multiply the amount by 26 (for the annual amount) and divide by 12. (The shortcut is to multiply by 2.167.)

When you are done, total up Column 4. This is your total monthly income.

C. Make a Budget or Spending Plan

After you've kept track of your expenses and income for a couple of months, you're ready to create a budget, or spending plan. (Although most people are more familiar with the term "budget," many people find it restrictive and prefer the term "spending plan." Use whichever is more comfortable for you.)

Your twin goals in making a budget are to control your impulses to overspend and to help you start saving money—an essential part of repairing your credit. You use the figures you entered on Forms F-2 and F-3 as the basis for your budget.

To make (and use) a monthly budget, follow these steps:

1. On a blank piece of paper, write down categories into which your expenses fall. (See list, below, for suggested categories.) Also, total up your two months' (or estimated

seasonal, annual, semi-annual or quarterly) expenses for the categories you create.

2. Starting on a second piece of paper, list your categories of expenses down the left side of the page. Use as many sheets as you need to list all categories. These are your budget sheets. (See the sample below.)

3. On the sheets containing your list of categories, make 13 columns. Label the first one "projected" and the remaining 12 with the months of the year. Unless today is the first of the month, start with next month.

4. Using your total actual expenses for the two months you tracked or your estimated seasonal, annual, semi-annual or quarterly expenses, project your monthly expenses for the categories you've listed. To find your projected monthly expenses, divide your actual two months' expenses by two, divide your total seasonal or annual expenses by 12, divide your semi-annual expenses by six and divide your quarterly expenses by four.

5. Enter your projected monthly expenses into the "projected" column of your budget sheets.

6. Add up all projected monthly expenses and enter the total into the "Total Expenses" category at the bottom of the projected column.

7. Enter your projected monthly income from Form F-3 below your total projected expenses.

8. Figure out the difference. If your expenses exceed your income, you will have to cut expenses or increase your income. One way to do this is to make more money—but let's assume that you are not likely to get a substantial raise, find a new (higher-paying) job, take on a second job, or make significant money by selling assets. This means you need to find ways to decrease your expenses without depriving yourself of items or services you truly need. Review your expenses with any eye toward reducing. Rather than looking to cut out categories completely, look for

categories you can comfortably reduce slightly. For example, let's say you need to cut $75 from your budget. You had planned to buy $25 in music each month, but you can reduce it by $10 easily. You had also planned on spending $55 a month to eat dinner out, but are willing to decrease that to $35, thereby saving $20. Keep looking for categories in which you can make similar, small adjustments.

9. Return to your budget and category by category make the kinds of small adjustments described above. Once you're done making your adjustments, enter your new total.

10. During the course of a month, use a pencil to write down your expenses in each category. At the end of the month, total up the amount you spent. How are you doing? Are you keeping close to your projected figures? (See the sample below.)

Don't think of your budget as etched in stone. If you do, and you spend more on an item than you've budgeted, you'll only find yourself frustrated. Use your budget as a guide. If you constantly overspend in an area, you need to change the projected amount for that category—don't berate yourself. Keep in mind that a budget is designed to help you recognize what you can afford—not to fill in the "correct" numbers. Check your figures periodically to help you keep an eye on how you're doing. If one month an annual payment comes due (such as your car registration), you'll need to cut back in other categories that month. If you never have enough money to make ends meet (you're using credit cards and not paying the balance in full each month), it's time to adjust some more. (See Section D, below, for suggestions of ways to control your spending.)

Categories of Expenses

Home
rent/mortgage
property taxes
insurance (renter's or
   homeowner's)
homeowner's association dues
telephone
gas & electric
water & sewer
cable TV
garbage
household supplies
housewares
furniture & appliances
cleaning
yard or pool care
maintenance & repairs

Food
groceries
breakfast out
lunch out
dinner out
coffee/tea
snacks

Wearing Apparel
clothing & accessories
laundry, dry cleaning &
   mending

Self Care
toiletries & cosmetics
haircuts
massage
health club membership
donations

Health Care
insurance
medications
vitamins
doctors
dentist
eyecare
therapy

Transportation
insurance
road service club
registration
gasoline

maintenance & repairs
car wash
parking & tolls
public transit & cabs
parking tickets

Entertainment
music
movies & video rentals
concerts, theater & ballet
museums
sporting events
hobbies & lessons
club dues or membership
film development
books, magazines & news-
   papers
software

Dependent Care
child care
clothing
allowance
school expenses
toys & entertainment

Pet Care
grooming
vet
food, toys & supplies

Education
tuition or loan payments
books & supplies

Travel

Gifts & Cards
holidays
birthdays & anniversaries
weddings & showers

Personal Business
supplies
photocopying
postage
bank & credit card fees
lawyer
accountant

Taxes

Insurance

Savings & Investments

Sample Monthly Budget

Expense Category	proj.	Aug.	Sept.	Oct.	Nov.	Dec.	Jan.	Feb.	Mar.	April	May	June	July
Home													
rent	650	650	650										
renter's insurance	12	0	24										
phone	55	53	50										
gas & electric	45	49	43										
water	30	30	30										
cable	25	25	25										
household supplies	20	35	28										
furniture & appliances	30	0	0										
cleaning	30	30	30										
maintenance & repairs	35	0	25										
Food													
groceries	200	250	197										
breakfast out	10	19	0										
lunch out	25	25	40										
dinner out	60	35	55										
coffee/tea	10	8	8										
snacks	10	15	12										
Wearing Apparel													
clothing & access.	20	30	0										
laundry	15	14	21										
Self Care													
toiletries & cosmetics	25	25	25										
haircuts	40	40	40										
donations	40	40	40										
Health Care													
medications & prescriptions	10	5	0										
vitamins	20	20	23										
insurance	100	100	100										

Sample Monthly Budget (cont'd)

Expense Category	proj.	Aug.	Sept.	Oct.	Nov.	Dec.	Jan.	Feb.	Mar.	April	May	June	July
Health Care (cont'd)													
dentist	10	0	0										
eyecare	10	0	0										
Transportation													
car insurance	80	80	80										
registration	15	180	0										
gasoline	35	35	34										
maintenance & repairs	20	0	12										
parking & tolls	30	30	25										
public transit & cabs	10	0	15										
Entertainment													
music	15	16	25										
movies & video rentals	20	10	7										
books, magazines & newspapers	25	20	35										
software	10	0	15										
Pet Care													
vet	30	0	45										
food & toys	30	30	15										
Travel	25	0	0										
Gifts & Cards	20	25	35										
Personal Business													
supplies	10	5	0										
postage	16	32	0										
bank & credit card fees	25	12	18										
Savings	35	35	35										
Total Expenses	1,988	2,008	1,862										
Total Income	2,100	2,100	1,950										
Difference	112	92	88										

D. Prevent Future Financial Problems

There are no magic rules that will solve everyone's financial troubles. But nine suggestions should help you stay out of financial hot water. If you have a family, everyone will have to participate—one person cannot do all the work alone. So make sure your spouse or partner, and the kids, understand that the family is having financial difficulties and agree together to take the steps that will lead to recovery.

1. **Create a realistic budget and stick to it.** This means periodically checking it and readjusting your figures and spending habits.

2. **Don't impulse buy.** When you see something you hadn't planned to buy, don't purchase it on the spot. Go home and think it over. It's unlikely you'll return to the store and buy it.

3. **Avoid sales.** Buying a $500 item on sale for $400 isn't a $100 savings if you didn't need the item to begin with. It's spending $400 unnecessarily.

4. **Get medical insurance if at all possible.** Even a stopgap policy with a large deductible can help if a medical crisis comes up. You can't avoid medical emergencies, but living without medical insurance is an invitation to financial ruin.

5. **Charge items only if you can afford to pay for them now.** If you don't currently have the cash, don't charge based on future income—sometimes future income doesn't materialize. An alternative is to toss all of your credit cards in a drawer and commit to living without credit for a while Or even better, cancel the cards that you really don't need. (To learn the correct way to cancel a credit card, see Chapter 6, Section C.5.)

6. **Avoid large rent or house payments.** Obligate yourself only to what you can now afford and increase your mortgage or rent payments only as your income increases. Consider refinancing your house if your payments are unwieldy.

7. **Avoid cosigning or guaranteeing a loan for someone.** Your signature obligates you as if you were the primary borrower. You can't be sure that the other person will pay.

8. **Similarly, avoid joint obligations with people who have questionable spending habits—even a spouse or significant other.** If you incur a joint debt, you're probably liable for all of it if the other person defaults.

9. **Don't make high-risk investments.** Invest conservatively, opting for certificates of deposit, money market funds and government bonds over riskier investments such as speculative real estate, penny stocks and junk bonds. ■

Handling Existing Debts

To repair your credit, you must pay attention to two different kinds of debts: debts that aren't overdue (such as current charges on your utility bill) and your past due accounts (such as an unpaid phone bill from last month or a doctor's bill from last year). You cannot repair your credit if you ignore your past due debts—those default notations will stand out in your credit report. In addition, if you repair your credit and later default on debts that are now current, you will have wasted the hard work you did repairing your credit in the first place.

Most important, stabilize your financial situation before you worry about repairing your credit. Focus your energy on finding a job or other income source and paying accounts in order to keep your home, car and other necessities. There are some things you can do to improve your credit even when your financial situation is still shaky (see Chapter 4 on how to clean up your credit report), but for the most part, your credit record will improve only after you demonstrate to creditors that your financial situation has changed.

More on past due bills. For more detail on paying your past due bills and contacting your creditors about accounts on which you are current, see *Money Troubles: Legal Strategies to Cope With Your Debts*, by Robin Leonard (Nolo).

Tips For Sending Letters

Throughout this chapter, you are advised to send various letters to your creditors, depending on your situation. When you send a letter, try to adhere to the following guidelines:

- type your letters or neatly fill in the blanks of the letters in Appendix 3 or on the CD-ROM, if possible
- keep a copy for yourself
- send by certified mail, return receipt requested, and
- if you are enclosing money, use a cashier's check or money order if you have any debts in collection; otherwise the recipient of the check could pass your checking account number on to any debt collector, which will make it easier for the collector to grab your assets to collect the debt.

A. Deal With Debts Current or Not Seriously Overdue

If you've already fallen behind on all your debts, jump ahead to Section C, below.

One important step in repairing and maintaining your credit is to stay current—or to not get too far behind—on your existing debts. If it looks like you can't pay, your best bet is to contact your creditors before you miss a payment.

Negotiating with your creditors for extra time or to change the terms of your agreement isn't particularly difficult. Creditors generally like to hear from people who anticipate having problems paying their bills. If you simply skip your payment, the creditor assumes the worst—that you're a deadbeat trying to get away with not paying. If you call or write in advance, however, your creditor will often help you through your difficulties. Merchants, lenders and other creditors are aware of unemployment rates,

Understand the Two Kinds of Debts

To successfully negotiate with your creditors, you must understand your options, which often depend on whether a debt is secured or unsecured. Knowing whether your debts are secured or unsecured will also help you decide which debts to pay first.

Secured debts are linked to specific items of property, called "collateral." One way for a debt to be secured is for you to sign an agreement to create a secured debt and specify the collateral. The collateral guarantees payment of the debt. If you don't pay, the creditor has the legal right to take the collateral. Because of this, these debts will usually be your highest priority (unless you don't care if you lose the collateral). The other way a debt becomes secured is for a creditor to record a lien (a notice that you owe the creditor money) against the property.

Common examples of secured debts include:

- mortgages and home equity loans (also called second mortgages)—loans to buy, refinance or fix up a house or other real estate
- loans for cars, boats, tractors, motorcycles, planes, RVs
- personal loans from finance companies where you pledge as collateral real estate or personal property, such as a paid-off motor vehicle
- department store charges when the store requires you to sign a security agreement in which you state that the item purchased is collateral for your repayment (most store charges are not secured), and

- tax liens, judgment liens, mechanic liens and child support liens.

Unsecured debts have no collateral. For example, when you charge a television set on your Visa card, the creditor can't take the television back if you don't pay your Visa bill. If the credit card company wants to be paid, it must sue you, get a judgment for the money you owe and try to collect. A creditor who wins a lawsuit typically can go after your wages, bank accounts and valuable property.

The majority of debts are unsecured. Some common ones are:

- credit and charge card purchases and cash advances (Visa, MasterCard, American Express, Discover Card)
- gasoline charges
- most department store charges
- student loans
- bills from doctors, dentists, hospitals, accountants and lawyers
- alimony and child support
- loans from friends or relatives unless you gave the person a note secured by some property you own
- rent, and
- utility bills.

Usually, paying unsecured debts should be a lower priority than paying secured debts. However, because collectors of some unsecured debts such as student loans and unpaid child support are allowed to use more aggressive collection tactics than the typical unsecured creditor, those debts deserve more attention.

underemployment trends, income reductions, corporate mergers and downsizing, and other sour economic realities. And when times turn good again, they're going to want—and need—your business. So they may be accommodating now.

As soon as it becomes clear to you that you're going to have trouble paying your bills, contact your creditors. Your goals are twofold: You want time to pay and you don't want the creditor to report your bill as past due to credit bureaus. Calling your creditors is faster than writing, but if you find it easier to express yourself on paper than over the phone, go ahead and write. If you call, follow up your call with a confirming letter so that you and the creditor have some evidence of what you agreed to. If you write, make sure your letter will get there before your payment is due. (Section B, below, explains how to use the form letters included in this book.)

Your success with your creditors will depend on the type of debt, the creditor's policies and your ability to negotiate. Follow these key points when dealing with your creditors:

Explain the problem clearly. Creditors can easily grasp accidents, job layoffs, emergency expenses for your child's health, costs of caring for an aged family member or a large back tax assessment.

Mention any development that points to an improving financial condition. Creditors like to hear about disability or unemployment benefits beginning, job prospects, an expense about to end (such as a child finishing school), the end of a strike, a job recall or a small inheritance on the way.

If you can afford it, send a token payment. This tells the creditor that you are serious about paying but just can't now. Of course, the creditor might also take your money and continue to refuse to negotiate with you.

Negotiation is often a good strategy, but it doesn't always work. Increasing numbers of creditors simply will not negotiate with debtors. Despite the fact that creditors get at least something when they negotiate settlements with debtors, many ignore debtors' pleas for help, continue to call demanding payment and leave debtors with few options other than filing for bankruptcy. In fact, nearly one-third of the people who filed for bankruptcy during the mid-1990s stated that the final straw that sent them into bankruptcy was the unreasonableness of their creditors or the collection agencies hired by their creditors. However, even if some creditors are unwilling to negotiate, you'll never know until you try.

➡ Skip ahead if you don't have these debts. Below is advice for dealing with specific types of debts: rent and mortgage payments, utility and telephone bills, car payments, secured loans, student loans, insurance policies, bills from professionals and credit card payments. Read only the sections that apply to you.

1. Rent Payments

Many landlords will let their tenants pay rent late for a month or two, especially if the tenant has been reliable in the past. You will have the best chance of working out a payment plan if you contact the landlord promptly.

If your rent is too steep for your budget, you could try asking for a reduction. Many landlords won't agree, but in areas where property values have declined or the vacancy rate has increased (there are many empty units on the market), it might work. The landlord may agree to accept a partial payment now and the rest later. The landlord may even temporarily lower your rent, rather than have to evict you or re-rent the place if you move out.

If your landlord agrees to a rent reduction or late payments, send by certified mail, or hand deliver, a letter confirming the arrangement. (See the sample, below.) Be sure to keep a copy for yourself. Once the understanding is written down, the landlord will have a hard time evicting you as long as you live up to your new agreement.

Sample Letter to Landlord

Frank O'Neill
1556 North Lakefront
Minneapolis, MN 67890

November 22, 2003

Dear Frank:

Thanks for being so understanding. This letter is to confirm the telephone conversation we had yesterday.

My lease requires that I pay rent of $750 per month. You agreed to reduce my rent to $600 per month, beginning December 1, 2003, and lasting until I find another job, but not to exceed six months. That is, even if I haven't found a new job, my rent will go back to $750 per month on June 1, 2004.

Thank you again for your understanding and help. As I mentioned on the phone, I am following all leads in order to secure another job shortly.

Sincerely,

Abigail Landsberg
Abigail Landsberg

If your landlord refuses to help out, your options are limited. If you don't pay the amount of rent you obligated yourself to pay, your landlord can—and no doubt will—evict you. You are usually better off trying to get a roommate or moving out before any eviction takes place.

If you have a month-to-month tenancy, you merely have to give your landlord the amount of notice required under your rental agreement before you move out (often 30 days). Of course, if moving out means living on the streets, you might as well stay and see what action the landlord takes. This is especially true in areas where evictions can take several weeks.

If you have a written lease, you will violate it by moving out before the lease term expires. If you know of someone who can take over your lease, recommend that person to your landlord. The landlord should accept her unless he has another tenant in mind, her rental history is poor or her credit is bad and the landlord is convinced she couldn't pay the rent. Even if you don't find someone to take over the lease, in most states the landlord has a duty to "mitigate" damages—he must use reasonable efforts to re-rent the place in order to collect the rent he's losing by your moving. If he re-rents the property, you'll have to pay only for the months in which the property is vacant. If you advanced one or two months' rent or paid a security deposit when you moved in, the landlord should put that money toward any rent you owe.

If you end up owing your landlord some money and don't pay it, your landlord might report the amount due to the credit bureaus or to tenant screening services, which provide the same function as credit bureaus but gather information for property owners and managers. Not all landlords report this information. But any time the landlord takes court action—files an eviction lawsuit or sues you for a balance owed—you can be sure it will appear in your credit file.

Tenant information. Complete information on your rights as a tenant can be found in *Every Tenant's Legal Guide*, by Janet Portman and Marcia Stewart (Nolo).

2. Mortgage Payments

You have a number of options for dealing with house payments.

- If you anticipate having trouble making payments for a few months, contact the lender. Lenders often defer or waive late charges, accept interest-only payments, apply prior prepayments to the current debt or temporarily reduce or suspend payments. (For more on these options, see *Money Troubles: Legal Strategies to Cope With Your Debts*, by Robin Leonard and Deanne Loonin (Nolo).)

- If your problem looks long-term, the lender may let you refinance the loan to reduce the amount of your monthly payments. Because you're looking to refinance with your original lender, the lender may waive many of the costs. Be realistic when considering this option. If you can't afford your new payments, refinancing won't help your financial situation, and may make it worse.

- If you can't refinance your loan with the original lender, you may be able to find another lender who will loan you money to pay off all or some of your first loan. Again, be aware of the potential costs involved. And read everything carefully before you sign on the dotted line. Many unscrupulous lenders try to take advantage of people with financial problems.

If you can't pay your mortgage and can't work out a deal with your original or a new lender, you have three options:

- **Sell the house.** This is usually the best option. Many investors and savvy buyers look to buy "distressed" houses—houses in or near foreclosure. You probably won't get top dollar, but you should be able to at least save some of the equity you have built up and avoid doing serious damage to your credit.

- **Walk away from your house.** Especially if you owe more than your house is worth, you may be best off moving out and giving the keys to the lender. *Money Troubles: Legal Strategies to Cope With Your Debts*, by Robin Leonard (Nolo), discusses steps to take if you plan to walk away from your home. To do this, you transfer your ownership interest in your home to the lender—called a deed in lieu of foreclosure. Lenders don't have to accept your deed in lieu, but many will. Keep in mind that with a deed in lieu, you won't get any cash back, even if you have lots of equity in your home. And it may have negative tax consequences. (For more on tax costs, see the caution icon in Chapter 1, Section C3.) The deed in lieu may also appear on your credit report as a negative mark. If you opt for a deed in lieu, try to get concessions from the lender—after all, you are saving it the expense and hassle of foreclosing on your home. For example, ask the lender to eliminate negative references on your credit report or give you more time to stay in the house.

- **Let the lender foreclose—force a sale of your house.** If this happens, you may still owe money. In most states, if the sale price doesn't cover what you owe, the lender gets something called a "deficiency balance." A deficiency balance is the difference between the amount you owe the foreclosing lender and the amount he sells the house for.

The U.S. Department of Housing and Urban Development (HUD) can give you the name of a reputable local housing counseling agency. If you'd like this referral, or if you are at risk of default on your mortgage or foreclosure, call 888-466-3487. For more information on predatory lenders, see the American Association of Retired Persons (AARP) website at www.aarp.org/homeloans and the HUD website at www.hud.gov.

How a Foreclosure Works

If you haven't been able to sell your house and you don't just walk away, your lender will probably foreclose. Here's generally what to expect (the exact process varies from state to state). After you miss a few payments, the lender will send you a letter reminding you that your payments are late and imposing a late fee. If you don't respond, the lender will wait another 60 days or so and then send you a notice telling you that your loan is in default and that it will begin foreclosure proceedings unless payment is received.

After getting this notice, you have about 90 days to "cure" the default and reinstate the loan—pay all your missed payments, late fees and other charges. If you can't bring the loan current, the only way to avoid foreclosure is to sell the house during this period. If you were being picky before, now is the time to accept any offer.

If you don't cure the default, the lender applies to a court for an order allowing it to sell your house at an auction. (Obtaining court approval is unnecessary when the lender issues a deed of trust, not a mortgage. The two documents are virtually the same, except that the holder of a deed of trust can forego court involvement.) Then the lender publishes a notice of the sale in a newspaper. Between the dates when the notice is published and the sale takes place, most lenders let you reinstate the loan by making up the back payments and penalties.

If you don't reinstate the loan or sell the house, the lender will "accelerate" the loan. This means you no longer can reinstate the loan. The only way you can keep your house is by paying the entire balance immediately.

If you don't pay the balance, your house will be sold at a foreclosure sale. Anyone with a financial interest in your house will attend. The house is sold to the highest bidder.

Even if your problem looks long-term, the lender may try to work with you to avoid foreclosure. In the past, lenders were quick to start foreclosure proceedings. In recent years, however, they have looked at new ways to work out mortgage delinquencies short of foreclosure.

If you want to try to work something out with your lender, begin negotiating as early as possible. Also, it's often a good idea to get help from a nonprofit debt counselor or lawyer with experience in mortgage workouts. For information on HUD-approved mortgage counseling agencies in your area, call 800-569-4287 or 800-877-8339 (TDD).

California foreclosures. For information on foreclosures in California, including how to avoid one, see *Stop Foreclosure Now in California*, by Lloyd Segal (Nolo).

When Your Loan Is Owned by the Federal Government

Millions of American homeowners' loans are owned by Fannie Mae or Freddie Mac. These are private corporations created by the United States government.

Both companies' default programs emphasize foreclosure prevention whenever feasible. They offer rate reductions, term extensions and other changes for people in financial distress, especially for people experiencing involuntary money problems due to things such as an illness, death of a spouse or job loss. One possible option would allow you to make partially reduced payments for up to 18 months.

If you can't get help from your loan servicer, contact Fannie Mae or Freddie Mac directly at:

- Fannie Mae......800-732-6643 www.fanniemae.com
- Freddie Mac......800-373-3343 www.freddiemac.com

3. Utility and Telephone Bills

Most electric, gas, water and telephone companies will let you get two or three months behind before turning off your service or taking other steps to collect what you owe.

Many utility companies offer reduced rates to elderly and low income people and have emergency funds to help pay the bills of low-income people. If you face high heating bills in the winter or air conditioning bills in the summer, you may want to see if your utility company offers "level payments." This means that the annual bill is averaged and paid in equal payments over 12 months. During a designated month of the year, the actual bills are calculated against your level payments and you are either billed for the balance owed or given a refund for any overpayment.

To find out if you qualify for reduced rates, level payments or other programs offered by the utility company, call and ask. In addition, in many areas, charitable groups—especially religious organizations—offer assistance to low-income people needing help with their utility bills. Take advantage of any assistance available to you. It can be a real hassle, and expensive, to get your utility service back after it's been shut off for nonpayment of your bill.

Keep in mind that most northern states prohibit termination of heat-related utilities during the winter months. Other states also have a limited prohibition against shutoffs for households with elderly or disabled residents and occasionally for households with infants. Usually, you must show financial hardship to qualify. But, even if you qualify for a prohibition against utility shutoff, you'll still owe the bill.

4. Car Payments

Handling car payments depends on whether you buy or lease your vehicle.

a. Purchase Payments

If you suspect you'll have trouble making your car payments for several months, your best bet is to sell the car, pay off the lender and use whatever is left to pay your other debts or to buy a used car that can get you where you need to go.

If you want to hold onto your car and you miss a payment, call the lender *immediately* and speak to someone in the customer service or collections department. Don't delay. Cars can be, and often are, repossessed within hours of the time payment was due. One reason is that the creditor doesn't have to get a court judgment before seizing the car. Another reason is that cars lose value fast—if the creditor has to auction it off, it wants the largest possible return.

If you present a convincing explanation as to why your situation is temporary, the lender will probably grant you an extension, meaning that you can make the delinquent payment at the end of your loan period. However, the lender probably won't grant an extension unless you've made at least six payments on time. Also, most lenders charge a fee for granting an extension, and don't grant more than one a year.

Instead of granting an extension, the lender may rewrite the loan to reduce the monthly payments. This means, however, that you'll make payments for a longer period of time and you'll pay more total interest.

b. Lease Payments

More than 30% of new car owners lease, rather than purchase, automobiles. The reasons are many—but most people like the low monthly payments which accompany vehicle lease contracts.

If you can't afford your lease payments, your first step is to review your lease agreement. If your total obligation under the lease is less than $25,000 and the lease term exceeds four months (virtually all car leases meet these two requirements), the federal Consumer Leasing Act (15 U.S.C. §§ 1667-1667e) requires that your lease include disclosures regarding the cost and terms of your lease agreement.

If you want to cancel your lease, look carefully at the provisions of your lease agreement describing what happens if you default and how you can terminate the lease early. There may be an early termination penalty.

If you can't figure out how much you'll owe, inform the dealer in writing that you want to cancel the lease early and ask how much you'll owe. The dealer will contact you with the amount. If the dealer has already assigned (sold) the lease, then contact the leasing company, such as Ford Motor Credit.

Some consumers have successfully challenged the amount owed or persuaded the leasing company to drop large penalties for early termination where the formula used to calculate the amount owed was not defined in a clear manner or not included in the lease agreement. If you want to pursue this option, you'll need to contact a lawyer. Not all courts agree as to what constitutes "confusing" in this context – the best way to find out how your local court has dealt with the issue is to speak with a lawyer who is experienced with auto leasing issues.

5. Loans Where You Pledged Collateral Other Than a Motor Vehicle

If a personal loan or store agreement is secured—for example, you pledged a refrigerator or couch as collateral for your repayment on that item—the lender probably won't reduce what you owe. Instead, it may threaten to send a truck over and take the property. Rarely do lenders repossess personal property other than motor vehicles, however, because appliances and furniture bring in little money at auctions. Thus, if you simply stop paying, the lender will probably sue you before grabbing your new couch.

If you propose something reasonable, the lender may extend your loan or rewrite it to reduce the monthly payments. This will keep the property from being repossessed and keep you from being sued.

6. Student Loans

Under certain circumstances, you may be able to cancel your obligation to repay your federally guaranteed student loans, defer your payments or enter into a payment schedule that fits with your income. If you're in default, you may be able to get out of default and avoid a lawsuit, wage garnishment or loss of your tax refund.

The student loan scheme is quite complex, depending on the type of loan you have and when you obtained it. Before taking action on your loan, you must understand what kind of loan it is. Your ability to negotiate with your lender, defer your payments or possibly cancel your loan may depend on the type of loan you have.

There are three primary kinds of federally guaranteed student loans: campus-based loans, bank loans, and Department of Education issued loans. The campus loans are called Perkins Loans, or the older National Direct/Defense Student Loans (NDSLs). The bank loans are called FFELP (Federal Family Education Loan Program) loans and include Stafford Loans (previously called Guaranteed Student Loans (GSLs)) and Federal Insured Student Loans (FISLs)), PLUS Loans (loans for parents), SLS Loans and consolidation loans. Loans issued directly by the Department of Education are called Direct Loans and include Stafford, PLUS and consolidation loans.

How to Get More Information About Your Student Loans

You can find information about your student loans through the National Student Loan Data Base at www.nslds.ed.gov. It will provide you with loan and grant amounts, outstanding balances, loan status and disbursements. Or, call 800-4-FED-AID.

If you've tried the above, and still have trouble getting information, call the Student Loan Ombudsman toll-free at 877-557-2575.

Student loan information. Further information on student loans may be found in the following:

- *Take Control of Your Student Loan Debt*, by Robin Leonard and Deanne Loonin (Nolo).
- *The Student Guide*, published by the U.S. Department of Education. You can obtain a copy from the Department of Education's Federal Student Aid Information Center (800-433-3243), the Department of Education's Debt Collection Services Office (800-621-3115) or the Department of Education's website (www.ed.gov).

a. Canceling a Student Loan

Depending on the type of loan you have and when you obtained it, you may be able to cancel all or a portion of your loan under one of the following circumstances:

- You become totally and permanently disabled.
- The former student has died.
- Your school closed before you could complete your program of study.
- Your school falsely certified that you were eligible for a student loan.
- You left school and were entitled to a refund, but never received the money.
- You teach in a Department of Education-approved school serving low-income students or in designated teacher shortage areas (other types of teacher cancellations are available for Perkins loans).
- You serve in the U.S. military (partial concellation for Perkins loans only).
- You're a full-time employee of a public or nonprofit agency providing services to low-income, high-risk children and their families (Perkins loans only).
- You're a full-time nurse or medical technician (Perkins loans only).
- You're a full-time law enforcement or corrections officer (Perkins loans only).
- You're a full-time staff member in a Head Start program (Perkins loans only).

- You're a Peace Corps or VISTA volunteer (Perkins loans only).

To cancel a student loan—or to determine if you qualify for cancellation—call the holder of your loan or the Department of Education's Debt Collection Services Office at 800-621-3115. Be aware that your loan holder may not inform you of all the options available to you. For this reason, it pays to first learn about your options using one of the resources listed in the suggested references icon above.

b. Obtaining a Deferment of Your Student Loan Payments

You may be able to defer (postpone) repayment of a federal student loan if you are not in default—that is, you have made your payments on time, are in the grace period after graduation or have been granted other deferments.

This section only lists deferments for loans disbursed after July 1, 1993. If you have loans disbursed at an earlier date, you can get more information from the Department of Education's website at www.ed.gov or by calling your loan holder. For more details on obtaining deferment on any type of loan, see *Take Control of Your Student Loan Debt*, by Robin Leonard and Deanne Loonin (Nolo).

You can request a deferment on any federal loan disbursed after July 1, 1993, if:

- You are enrolled in school at least half-time.
- You are enrolled in an approved graduate fellowship program or a rehabilitation program for the disabled.
- You are unable to find full-time employment.
- You are suffering from economic hardship.

In addition, you can defer a Perkins loan for most of the reasons listed in Section a, above.

To obtain a deferment of a federal student loan, contact the current holder of your loan. If you don't know who currently holds your loan, contact the financial or educational institution you initially borrowed from. If that institution has sold your loan or sent it elsewhere, it will tell you.

Ask the holder of your loan to send you a deferment application form. Fill it out thoroughly. The holder of your loan may require that you submit supporting documentation, such as periodic verifications of your job search if you obtain an unemployment deferment. Be sure to comply. Deferment forms are available on the Department of Education's website at www.ed.gov.

c. Obtaining a Forbearance of Your Student Loan Payments

If you don't qualify for a deferment, but are facing hard times financially, your lender may still allow you to postpone payments or temporarily reduce them. An arrangement of this sort is called a forbearance. Although forbearances are easier to obtain than deferments—you may be able to obtain a forbearance even if your loan is in default—they are less attractive because interest continues to accrue during the time when you are not making payments, no matter what type of loan you have.

Lenders typically have the authority to grant forbearances in six-month increments for up to two years. There is no stated condition for qualifying—it's usually just up to the lender. Call your lender and ask.

d. Consolidating Your Student Loans

If you want to repay your loans but can't afford the payments and don't qualify for cancellation, deferment or forbearance, you may be able to consolidate your loans.

When you consolidate, you lower your monthly payments by combining multiple loans into one packaged loan and extending your current repayment period. You may also be able to refinance several loans, or just one loan, at a lower interest rate. But be aware that if you extend your repayment period, you will increase the amount of money you pay in interest over the life of your loan—sometimes dramatically. Even so, consolidation is one way to keep your head above water and avoid default. And if you've already defaulted, consolidation can help you get back on track.

e. Requesting a Flexible Payment Option

If you have a direct or FFELP Stafford loan, you can pay it back in any of the four ways listed below. If you have a direct PLUS loan, you can pay it back in any of the first three ways:

- the standard ten-year repayment schedule
- an extended repayment schedule—the length of your payback period depends on the amount of your loan—from 12 years for loans under $10,000 to 30 years for loans over $60,000
- a graduated repayment schedule—you can pay off your loan in as many as 30 years by making lower payments in the early years of the loan and higher payments later, and
- an income-contingent repayment plan (for Direct loans) or an income-sensitive repayment plan (for FFELP loans)—your payments change each year based on the amount of your income, the amount of your student loan and your family size.

While these payment options can offer much relief, opting for one could cost you a lot. For example, if you stretch your payments out for 20 or 30 years, you will wind up paying thousands—possibly tens of thousands—of dollars more in interest than you would have if you paid your loans off in ten years. While financial institutions are not obligated to offer extended, graduated or income-contingent repayment plans, many do so in order to remain competitive with the government direct lending program.

Many websites have calculators to help you figure out your monthly payments under different payment plans. Check out the calculators on the Department of Education's website at www.ed.gov.

Many loan servicers also have online payment calculators.

f.   Getting Out of Default

You can get out of default on any government loan if you make a certain number of payments under a "reasonable and affordable" payment plan and then rehabilitate the loan. This is how it works: You have the right to get on a payment plan that is "reasonable and affordable" based on your financial circumstances. If you make six consecutive timely payments under this plan, you will become eligible for new student loans and grants. Only enter into this payment arrangement if you can truly afford it. If you default, you won't get another chance to get out of default this way.

If you make twelve consecutive timely payments and jump through a few other hoops, you will be able to "rehabilitate" your loan – this means you'll no longer be in default.

Once you're out of default, and if you don't qualify for a deferment of the loan, you will have to repay the loan within ten years. So, if you've been paying very small amounts under the "reasonable and affordable" payment plan, when you get out of default, your monthly payment amount may rise dramatically. If you can't afford the new amount, you should request one of the flexible repayment options described above.

7.   Insurance Policies

Most insurance policies have 30-day grace periods—that is, if your payment is due on the tenth of the month and you don't pay until the ninth of the following month, you won't lose your coverage. A few companies won't terminate your policy as long as you pay your premium within 60 days of when it's due. If you don't pay within 60 days, your policy will surely be canceled.

If you want to keep your insurance coverage, contact your insurance agent. You can reduce the amount of your coverage or increase your deductible, thereby reducing your premiums. This can usually be done easily for auto, medical, dental, renter's, life and disability insurance. It will be harder for homeowner's insurance, because you'll probably have to get authorization from your mortgage lender, who won't want your house to be under-insured.

If you have a life insurance policy with a cash value—an amount of money building up that you'll receive if you cancel the policy before it pays out—you usually can apply the money that represents the cash value toward your premiums. The company will treat the use of the cash value as a loan. Your policy's cash value won't decrease, but you are theoretically required to repay the money. (If you don't repay it, when you die, the proceeds your beneficiaries receive will be reduced by what you borrowed.) Or, you can simply ask that the cash reserves be used to pay the premiums. This will reduce your cash value, but you won't have to repay anything.

Perhaps the best way to keep life insurance coverage while reducing the payments is to convert a whole or universal policy (with relatively high premiums and a cash value build-up) into a term policy (with low premiums and no cash value.) You may lose a little of the existing cash value as a conversion fee, but it may be worthwhile if you get a policy that costs far less to maintain.

8.   Doctors', Dentists', Lawyers' and Accountants' Bills

Many doctors, dentists, lawyers and accountants are accommodating if you communicate how difficult your financial problems are and try to get their sympathy. They may accept partial payments, reduce the total bill, drop interest or late fees and delay sending bills to collection agencies.

9.   Credit and Charge Card Bills

If you can't pay your credit card bill (including a department store or gasoline card bill), contact the credit card company. Most will insist that you make the minimum monthly payment, usually 5% of the outstanding bill, but in no event less than $20. If you convince the company that your financial situation is bleak, it may reduce your payments to 2%-2.5% of the outstanding balance. And if you have an excellent payment history, the company may let you skip a month or two altogether.

⚠ **It's important not to pay your credit card bills late.** That can result in a hefty late fee (sometimes $35), an increase in the interest rate in your account (the new rate can be as high as 25%) and a negative entry on your credit report. All of those can cause other creditors to increase their interest rates as well. By paying less than the full bill, you also incur interest charges. This is a strategy you should employ only temporarily. Otherwise, your balance may increase faster than you will be able to pay it off.

While you are paying off your balance, some credit card companies will help by waiving late fees. It's almost impossible to get a credit card company to reduce interest that has already accumulated. Some will stop the addition of future interest charges, however, if you get assistance from a credit or debt counseling agency. (See Appendix 1.) The company also will probably freeze your credit line—that is, not let you incur any more charges—if you pay less than the minimum.

Ask the company to report your payments to a credit bureau as on time while you pay off your balance. If you keep to the new schedule, the credit card company shouldn't report the debt as past due.

If you can't pay a charge card bill—such as American Express or Diners' Club—you must approach the creditor differently than with a credit card. Normally, you are required to pay off your entire charge card balance when your bill arrives. If you don't, you'll get one month in which no interest is charged. After that, you'll be charged interest in the neighborhood of 20%. Call the charge card company and ask that you be given a monthly repayment plan for paying off the bill. Offer to pay only

what you can afford. But remember, if you pay only a very small amount, interest will accumulate and your balance will go up faster than you're able to pay it off. The company usually doesn't report this arrangement to credit bureaus if you pay the monthly amount you agreed to.

a. If You Dispute a Credit or Charge Card Bill

If you buy a defective item or service and pay for it with your credit or charge card, you can often withhold payment if the seller refuses to replace, repair or otherwise correct the problem. (15 U.S.C. §1666i).

However, there are conditions in order to use this law. First, you must make a good faith effort to resolve the dispute with the seller. Second, you are required to explain to the credit or charge card company in writing why you are withholding payment. Third, if you used a Visa, MasterCard or other card not issued by the seller, you can refuse to pay only if: (1) the purchase was for more than $50, and (2) you made the purchase in the state where you reside or within 100 miles of your home. These conditions do not apply if the credit or charge card was issued by the seller, such as a department store or gas station card, or the seller obtained your order by mailing you an advertisement in which the card issuer participated and urged you to use the card for the purchase.

If you conclude that you are entitled to withhold payment, write to the credit card company and explain why you aren't going to pay. Detail how you tried to resolve the problem with the merchant. Before you mail the letter, look at the fine print on the back of your bill or call the credit card company and find out where to send it. Credit card companies have special addresses for mailing these types of letters. If you don't send it to the correct address, the company can disregard your letter. Use *Form F-4: Dispute Credit Card Bill* in Appendix 3 or on the CD-ROM. Always keep a copy for your own records.

b. If Your Bill Contains an Error

If you find an error in your credit or charge card statement, immediately write a letter to the company that issued the card; don't just scribble a note on the bill. The credit or charge card company must receive your letter within 60 days after it mailed the bill to you. You can use *Form F-5: Error on Credit Card Bill* in Appendix 3 or on the CD-ROM. Give your name, account number, an explanation of the error and the amount involved. Also enclose copies of supporting documents, such as receipts showing the correct amount of the charge. Send the letter to the particular address designated by the creditor for this purpose. Check the back of your statement for this address or call the company to get it.

What Is a Billing Error?

Most people think the definition of "billing error" only includes a mistake in the amount you owe. In fact, for purposes of the remedies described in this section, it also includes:

- an extension of credit to someone who was not authorized to use your card
- an extension of credit for property or services that was never delivered to you
- the company's failure to credit your account properly, and
- an extension of credit for items that you returned because they were defective.

The credit or charge card company must acknowledge receipt of your letter within 30 days, unless it corrects the bill within that time. The card issuer must, within two billing cycles (but in no event more than 90 days from when it receives your letter), correct the error or explain why it believes the amount to be correct. If the card company does not comply with these time limits, it must credit you $50 of the disputed balance, even if you are wrong.

During the two-billing-cycle/90-day period, the card issuer cannot report to a credit bureau or other creditors that the disputed amount is delinquent. Likewise, the card issuer cannot threaten or actually take any collection action against you for the disputed amount. But it can include the disputed amount on your monthly billing statements. And it can apply the amount in dispute to your credit limit, thereby lowering the total credit available to you. Furthermore, the credit or charge card company can add interest to your bill on the amount you dispute, but if the company later agrees you were correct, it must drop the interest accrued.

If the card company sends you an explanation but doesn't correct the error and you are not satisfied with its reason, you have ten days to respond. Send a second letter explaining why you still refuse to pay. If the card company then reports your account as delinquent to a credit bureau or anyone else, it must also state that you dispute that you owe the money.

Check your credit file following a billing dispute or error. Despite laws designed to protect consumers, a credit card company may negligently report an outstanding balance it removed from your card or fail to report that you dispute a charge. Be sure to check your credit file. (See Chapter 4, Sections B, C and D.)

c. If Someone Uses Your Credit Card Without Your Permission

Unauthorized credit card use—when someone steals your credit card number or otherwise uses it without your permission—is a growing problem, due in part to the huge volume of credit card business transacted over the phone and Internet. Fortunately, federal law offers some protection if this happens to you.

Your liability for unauthorized use of your credit card is limited to $50. So, if someone steals your card and uses it, your credit card lender cannot require you to pay more than $50 of those charges.

Some credit card issuers waive the $50, especially for Internet transactions.

It is very important to report unauthorized credit card use as soon as you know about it. If you call before any charges are incurred, you are not liable for anything—not even $50. If there is an unauthorized charge on your bill, you can dispute the charge the same way you dispute a billing error.

⚠ **Be careful using debit cards.** The protections discussed above don't always apply to charges made with debit cards.You may be liable for $500 or more if you don't notify the bank within two days after you realize your card is missing. Some card issuers, and some states, cap your potential loss at $50.

10. Debts You May Not Owe

This chapter focuses on handling debts that you do owe, not on ones you think you don't owe. If you've been cheated by dishonest creditors or the product you bought was defective, there may be consumer laws that will help you eliminate the underlying debt. For more information on what to do with debts you dispute, see *Money Troubles: Legal Strategies to Cope With Your Debts*, by Robin Leonard (Nolo).

B. Use the Form Negotiation Letters Provided in This Book

Negotiating with your creditors to request a reduction, extension or other repayment program can be somewhat intimidating. Fortunately, sending a short letter can simplify the process considerably. Appendix 3 and the CD-ROM include several form letters you can send to creditors. Use these to confirm telephone conversations or to start the negotiation process. You can fill in the blanks and send the forms,

or, if you prefer, retype the letters. Be sure to keep a copy of whatever you send.

At the top of the form you're using, above the "Attn: Collections Department" line, type or write the creditor's name and address. Most items on the forms are self-explanatory. At the bottom, be sure to sign your name and provide the address that appears on your bill. If you are asking the creditor to get in touch with you, include your home phone number.

If you use Forms F-7, F-8, F-9, F-10 or F-11 (see Appendix 3) you will need to state reasons why you can't make full payment. Here are what creditors and lenders look for:

- job layoff, reduction in hours, sporadic employment or pay cut, coupled with a good faith effort to find work or increase income
- large and unexpected tax assessment
- divorce or separation—your responsibility for paying bills or your ex-spouse fails to pay bills the court ordered him or her to pay
- permanent or temporary disability—temporary disabilities may include a heart attack, stroke or cancer, or something less drastic like repetitive motion syndrome, or
- inadequate medical insurance coverage following a major illness or accident.

C. Deal With Creditors on Past Due Accounts

It's important to know if the person trying to collect your past due debt works for the business or person who first extended you credit (the creditor) or for a company or lawyer hired by a creditor to collect the creditor's debt (a collection agency). A collection agency also includes a creditor who sets up a separate office (operated under a different name) to collect its debts. Depending on who is trying to collect, you have different legal rights and may want to employ different strategies. If any of your debts are being pursued by a collection agency, read Section D, below.

⚠️ Don't assume you must deal with a collector. If you have no money, plan to file for bankruptcy or just don't feel like paying right now, you can opt to not speak with the collector at all. Or you may want to seek outside help. Depending on the complexity of your situation and your negotiating skills, negotiating with your creditors on your own may not always be wise. A savvy lender who refuses to rewrite your car loan may think twice if he hears from a credit or debt counselor or lawyer. (See Appendix 1.)

If you have past due accounts, you may be able to take care of the debts and start repairing your credit. Here are two requests you can make to a creditor using *Form F-6: Make Payment If Negative Information Removed or Account Re-aged* in Appendix 3 or on the CD-ROM:

- Ask that an unpaid debt and negative information in your credit file associated with the debt be removed from your credit file in exchange for full or partial payment. Some creditors will agree to report your account as "nonevaluated" rather than as past due or formerly past due.

- If the creditor puts you on a new schedule for repaying the debt, ask the creditor to "re-age" your account, meaning it makes the current month the first repayment month and shows no late payments. Sometimes, the creditor won't re-age the account until you make two or three monthly payments first.

Not all creditors remove negative marks or re-age accounts, but it never hurts to ask. Contact the creditor's collections or customer service department and make an offer. Tell whomever you speak to that you cannot afford to pay more, but that you'd really like to pay a good portion of the bill. Explain your financial problems—be bleak, but never lie. Get the creditor's agreement in writing (send your own confirming letter if need be) before sending any money.

When negotiating, it's helpful to know at what stage you stand in the collection process. Collection efforts almost always begin with past due invoices

or letters. One day, you open your mail box and find a polite letter from a creditor reminding you that you seemed to have overlooked the company's most recent bill. "Perhaps it's already in the mail. If so, please accept our thanks. If not, we'd appreciate prompt payment," the letter or invoice states.

This "past due" form letter is the kind that almost every creditor sends to a customer with an overdue account. If you ignore it, you'll get a second one, also automatically sent. In this letter, most creditors remain friendly, but want to know what the problem is. "If you have some special reason for withholding payment, please let us know. We are here to help." Some creditors also suspend your credit at this point; the only way to get it back is to send a payment.

If you don't answer the second letter, you'll probably receive three to five more form letters. Each will get slightly firmer. By the last letter, expect a threat: "If we do not receive payment within ten days, your credit privileges will be canceled. Your account will be sent to a collection agency and your delinquency will be reported to a credit reporting agency. You could face a lawsuit, wage attachment or lien on your property."

After you've received a series of collection letters, you may conclude that you no longer have leverage to negotiate. Nonsense. You always have leverage because you have what they want—money.

Appendix 3 and the CD-ROM include several form letters you can use to send to creditors for your past due accounts. The forms are described below. Find the form that fits your situation and send it off.

If the creditor rejects your proposal or wants more evidence that you are genuinely unable to pay, consider contacting a nonprofit credit or debt counseling agency. (See Appendix 1.)

Or, if the debt is quite large, or one of many, consider hiring a lawyer to write a second letter asking for additional time. The lawyer won't say anything different than you would, but a lawyer's stationery carries clout. And it especially may be

Tips on Negotiating With Creditors

You are most vulnerable at this time. Be sure you truly understand any new loan terms and can afford to make the payments under a new agreement.

- Get outside help negotiating if you need or want it.
- If you're told "no" in response to any request, ask to speak to a supervisor.
- Adopt a plan and stick with it. If you owe $1,100 but can't afford to pay more than $600, don't agree to pay more.
- Try to identify the creditor's bottom line. For example, if a bank offers to waive two months' interest if you pay the principal due on your loan, perhaps the bank will actually waive three or four months of interest. If you need to, push it.
- Don't split the difference. If you offer a low amount to settle a debt and the creditor proposes that you split the difference between a higher demand and your offer, don't agree to it. Treat the split-the-difference number as a new top and propose an amount between that and your original offer.
- Don't be intimidated by your creditors. If they think you can pay $100, they will insist that $100 is the lowest amount they can accept. Don't believe them. It's fine to hang up and call back a day later. Some of the best negotiations take weeks.
- Try to settle with a lump sum. Many creditors will settle for less than the total debt if you pay in a lump sum, but will insist on 100% if you pay over time. If so, try to get the money to settle the matter. (See Chapter 1, Section C.2.)
- Get a signed release. If you settle for less than the full amount owed, make sure the creditor signs a release stating that your partial payment excuses you from the remaining balance.
- Be careful not to give up more than you get. A creditor may waive interest, reduce your payments or let you skip a payment and tack it on at the end. But tread cautiously. The creditor is likely to ask for something in exchange, such as getting a cosigner (who will be liable for the debt if you don't pay, even if you erase the debt in bankruptcy), waiving the statute of limitations (the number of years the lender has to sue you if you stop making payments), paying higher interest, paying for a longer period or giving a security interest in your house or car.

Forms for Negotiating With Creditors

No.	Form Name	Use if ...
F-7	Request Short-Term Small Payments	You need a few months to make reduced payments but then intend to resume full payments.
F-8	Request Long-Term Small Payments	You need to make reduced payments indefinitely.
F-9	Request Short-Term Pay Nothing	You can't make any payment for a few months but intend to resume full payments shortly.
F-10	Request Long-Term Pay Nothing	You've concluded that your situation is bleak and you cannot make any payment for an indefinite period.
F-11	Request Rewrite of Loan Terms	You would like the lender to rewrite the loan to permanently reduce the amount of each payment.
F-12	Offer to Give Secured Property Back	You want the lender to take the collateral back, making sure you won't owe any balance on the debt after the property is taken back.
F-13	Cashing Check Constitutes Payment in Full (Outside of California)	You live outside of California and plan to send the creditor part of what you owe with a notation on the check, "cashing this check constitutes payment in full."
F-14 & F-15	Cashing Check Constitutes Payment in Full (California)	You live in California and want to send the creditor part of what you owe with a notation on the check, "cashing this check constitutes payment in full."
		You must send two forms. The first (Form F-14) is to let the creditor know you intend to send a partial check. In that letter you must identify a dispute you have with the creditor. If the creditor does not object within 15 days, you send the second (Form F-15) along with the check. The second must be sent between 15 and 90 days after the first.
F-16	Inform Creditor of Judgment Proof Status	You have no property that can be taken by your creditors to pay what you owe them, even if you file for bankruptcy or they sue you. (This is called being judgment proof.) You are judgment proof if your only source of income is exempt government benefits or disability, you have little or no equity in a house or car, and you have limited personal property.
F-17	Inform Creditor of Plan to File for Bankruptcy	You plan to file for bankruptcy. Incur no more charges on the account after sending the letter. If you do, you will not be able to erase those debts in bankruptcy, because the creditor will argue that you knew you were going to file and incurred debts anyway, never intending to pay.

worth the few hundred dollars if you have many outstanding debts and need substantial help. When a creditor learns that a lawyer is in the picture, the creditor may be willing to compromise, assuming that you'll file for bankruptcy if he isn't accommodating.

⚠ Be specific with the lawyer about what you want done. If you're not clear that you want the lawyer only to write a letter to your creditors on your behalf, the lawyer may do much more and send you a bill for work you didn't authorize and can't afford, giving you one more debt to add to your pile.

D. Deal With Collection Agencies

If you ignored (or didn't receive) the creditor's letters and phone calls, or you failed to make payments as promised on a new repayment schedule, your bill was probably turned over to a collection agency.

In dealing with collection agencies, remember this: A person who works at a collection agency is not your friend and does not have your best interest at heart. *He wants your money.* To get it, he may ask you to take him into his confidence regarding your personal problems. He may claim that he's trying to save you from ruining your credit. Or he may pose as your friend and counselor. Don't believe him. A collection agent doesn't really care about your problems or your credit rating. His only goal is to get you to send him money.

By taking some time to understand how collection agencies operate, you'll know how to respond when they contact you.

Point 1. A collection agency takes its cues from the creditor that hired it. The collection agency can't sue you without the creditor's authorization, although that authorization is routinely granted. Similarly, if the creditor insists that the agency collect 100% of the debt, the agency cannot accept less

from you, although it can agree to accept installment payments. To reduce the total amount you pay, the collection agency must get the creditor's okay, or you'll have to contact the creditor yourself.

Contacting the creditor directly can often be to your benefit because the creditor has broader discretion in negotiating than does the collection agency. Unfortunately, however, some creditors won't deal with you after your debt has been sent to a collection agency, unless you raise a legitimate dispute with the creditor or make three consecutive monthly payments to the collection agency first. (See Point 4, below.) Even if you don't have a dispute, try negotiating with the creditor before negotiating with a collection agency. Send *Form F-18: Request Direct Negotiation With Creditor* in Appendix 3 or on the CD-ROM to the collection agency, with a copy to the creditor.

Point 2. A collection agent will try to contact you very soon after the creditor hires the agency. Professional debt collectors know that the earlier they strike, the higher the chance of collecting. For example, if an account is three months overdue, bill collectors typically have a 75% chance of collecting it. If it's six months late, the chances of collecting drop to 50%. And if the bill's been owed for more than a year, collectors have only a one in four chance of recovering the debt.

Point 3. A collection agency usually keeps between 25% and 60% of what it collects. The older the account, the higher the agency's fee. Sometimes, the agency charges per letter it writes or phone call it places—usually about 50¢ per letter or $1 per call. Thus, some collection agencies are very aggressive about contacting debtors.

Point 4. If you're contacted by a collection agency, you can delay collection efforts if you raise legitimate questions about the debt. For example, if you question the accuracy of the balance owed or the quality of the goods you received, the agency will have to verify the information with the creditor. If you raise a legitimate concern, the collection agency will send the debt back to the creditor— collection agencies don't pursue debtors who have a beef with creditors. Getting the debt sent back to the creditor should remove any "sent to collection agency" notation in your credit file.

Use *Form F-19: Dispute Amount of Bill or Quality of Goods or Services Received* in Appendix 3 and on the CD-ROM to raise a legitimate concern about the amount of a bill or the quality of goods or services received.

1. Getting a Collection Agency Off Your Back

You have the legal right to tell a collection agency to leave you alone. Simply write to the collection agency and tell it to cease all communications with you. Use *Form F-20: Collection Agency: Cease All Contact* in Appendix 3 and on the CD-ROM. By law, the agency must then stop contacting you, except to tell you that:

- collection efforts against you have ended, or
- the collection agency or creditor will invoke a specific remedy against you, such as suing you.

If a collection agent contacts you to tell you that she intends to invoke a specific remedy, she must truly plan to do so. The agent cannot simply write to you several times saying "We're going to sue you" and then drop the matter.

2. Negotiating With a Collection Agency

Although most creditors initially insist that collection agencies collect 100% of a debt, if you make a sweet enough offer, the collection agency may convince the creditor to accept less. Often, the creditor has all but given up on you and will be thrilled if the collection agency can collect anything. Knowing that, keep in mind the following:

- The collection agency didn't lay out the money initially. It doesn't care if you owe $250 or $2,500. It just wants to maximize its return, which is usually a percentage of what it collects.

- Time is money. Every time the collection agency writes or calls you, it spends money. The agency has a strong interest in getting you to pay as much as you can as fast as possible. It has less interest in collecting 100% over five years.

3. Offering a Lump-Sum Settlement

A collection agency has more incentive to settle with you if you can pay all at once. If you owe $500 and offer $300 on the spot to settle the matter, the agency can take its fee, pass the rest on to the creditor (who writes off the difference on its tax return as a business loss) and close its books.

If you decide to offer a lump sum, understand that no two collection agencies accept the same amount to settle a debt. Some want 75%-80%. Others—especially when they are the second or third agency to try to collect your debt—will take 50¢ on the dollar. But be careful. Once the agency sees you are willing to pay something, it will assume it can talk you into paying more. Which of course is a good reason to start by offering less than you know you can pay.

Although you don't want to agree to pay more than what you initially decided was your top amount, if you can get the debt removed from your credit file in exchange for paying a little more, it may be worth it. But don't let the collection agency know where that money is coming from. If you mention a parent, friend or distant relative who "may be able to help you out," the collection agent will sit back and wait for the entire amount. And never agree to more than you can truly pay. Whatever you agree to over the phone, be sure to send a confirming letter and keep a copy for your records. The letter should state that the creditor is accepting the lump-sum payment in settlement of the entire amount that you owe. You could use *Form F-13: Cashing Check Constitutes Payment in Full* and describe your agreement in the blank space above "Sincerely." For example, "This check is being sent per our agreement of October 2, 20xx, in which you agreed to accept $565 as payment in full for my outstanding bill."

4. Offering to Make Payments

If you offer to make monthly payments, the agency has little incentive to compromise for less than the full amount. It still must chase you for payment, and statistically there's a good chance that after a month or two, you'll stop paying. If you succeed in convincing the creditor (through the collection agency) to remove the "past due" notation in your credit file in exchange for paying off the debt or to re-age your account in agreement for paying under a new schedule, remember that as soon as you miss a payment under your new agreement the past due notation goes back into your file.

But if you have no choice—you simply can't afford a lump sum—offer installments. If the creditor (through the collection agency) won't remove the negative credit file notation right away, get back in touch after you've made six months of payments and again ask them to remove the notation. State that the negative marks are keeping you from getting good credit, a place to live, a good job or anything else you've been denied, and that with better credit/place to live/job, you will be more secure and better able to pay off the debt. Be sure to keep a copy of the letter for your records.

⚠️ **Don't offer more than you can afford.** Make sure you can afford any lump-sum payment or installment arrangement that you offer. And be sure that making these payments won't keep you from paying higher priority debts (like your mortgage).

5. When the Collection Agency Gives Up

If collection efforts by the collection agency fail, the creditor and agency will put their heads together and decide whether or not to pass your debt on to an attorney for collection. They will consider the following:

- the likelihood of winning
- the likelihood of collecting—are you currently employed or apt to become employed, or do you have other assets from which the creditor could collect (such as a bank account or a house on which the creditor could record a lien)
- whether the contract calls for the collection of the lawyer's fees (most loan agreements and credit contracts do)—which means the collection agency can tack its lawyer's fee onto the judgment against you, and
- whether or not you recently filed for bankruptcy (you may have to wait six years to file again).

6. Illegal Debt Collection Practices

The federal Fair Debt Collections Practices Act (FDCPA) prohibits a collection agency from engaging in many kinds of activities. (15 U.S.C. § 1692 et seq.) If a collection agency violates the law, you have the right to sue both the agency and the creditor that hired the agency. If the behavior is truly outrageous, the creditor may waive the debt and remove the negative marks from your credit file in exchange for your agreement not to sue.

Under the FDCPA, a collection agency cannot legally engage in any of the following:

Communications with third parties. With a few exceptions, a collection agent cannot contact other people except to locate you. When contacting other people, the agent must state her name and that she's confirming or correcting location information about you. She cannot:

- give the collection agency's name, unless asked
- state that you owe a debt, or
- contact the person more than once unless he requests it or the agent believes his first response was wrong or incomplete.

There are a few exceptions to this general rule. Collectors are allowed to contact:

- **Your attorney.** If the collector knows you are represented by an attorney, it must only talk to the attorney, not you, unless you give it permission to contact you or you attorney doesn't respond to the collector's communications.
- **A credit reporting agency.**
- **The original creditor.**

Collectors are also allowed to contact your spouse, your parents (only if you are a minor) and your co-debtors. But collectors cannot contact these people if you have already told them (in writing) to stop contacting you.

Communications with you. A collection agent cannot contact you:

- at an unusual or inconvenient time or place—the debt collector must assume that calls before 8 a.m. and after 9 p.m. are inconvenient unless she knows otherwise, or
- at work, if she knows that your employer prohibits you from receiving collections calls at work—if you are contacted at work, tell the collector that your boss prohibits such calls.

Harassment or abuse. A collection agent cannot engage in conduct meant to harass, oppress or abuse you. The agent cannot:

- use or threaten to use violence or harm you, another person, or your or another person's reputation or property
- use obscene or profane language
- publish your name as a person who doesn't pay bills, such as in a "deadbeats" list
- list your debt for sale to the public
- call you repeatedly, or
- place telephone calls to you or any other person without identifying herself.

False or misleading representations. A collection agent cannot:

- claim to be a law enforcement officer, suggest that she is connected with the government or send you a document that looks like it's from a court or government agency

- falsely represent the amount you owe or the amount of compensation she will receive
- falsely claim to be an attorney or send you a document that looks like it's from a lawyer
- threaten to take action that isn't intended or can't be taken
- communicate false credit information, including failing to tell someone you dispute a debt
- use a false business name, or
- claim to be employed by a credit bureau, unless the collection agency and the credit bureau are the same company.

Unfair practices. A collection agent cannot engage in any unfair or outrageous method to collect a debt. Specifically, she can't:

- add interest, fees or charges not authorized in the original agreement or by state law
- solicit a postdated check by threatening you with criminal prosecution
- accept a check postdated by more than five days unless she notifies you between three and ten days in advance of when she will deposit it
- deposit a postdated check prior to the date on the check, or
- call you collect or otherwise cause you to incur communications charges.

7. If a Collection Agency Violates the Law

More than a few collection agencies engage in illegal practices when attempting to collect debts. Low income and non-English speaking debtors are especially vulnerable. Some collectors send fake legal papers and visit debtors, pretending to be sheriffs. The collectors tell debtors to pay immediately or threaten to take the debtors' personal possessions. Other collectors use vulgarity and profanity to threaten debtors. Another favorite tactic is to harass the debtor's parents or adult children.

If a collection agent violates the law—be it a large or small violation—complain loud and clear. If you're loud enough about the abuse you suffered—and you've got a witness backing you up—you have a chance to get the whole debt canceled in exchange for dropping the matter. Use *Form F-21: Complaint About Collection Agency Harassment* in Appendix 3 and on the CD-ROM to write and complain about a collection agency.

Here are some suggestions of where to send your complaint letter:

- **The creditor.** The creditor may be disturbed by the collection agency's tactics and concerned about its own reputation.
- **The Federal Trade Commission.** (Addresses and phone numbers are in Chapter 4, Section D.)
- **Your state consumer protection office.** (See Appendix 1.)

You also have the right to sue a collection agency for harassment. You can represent yourself in small claims court or hire an attorney; you can recover attorney's fees and court costs if you win.

You're entitled to any actual damages (including pain and suffering) and, even if you didn't suffer damages, up to $1,000 for any FDCPA violation. You might also get punitive damages if the collector's conduct was particularly horrible. To win, you'll probably need to have a witness and to produce documentation of repeated abusive behavior. If the collector calls five times in one day and then you never hear from him again, you probably don't have a case.

Some attorneys specialize in debt collection abuse cases. For a list of consumer-oriented lawyers, see the National Association of Consumer Advicates website, www.naca.net.

State debt collection laws. For more information on debt collectors—including state laws that govern collection agencies and creditors collecting their own debts—see *Money Troubles: Legal Strategies to Cope With Your Debts*, by Robin Leonard (Nolo). ■

Cleaning Up Your Credit File

Credit bureaus are profit-making companies that gather and sell information about a person's credit history. They sell credit files to banks, mortgage lenders, credit unions, credit card companies, department stores, insurance companies, landlords and even a few employers. These companies and individuals use the credit files to supplement applications for credit, insurance, housing and employment.

Credit bureaus may also provide identifying information concerning a consumer—including name, address, former address, place of employment and former place of employment—to government agencies. If a government agency is consider-ing extending credit, reviewing the status of an account or attempting to collect a debt, the agency is entitled to the complete credit report.

There are three major credit bureaus—Equifax, Experian and Trans Union. There are also thousands of smaller credit bureaus, known as "affiliates." Open up your Yellow Pages and look under "Credit Reporting Agencies." You may see none, one, two or all three of the three major credit bureaus. You will probably also see dozens of affiliates. The affiliated companies get their information from Equifax, Experian and Trans Union, so this chapter focuses on the reports issued by those companies.

Expanding Credit Checks

We expect credit card issuers and other lenders to conduct a credit check before approving an application. But employers? Insurance companies? What could your credit history have to do with job performance or insurability? A lot, say the companies that do pre-employment and pre-issuance (of insurance policies) screening. In fact, tens of thousands of employers review credit reports as part of evaluating a job candidate. Employers use this information to judge financial honesty and integrity, as well as the risk of bribery of people with a lot of debt. And, once you're hired, employers can use the report for just about anything related to the job, including promotion and reassignment decisions.

Federal law requires that an employer obtain your written approval before conducting a credit check. Once it gets your approval, and as long as it provides proper notice, your employer can continue to get your credit report without obtaining another authorization form from you.

Deciding whether to authorize an employer to get your credit report leaves many employees and job applicants in a bind. If you say no, you may look like you're hiding something and be turned down for the job. If you say yes, and the employer doesn't like what it sees, you have the right to see your report and dispute any inaccuracies before being rejected for the job. But what if the contents aren't inaccurate? The best you can do is claim that your problems are behind you and have little or no bearing on job performance.

Insurance companies, too, routinely check on applicants before issuing a policy. Most health and life insurers request information on your medical history—mostly about major illnesses—from the Medical Information Bureau (MIB) in Boston (www.mib.com). Other insurers are permitted to check reports, although their use is infrequent and questionable.

MIB isn't the only noncredit bureau that provides information to creditors, employers, landlords or insurance companies. U.D. Registry and other similar companies provide information to landlords about evictions (also called unlawful detainer actions). A few companies provide check account histories (check bouncing, ATM use, debit card payment) to banks reviewing checking account applications. All of these companies are governed by the federal and state laws regulating credit bureaus.

A. The Contents of a Credit Report

Information in your credit report can be broken down into five main categories:

- personal information about you
- accounts reported monthly
- accounts reported when in default
- public records, and
- inquiries.

Most credit reports also contain a credit score (see Chapter 5). Finally, some special credit reports, called investigative reports, contain even more information.

1. Personal Information

A credit file usually includes your name and any former names, past and present addresses, Social Security number and employment history (including salary). Credit bureaus get this information from creditors, who get it from you every time you fill out a credit application. For this reason, it is very important that your credit applications be accurate and complete.

Whether you are married, separated, divorced or single, your credit file should contain information about you only. Information about both spouses should appear in both files only if both spouses are permitted to use or obligated to pay an account. For example, information about joint accounts should appear on both spouses' credit reports.

2. Accounts Reported Monthly

The bulk of information in your credit file is your credit history. Certain creditors (see below) provide monthly reports to credit bureaus showing the status of your account with them. Your credit report will contain the following information on these accounts:

- name of the creditor
- type of account

- account number
- when the account was opened
- your payment history—that is, whether you take 30, 60, 90 or 120 days to pay, whether the account has been turned over to a collection agency, whether the account has been discharged in bankruptcy or whether you are disputing any charges
- your credit limit or the original amount of a loan, and
- your current balance.

Creditors who provide monthly reports generally include:

- banks, savings and loans, credit unions, finance companies and other commercial lenders that issue credit cards and make mortgage, personal, car and student loans
- nonbank credit and charge card issuers (such as American Express, Discover and Diner's Club)
- large department stores
- oil and gas companies, and
- other creditors receiving regular monthly installments.

3. Accounts Reported When in Default

Many businesses provide information to credit bureaus only when an account is past due or the creditor has taken collection action against you, including turning the account over to a collection agency. In these situations, your credit report will generally include the following:

- name of the creditor
- type of account
- account number, and
- your delinquency status—whether you're 60, 90 or 120 days late, whether the account has been turned over to a collection agency or you've been sued, or whether the account has been discharged in bankruptcy.

Creditors who generally report accounts only when they are past due or in collection include:

- landlords and property managers
- utility companies
- local retailers
- insurance companies
- magazines and newspapers
- doctors and hospitals, and
- lawyers and other professionals.

While creditors tend to report these accounts only when they are past due, credit bureaus increasingly gather monthly information from utility companies, phone companies and local retailers to add to credit reports. The goal is to increase the data contained in files of people who don't have much traditional credit history, such as young people and immigrants.

4. Public Records

Public records are maintained by government agencies and are accessible to anyone. Local, state and federal court filings are public records. So is the data kept at land records offices. Credit bureaus use private companies to search public records for information such as:

- lawsuits (including a divorce)
- court judgments and judgment liens
- foreclosures
- bankruptcy filings
- tax liens
- mechanic's liens, and
- criminal arrests and convictions.

In addition, federal law requires child support enforcement agencies to report child support delinquencies to credit bureaus.

5. Inquiries

The final items in your credit report are called "inquiries." These are the names of creditors and others (such as a potential employer) who requested a copy of your report during the previous year or two.

Credit inquiries usually fall into two categories. The first category contains inquiries that show up only on the report that you see, not on the report that creditors get. There are several types of inquiries in this category, including creditors that request your credit report for promotional purposes (think of all those pre-approved credit card applications you get in the mail), current creditors that review your report periodically to check up on you and notations when you've requested a copy of your own credit report.

The second category of inquiries appears on the report sent to prospective creditors and employers (they also appear on the report you get). These inquiries consist of creditors that have requested your report after you have applied for credit with them. Creditors don't like to see a credit report with lots of inquiries in this second category. It makes you look like you're desperately applying for new credit. This is why it's important to be careful when shopping for new credit. Used car dealers, in particular, often try to get you to sign a form allowing them to look at your credit report, even if you're just window-shopping. Don't agree to this until you are serious about entering into a deal.

6. Investigative Reports

Some special credit reports, called investigative reports, have even more information than do regular credit reports. The big difference is that they include information from interviews with third parties such as your neighbors or friends. Because this information is personal and invasive, there are additional rules that apply to these reports.

Luckily, creditors do not usually request these investigative reports. Insurers and employers are the most likely to ask for them, but others can too as long as they give proper disclosures and have a legitimate reason to make the request.

B. Get a Copy of Your Credit Report

The major step in repairing your credit is cleaning up your credit report. You can't do that unless you know exactly what's in it. You start by getting a copy. Then you review it and challenge the incorrect items.

You can get your credit report by asking Equifax, Experian, Trans Union or all three companies to send you one. (Addresses appear at the end of this section.)

Develop Good Habits

Now is the time to develop good habits. Even after you have cleaned up your credit report, you should still get a copy of your report each year. Look for old or inaccurate information. Also check for anything that looks fishy—if someone has stolen your identity, you want to know as soon as possible. (See Chapter 4, Section H for more on avoiding identity theft.)

Tips for Sending Letters

Throughout the rest of this chapter, you are advised to send various letters to credit bureaus, and in some cases, your creditors. When you send a letter, try to adhere to the following guidelines:

- type your letters or neatly fill in the blanks of the letters in Appendix 3 or on the CD-ROM
- keep a copy for yourself
- send by certified mail, return receipt requested, and
- if you are enclosing money, use a cashier's check or money order if you have any debts in collection; otherwise the recipient of the check could pass your checking account number to any debt collector, which will make it easier for the collector to grab your assets to collect the debt.

1. How Much Does a Credit Report Cost?

You are entitled to a copy of your credit report for free if any one of the following is true:

- **You've been denied credit because of information in your credit file.** You are entitled to a free copy of your file from the bureau that reported the information. (A creditor that denies you credit in this situation will tell you the name and address of the credit bureau reporting the information that led to the denial.) You must request your copy within 60 days of being denied credit.
- **You haven't requested a copy in the last year.** You can get a free copy of your credit report once a year from any credit bureau if you live in Colorado, Georgia, Maryland, Massachusetts, New Jersey or Vermont.

- **You are unemployed and planning to apply for a job within 60 days** following your request for your credit report. You must enclose a statement swearing that this is true information. It might also help to include a copy of a recent unemployment check, layoff notice or similar document verifying your unemployment.

- **You receive public assistance.** Enclose a statement swearing that this is true information and a copy of your most recent public assistance check as verification.

- **You reasonably believe your credit file contains errors due to someone's fraud,** such as using your credit cards, Social Security number, name or something similar. Here, too, you will need to enclose a statement swearing that this is true information.

For additional copies—or if you don't qualify for a free copy—you'll have to pay a fee of $9 except in California ($8), Connecticut ($5), Maine ($3), Minnesota ($3), Montana ($8.50) or the U.S. Virgin Islands ($1). Many websites offer a free copy with a 30-day trial membership. (Be sure to cancel the trial membership!) You should receive the report in a week to ten days.

2. From Which Company Should I Get My Credit Report?

You can request your credit report from just one or two bureaus. But it's best to order one from all three. (You can order a three-in-one report at many websites for about $35.) If you've been denied credit, at the very least, get a copy of your credit report from the bureau that reported the information leading to the denial. If you haven't been denied credit, request a copy from the company closest to where you live. If you find errors in the first credit file, obtain copies of your file from the other two bureaus.

Use *Form F-22: Request Credit File* in Appendix 3 or on the CD-ROM to request your credit file. The following instructions explain what information must be provided and whether any of it is optional.

Full name. A credit bureau cannot process your request without your name. It's important that you provide your full name, including generations (Jr., Sr., III) and any other versions of your name that you use, such as "Trevor J. (aka T.J.) Williams."

Date of birth. A credit bureau may provide your report without your date (or at least year) of birth. But this information helps distinguish you from anyone else with a similar name, so you should include it.

Social Security number. Most credit bureaus require this. They use it to distinguish between people with the same or similar last names.

Spouse's name. It's not absolutely necessary, but again, it helps distinguish you from anyone else with a similar name.

Telephone number. You may not get your report if you don't include your telephone number. You may hesitate to include it, knowing that bill collectors can get it by getting a copy of your credit file. But unless it's unlisted, they can also call Directory Assistance and get it. If you're trying to repair your credit, you will want to make sure your phone number is in your file. It is one sign of stability your future creditors look for.

Current address. You won't get a copy of your credit report if you don't include your address.

Previous addresses. Credit bureaus ask for this if you've been at your current address fewer than two to five years. Again, it helps distinguish you from other people with similar names. If you don't want the bureau to have this information, you can leave it off, but your request may be rejected.

C. Review Your Credit Report

Review your report carefully. One of the biggest problems with credit files is that they contain incorrect or out-of-date information. In a 1998 investigation by the U.S. Public Interest Research Group, 70% of the credit reports contained an error.

Sometimes credit bureaus confuse names, addresses, Social Security numbers or employers. If you have a common name, say John Brown, your file may contain information on other John Browns, John Brownes or Jon Browns. Your file may erroneously contain information on family members with similar names.

On the pages that follow are copies of sample credit reports from Equifax, Trans Union and Experian. You will notice that the three credit bureaus report the information in very different formats, and furthermore, contain different information.

1. Review the Sample Reports

Here's how to read each credit report.

Equifax. Equifax is the only credit reporting agency that provides consumers with a credit report in column format. (All three credit bureaus used to report the information this way.) Nevertheless, the Equifax report is not difficult to read. At the top of the first page, you'll find a unique confirmation number, the date of the report, and your name, address, previous addresses, Social Security number, age and employer.

The only other information is the credit history. The report begins with public record information obtained from local, state and federal courts and offices, such as lawsuits, bankruptcies and liens.

Next, Equifax often separates out accounts with collection agencies.

In the next section, the report lists each account reported to Equifax. Here's what you see:

- **Company Name** is the name of the business reporting the information. In many cases, just below the company name, Equifax includes a description of the type of account (such as student loan, credit card or line of credit), some payment history and/or the account's status (such as charge off, collection account, payment deferred, account transferred or account closed by consumer).
- **Account Number** is your account number with the company reporting the information.

- **Whose Acct** indicates who is responsible for the account and the type of obligation you have. The possibilities are:
  A = Authorized user (of someone else's account)
  B = On behalf of another person
  C = Comaker/Cosigner
  I = Individual
  J = Joint
  M = Maker
  S = Shared
  T = Terminated
  U = Undesignated
- **Date Opened** is the month and year you opened the account.
- **Date of Last Activity** is the most recent month and year that something happened on the account. This may be the last time you made a payment (if you are currently paying) or when the account was charged off or sent to collections. This date is important because negative information (other than bankruptcies) can stay on your report for up to seven years after the date of the last activity.
- **Status** indicates both the type of account and your payment history.

  Type of Account
  I = Installment (payment amount is fixed each month)
  O = Open (entire balance is due each month)
  R = Revolving (payment amount is variable each month)
- **High Credit** is the amount of any loan you took out, your credit limit or possibly the highest amount you have ever charged on the account.
- **Terms** indicates either the number of installments you have (indicated by an M) to pay off the debt or the amount of your monthly payment.
- **Balance** is the amount you owed on the account when the creditor last provided Equifax with information.

- **Past Due** is the amount past due on the account when the creditor last provided Equifax with information.
- **Date Reported** is the date the creditor last provided Equifax with information.
- **Prior Paying History** includes information on late or past due payments.

Creditors who have requested a copy of your report are listed in the final section with the date they requested your report. Some of these creditors are coded (under Equifax's own policies, coded inquiries are given only to you; other creditors don't see them):

  ACIS = This indicates that Equifax responded to your request for a copy of your credit report or to verify information in your account.
  AM = This is one of your existing creditors who requested your file for periodic review. This inquiry remains for one year.
  AR = Same as AM.
  EQUIFAX = Same as ACIS.
  PRM = This indicates that a creditor wanted your file to send you an application for credit. Only your name and address was given out. This inquiry remains for one year.
  UPDATE = Same as ACIS.

Trans Union. The top of each Trans Union report contains identifying information. This information includes a unique file number, the date of the report, and your name, former names (AKA), address, former addresses, employment, Social Security number, birthdate and phone number.

Trans Union breaks down the credit information into several subsections:

- **Public records.** This section includes information obtained from local, state and federal courts and offices, such as lawsuits, bankruptcies and liens.
- **Adverse Account Information.** Trans Union separates out accounts that "contain information which some creditors may consider to be adverse" and further highlights the negative information (for you, not your creditors) by

enclosing it in >brackets<. The bracketed information usually includes the account's status, any past due amount and information on late payments.

- **Satisfactory Account Information.** Immediately following the negative accounts, Trans Union lists the accounts that are "reported with no adverse information."

  Both the accounts with negative notations and the accounts without negative notations contain the following information:
  - name of the company
  - account number (these are deleted on the sample report)
  - type of credit extended:
    - Check credit (line of credit drawn on by writing checks)
    - Collection account (sent out to a collection agency)
    - Installment (payment amount is fixed each month)
    - Mortgage (installment credit extended to purchase a home)
    - Open (entire balance is due each month)
    - Revolving (payment amount is variable each month)
  - the date the creditor last provided Trans Union with information (updated)
  - the amount you owed on the account when the creditor last provided Trans Union with information (balance)
  - who is responsible for the account, such as individual account, joint account, account relationship terminated, cosigner account
  - the month and year you opened the account (opened)
  - the amount of any loan you took out or the highest amount you have ever charged on the account (most owed)
  - your credit limit on a revolving or open account (credit limit) or the amount of your monthly payments and number of

months you have to pay off an installment debt (pay terms)
  - the month and year you or the creditor closed the account (closed)
  - the status of your account as of the date the account was updated:
    - charged off as bad debt
    - collection account
    - paid as agreed
    - payment after charge off/collection (you began repaying the debt after the creditor had already written it off)
    - unrated (a creditor usually does not rate accounts for which they have no payment history—for example, when your payments have been deferred or an account which has been transferred to another creditor or closed)

- **Inquiries.** Trans Union divides the inquiries (companies or people that have requested a copy of your report) into different sections. The first section, "Regular Inquiries," lists creditors that have received your full credit report. These inquiries stay on your report for two years. The second section, "Promotional Inquiries," includes names of creditors seeking information about you to offer you credit or insurance. These creditors do not receive your full credit report, but only your name, address, and other limited information. Promotional inquiries are not seen by anyone but you. The third section, "Account Review Inquiries," contains names of creditors that received information about you to review an existing account or for certain other types of business transactions. As with promotional inquires, these inquires are not seen by anyone but you.

The final sections of the Trans Union report contain consumer statements (see Section E for an explanation of consumer statements) and other special messages.

In addition, all Trans Union reports now provide your Trans Union Personal Credit Score and an explanation of the factors affecting your score. (For more on credit scores, see Chapter 5, Section B.2).

Experian. On the first page of the report, Experian summarizes the contents into two categories—potentially negative items (public records and accounts with creditors and others) and accounts in good standing. On this and all other pages, the consumer's name and a unique report number appear in the top banner.

On the second page, Experian provides you with "information affecting your creditworthiness." As explained, the items listed with dashes before and after the number, such as —3—, may have a negative effect on your credit. The sample report includes a statement that the consumer was a victim of identity theft. (See Section H for more on identity theft.)

Those items are listed first, beginning with public records and followed by credit accounts. After the negative entries come the items for which there is no negative information.

For all accounts, negative or positive, Experian includes the creditor's name and address and the account or court case number. To protect your identity and lessen your risk of identity theft, Experian does not include the full account number—the final few digits are missing.

Next, Experian notes the date the account was opened and how long the account has been reported with Experian, date of last activity on the account, the type of account, your payment terms, your monthly payment amount, who is responsible for paying, the original amount borrowed, your credit limit or your highest balance, and any recent balance or payment. Finally, the comments paragraph tells the status of the account (such as in collection or never late) and for past due accounts, when the information is scheduled to come off your report.

Following the list of credit accounts, Experian provides more detailed information for certain accounts. This detail includes your monthly balances for up to 24 months and your credit limit, high balance or original loan amount.

Toward the end of the report, Experian separates out credit inquiries into two sections: creditors who reviewed your report for the purpose of offering you credit (these inquiries are included in the credit report provided to other creditors) and creditors reviewing their own accounts or who reviewed your report for marketing purposes (these inquiries are not included in the credit report provided to other creditors). For the first set of inquiries, each entry indicates how long the item will remain in your report.

The end of the report contains identification information, including your name and all other names you have used, your current and previous addresses, your Social Security number, year of birth, and current and previous employers.

2. How Long Items Can Stay in a Credit Report

Once a credit bureau gathers information about you, it can report that information (that is, include it in a credit report) as follows:

- Bankruptcies from the date of the last activity may be reported for no more than ten years. Although the date of the last activity for most bankruptcies is the date you receive your discharge or the date your case is dismissed, credit bureaus usually start counting the ten-year period from the earlier date of filing.
- Lawsuits and judgments may be reported from the date of the entry of judgment against you for up to seven years or until the govern-

CLEANING UP YOUR CREDIT FILE

ing statute of limitations has expired, which-ever is longer.

- Paid tax liens from the date of the last activity for up to seven years.

- Most criminal records, such as information about indictments or arrests, may be reported for only seven years. But records of criminal convictions may be reported indefinitely.

- Accounts sent to collection (internally or to a collection agency), accounts charged off or any other similar action may be reported from the date of the last activity on the account for up to seven years. The date of last activity is no later than 180 days from the delinquency itself. Creditors must include the date of the delinquency when they report past due accounts to credit bureaus. The clock does not start ticking again if the account is sold to another collection agency.

- Bankruptcies, lawsuits, paid tax liens, accounts sent out for collection, criminal records and any other adverse information may be reported beyond the usual time limits if you apply for $150,000 or more of credit or insurance, or if you apply for a job with an annual income of at least $75,000. As a practical matter, however, credit bureaus usually delete all items after seven or ten years.

Laws Regulating Credit Bureaus

Credit bureaus are regulated by the Federal Trade Commission under the provisions of the 1971 Federal Fair Credit Reporting Act (FCRA) (15 U.S.C. §1681 and following). The FCRA is designed to bar inaccurate or obsolete information from appearing in credit reports, and it requires credit bureaus to adopt reasonable procedures for gathering, maintaining and distributing information. The FCRA also regulates who can access credit reports. Most states have passed similar laws, some imposing more limitations on creditors and credit bureaus.

Appendix 2 contains the text of the FCRA. To get a copy of your state law governing credit bureaus, contact your state consumer protection agency (listed in Appendix 1, Section F).

3. Review Your Report

As you read through your credit report, make a list of everything that is inaccurate, incomplete or not authorized to be in your file. In particular, look for the following:

- incorrect or incomplete name, address or phone number
- incorrect Social Security number or birthdate
- incorrect, missing or outdated employment information
- incorrect marital status—a former spouse listed as your current spouse

- bankruptcies older than ten years or not iden-tified by the specific chapter of the bankruptcy code
- lawsuits or judgments reported beyond seven years or beyond the expiration of the statute of limitations
- paid tax liens or criminal records older than seven years, delinquent accounts older than seven years or which do not include the date of the delinquency
- credit inquiries by automobile dealers from times you simply test drove a car or from other businesses when you were only com-parison shopping (creditors cannot pull your credit report without your permission until you indicate a desire to enter into a sale or lease)
- commingled accounts—credit histories for someone with a similar or the same name
- duplicate accounts—for example, a debt is listed twice, once under the creditor and a second time under a collection agency

- premarital debts of your current spouse attributed to you
- lawsuits you were not involved in
- incorrect account histories—such as a late payment notation when you've paid on time or a debt shown as past due when it's been discharged in bankruptcy
- voluntary surrender of your vehicle listed as a repossession
- paid tax, judgment, mechanic's or other liens listed as unpaid
- a missing notation when you disputed a charge on a credit card bill
- closed accounts incorrectly listed as open—it may look as if you have too much open credit, and
- accounts you closed that don't indicate "closed by consumer"—it looks like your creditors closed the accounts.

Sample Equifax Credit Profile

Your Credit Profile as of 04/09/2001

This Credit Profile will be available for review for 30 days. If you would like a current Credit Profile you should order another Credit Profile from the Member Center under Other Equifax Products and Services.

Personal Data

John Q. Public
2351 N 85th Ave
Phoenix, AZ 85037

Social Security Number: 022-22-2222
Date of Birth: 1/11/1960

Previous Address(es):

133 Third Avenue
Phoenix, AZ 85037

Employment History

Cendant Hospitality FR	Location: Phoenix, AZ	Employment Date: 2/1/1989	Verified Date: 1/3/2001
Previous Employment(s):			
SOFTWARE Support Hospitality Franch	Location: Atlanta, GA	Employment Date: 01/3/2001	Verified Date: 01/3/2001

Public Records

No bankruptcies on file
No liens on file
No judgements on file
No garnishments on file
No secured loans on file
No marital statuses on file
No financial counseling on file
No foreclosures on file
No non-responsibility entries on file

Collection Accounts

No collections on file.

Credit Information

Company Name	Account Number and Whose Account	Date Opened	Last Activity	Type of Account and Status	High Credit	Items as of Date Reported Terms	Balance	Past Due	Date Reported
Americredit Financial Services	40404XXXX JOINT ACCOUNT	03/1999	03/2000	Installment REPOSSESION	$16933	$430	$9077	$128	2/2000

Prior Paying History

30 days past due 07 times; 60 days past due 05 times; 90+ days past due 03 times

INVOLUNTARY REPOSSESION AUTO

Capital One	412174147128XXXX INDIVIDUAL ACCOUNT	10/1997	01/2001	Revolving PAYS AS AGREED	$777	15	$514		01/2001

Prior Paying History

30 days past due 02 times; 60 days past due 1 times; 90+ days past due 00 times
CREDIT CARD

Desert Schools FCU	423325003406XXXX INDIVIDUAL ACCOUNT	07/1997	06/1998	Revolving PAYS AS AGREED	$500		$0		07/1999

Prior Paying History

30 days past due 02 times; 60 days past due 00 times; 90+ days past due 00 times
ACCOUNT PAID
CLOSED ACCOUNT

Sample Equifax Credit Profile

Heilig-Meyers Company	7360300XXXX INDIVIDUAL ACCOUNT	03/1998 07/1999	Revolving PAYS AS AGREED	$1000	$0		07/1999

Prior Paying History

30 days past due 02 times; 60 days past due 1 times; 90+ days past due 00 times
CREDIT CARD
AMOUNT IN H/C COLUMN IS CREDIT LIMIT

Sears	806050211XXXX INDIVIDUAL ACCOUNT	09/1998 07/1999	Revolving PAYS AS AGREED	$720	$0		07/1999

Prior Paying History

CHARGED
AMOUNT IN H/C COLUMN IS CREDIT LIMIT

Wells FARGO	503830276150XXXX INDIVIDUAL ACCOUNT	11/1996 12/2000	Installment PAYS AS AGREED	$17146	$401	$4058	12/2000

Prior Paying History

AUTO

Credit Inquiries

Companies that Requested your Credit File

04/29/2001 EFX Credit Profile Online
06/30/2001 Automotive
06/16/2000 AR-Associates National Bank
01/18/2000 Desert Schools Federal Cu.
01/15/2000 Desert Schools Federal C.U.
07/02/1999 Time Life, Inc

THE FOLLOWING INQUIRIES ARE NOT REPORTED TO BUSINESSES:
PRM - This is a promotional inquiry in which only your name and address were given to a credit grantor so you could be solicited you with an offer such as a credit card. (PRM inquiries remain on file for 12 months.)
AM or AR - These inquiries indicate a periodic review of your credit history by one of your creditors (AM and AR inquiries remain on file for 12 months.)
EQUIFAX, ACIS or UPDATE - These inquiries indicate Equifax's activity in response to your contact with us for either a copy of your credit file or a request for research.
PRM, AM, AR, INQ, EQUIFAX, ACIS and UPDATE inquiries do not show on credit files that businesses receive, only on copies provided to you.

- Your confirmation number is 109933931. **Please keep this number in your records for future communication with us.**

Equifax Consumer Services, Inc.

Sample Trans Union Credit Report

DOE, JOHN J.
123 NOWHERE ST.
WONDERLAND, IL 12345

Date of Report: 10/02/2001
File Number: 104452642

Personal Data:

Former Address Reported:
321 NOPLACE RD.
GREATWORLD, MN 54321

Social Security Number: 999-99-0000

Estimated Date of Birth: 08/01/1970

You have been in our files since: 10/01/1988

Phone Number: 123-4567

Employment Data:

Employer:	NONAME INC.	**Address:**	123 MAIN STREET ANYWHERE, IL
Position:	MANAGER	**Date Verified:**	10/18/2001

Public Record:

The following items obtained from public records appear on your report. You may be required to explain public record items to potential creditors. Any bankruptcy information will remain on your report for 10 years from the date of filing. Unpaid tax liens may generally be reported for an indefinite period of time depending on your state of residence. Paid tax liens may be reported for 7 years from date of payment. All other public record information, including discharged Chapter 13 Bankruptcy and any accounts containing adverse information remain for 7 years. All other public record information including discharged Chapter 13 Bankruptcy, may be reported for 7 years.

Docket Number#: SM102030 Small Claims SOMEONE CORP.

Plaintiff:

Plaintiff Attorney: PRO SE

Paid civil judgement
Entered: 01/01/1993

Assets:

Liabilities: $819
Paid: 09/01/1993

Sample Trans Union Credit Report

Adverse Account Information Section

The following accounts contain information which some creditors may consider to be adverse. Adverse account information may generally be reported for 7 years from the date of the first delinquency, depending on your state of residence. The adverse information in these accounts has been printed in >brackets< for your convenience, to help you understand your report. They are not bracketed this way for creditors. (Note: the account # may be scrambled by the creditor for your protection).

XYZ INC.   **Acnt#:** 1010101010101010   Installment account

>Included in bankruptcy<   Automobile

Updated date:	10/18/2001	**Balance:**	$0		Individual account
Opened:	05/01/1989	**Most Owed:**	$939	**Payment Terms:**	60 Monthly $80
Closed:	12/01/1995				
		Past Due:	$0	**Credit Limit:**	$0

>Status as of 12/01/1995: Collection account<

Satisfactory Account Information Section

The following accounts are reported with no adverse information.

ABCD BANK   **Acnt#:** 1010101010101010   Revolving account

Credit Card

Updated date:	10/01/2001	**Balance:**	$3678		Joint Account
Opened:	03/01/1996	**Most Owed:**	$3907		
Closed:				**Payment Terms:**	
		Past Due:	$0	**Credit Limit:**	$5000

>Status as of 10/01/2001: Paid or paying as agreed<

Regular Inquiry Section

The following companies have received your credit report. Their inquiries remain on your credit report for two years. (Note: TransUnion consumer disclosure inquiries are not viewed by creditors.)

Date	Inquiry Type	Subscriber Name
09/13/2001	Individual	ZYX FINANCIAL CORP
09/21/2001	Individual	TU CONSUMER DISCLOSURE
08/06/2001	Joint	CREDIT DATA/SOMEONE CORP.

Sample Trans Union Credit Report

Promotional Inquiry Section

The companies listed below received your name, address and other limited information about you so they could make a firm offer of credit or insurance. They did not receive your full credit report, and these inquiries are not seen by anyone but you.

Date	Subscriber Name
09/13/2001	NONAME BANK
09/21/2001	XXYY FINANCIAL

Account Review Inquiry Section

The companies listed below obtained information from your consumer report for the purpose of an account review or other business transaction with you. These inquiries are not displayed to anyone but you and will not affect any other creditor's decision or any score.

Date	Subscriber Name
10/18/2001	TRANS UNION SCORE
10/01/2001	ABCD BANK

Consumer Statement Section

No Consumer Statements on file

Special Messages Section

No Special Messages on file

End of Report Section

If you believe any of the information in your credit report is incorrect, please let us know. Please address all correspondence regarding your credit report to:

Contact Bureau: TRANS UNION LLC

Bureau Address: 2 BALDWIN PLACE, P. O. BOX 2000
CHESTER, PA. 19022
800-916-8800

Our Business Hours in Your Time Zone Area: 8:30 A.M. TO 4:30 P.M. Monday thru Friday, except on major holidays

Sample Trans Union Credit Report

▶ TransUnion Personal Credit Score

NAME: DOE, JOHN J.	**DATE OF CREDIT SCORE:** 10/02/2001
ADDRESS: 123 NOWHERE ST.	**FILE NUMBER:** 104452642
WONDERLAND, IL 12345	

About your credit score:

A credit score is a computer generated mathematical calculation of the information which appears in a credit report. It represents your credit worthiness as a number or numerical value. The credit score is based on data about your credit history and payment behavior. Credit scores are used to assist a lender or insurance company in determining the level of risk associated with granting you a loan, or evaluating an insurance policy. Credit scores may change over time, depending on how your credit history and payment behavior changes and how well you manage your credit obligations.

Since the credit score is based on information in your credit history, it is important that you review the credit report that is being furnished with this document to make sure it is complete and accurate.

The credit score, displayed below, is created by TransUnion. A higher credit score means a lower likelihood of delinquency in the next two years on a new account. The credit score is presented with up to four key factors. These factors will print in the order of importance as to the reasons your credit score is not higher.

Please note that this credit score may be different than a credit score used by a lending institution or insurance company. The credit industry and the insurance industry use many different types of credit scores. For more information, visit www.transunion.com.

Personal Credit Score

Your Credit Score:	+800
Minimum Score:	+150
Maximum Score:	+934

Factor Description

Factor 1: COLLECTION AMOUNTS EVER OWED ARE TOO HIGH CONSUMERS WITH COLLECTION ACTIVITY ARE MORE LIKELY OF FUTURE DELINQUENCY. MAKING PROMPT PAYMENTS OVER A LONGER PERIOD OF TIME MAY IMPROVE YOUR SCORE.

Factor 2: TOO MANY SERIOUS DELINQUENCIES YOUR CREDIT REPORT REFLECTS ONE OR MORE ACCOUNTS WITH A DELINQUENT PAYMENT HISTORY OF 90 DAYS OR MORE DELINQUENT. MAKING PROMPT PAYMENTS OVER TIME MAY IMPROVE YOUR CREDIT SCORE.

Factor 3: AVERAGE BALANCE OF REVOLVING ACCOUNTS IS TOO HIGH LOWERING YOUR BALANCES ON THESE ACCOUNTS MAY IMPROVE YOUR CREDIT SCORE.

Factor 4: TOO MANY DELINQUENCIES YOUR CREDIT REPORT REFLECTS DELINQUENT PAYMENT HISTORY ON ONE OR MORE ACCOUNTS. MAKING PROMPT PAYMENTS OVER TIME MAY IMPROVE YOUR CREDIT SCORE.

experian

Prepared for
JOHN Q CONSUMER
Report number
1687771839

Report date
June 01, 1999

Page 1 of 8

Personal Credit Report

About this report

Experian collects and organizes information about you and your credit history from public records, your creditors and other reliable sources. We make your credit history available to your current and prospective creditors and employers as allowed by law. We do not grant credit or evaluate your credit history. Personal data about you may be made available to companies whose products and services may interest you.

Important decisions about your creditworthiness are based on the information in this report. You should review it carefully for accuracy.

Experian
PO Box 9595
Allen TX 75013-9595

Information affecting your creditworthiness

Below is a summary of the information contained in this report.

Potentially negative items listed

Public records

Accounts with creditors and others

Accounts in good standing

If you have questions

For all questions about this report, please call us at:
1 888 XXX-XXXX
M thru F 9 am – 5 pm in your time zone

To learn more about
2   Experian or for other helpful information,
2   including tips on how to improve your credit-
3   worthiness, visit our web site:
http://www.experian.com

experian

Prepared for	**Report date**
JOHN Q CONSUMER	June 01, 1999
Report number	**Questions?**
1687771839	Call 1 888 XXX XXXX

Information affecting your creditworthiness

Items listed with dashes before and after the number, for example - 1- may have a potentially negative effect on your future credit extension and are listed first on the report.

Credit grantors may carefully review the items listed below when they check your credit history. Please note that the account information connected with some public records, such as bankruptcy, also may appear with your credit accounts listed later in this report.

Your statement

At your request, we've included the following statement every time your credit report is requested.

"My identification has been used without my consent on applications for credit. Please call me at 999 999 9999 before approving credit in my name."

Public record information about you

Source/ Identification number	Location number	Date filed/ Date resolved	Responsibility	Claim amount/ Liability amount	Comments
-1- Holly CO DIST CT 305 MAIN STREET HOLLY NJ 08060	B312P7659	3-1997/ NA	Joint	$3,756/ NA	Status: civil claim judgment filed. Plaintiff: Dime Savings. This item is scheduled to continue on record until 3-2004. This item was verified on 8-1997 and remained unchanged.
-2- BROWN TOWN HALL 10 COURT ST BROWN NJ 02809	BK443PG14	11-1997/ 10-1998	Joint	$57,786/ NA	Status: chapter 7 bankruptcy discharged. This item is scheduled to continue on record until 11-2007. This item was verified on 8-1997 and remained unchanged.

experian

Prepared for
JOHN Q CONSUMER
Report number
1687771839

Report date
June 01, 1999
Questions?
Call 1 888 XXX XXXX

Page 3 of 8

Credit Information about you

Source / Account number (except last few digits)	Date opened / Reported since	Date of status / Last reported	Type / Terms / Monthly payment	Responsibility	Credit limit or original amount / High balance	Recent balance / Recent payment	Comments
-3- FIDELITY BK NA 300 FIDELITY PLAZA NORTHSHORE NJ 08902 46576000024.....	6-1994/ 6-1994	12-1996/ 12-1996	Installment/ 10 months/ $0	Individual	$4,549/ NA	$4,549 as of 12-1996	Status: charge off. $4,549 written off in 12-1996. This account is scheduled to continue on record until 12-2003
-4- B.B. CREDIT 35 WASHINGTON ST. DEDHAM MA 547631236	10-1990/ 4-1995	4-1998/ 4-1998	Installment/ 80 months/ $34	Individual	$8,500/ $8,500	$0 as of 4-1998/ $34	Status: Debt re-included in chapter 7 bankruptcy. $389 written off in 3-1998. Account history: Collection as of 9-1995 thru 6-1996 90 days as of 7-1995 60 days as of 11-1994, 6-1995 30 days as of 9-1994, 1-1995 and 2 other times This account is scheduled to continue on record until 2-2001. This item was verified and updated on 6-1996

Original creditor: Bally's Health Club/Personal Services.

experian

Prepared for	Report date
JOHN Q CONSUMER	June 01, 1999
Report number	Questions?
1687771839	Call 1 888 XXX XXXX

Page 4 of 8

Credit Information about you *continued*

Source/ Account number (except last few digits)	Date opened/ Reported since	Date of status/ Last reported	Type/ Terms/ Monthly payment	Responsibility	Credit limit or original amount/ High balance	Recent balance/ Recent payment	Comments
5 **FIRST CREDIT UNION** 78 WASHINGTON LN LANEVILL TX 76362 129474 Mortgage: 74848347834	3-1996/ 3-1996	11-1998/ 11-1998	Installment/ 48 Months/ $420		$17,856/ NA	$0 as of 11-1998/ $420	Status: open/never late.
AMERICA FINANCE CORP PO BOX 8633 COLLEY IL 60126 6376001172.....	6-1993/ 7-1993	11-1998/ 11-1998	Revolving/ NA/ $400		$0/ $18,251	$0 as of 11-1998/	Status: card reported lost or stolen. This account is scheduled to continue on record until 11-2000.
NATIONAL CREDIT CARD 100 THE PLAZA LANEVILLE NJ 08905 420000638.....	6-1993/ 6-1993	11-1998/ 11-1998	Revolving/ NA/ $0	Joint with JANE CONSUMER	$8,000/ $8,569	$0 as of 11-1998/	Status: open/never late.

Purchased from **CITIBANK VISA**

experian

Prepared for	Report date	Page 5 of 8
JOHN Q CONSUMER	June 01, 1999	
Report number	**Questions?**	
1687771839	Call 1 888 XXX XXXX	

Page 5 of 8
Your use of credit

The information listed below provides additional detail about your accounts, showing up to 24 months of balance history and your credit limit, high balance or original loan amount. Not all balance history is reported to Experian, so some of your accounts may not appear. Also, some credit grantors may update the information more than once in the same month.

Source/Account number   *Date/Balance*

6 AMERICA FINANCE CO CORP 11-1998/$0 10-1998/$4,329 8-1998/$0 5-1998/$0 2-1998/$250 1-1998/$0 12-1997/$2,951
6376001172....... 9-1997/$3,451 7-1997/$4,251 5-1997/$4,651 2-1997/$5,451 1-1997/$5,851; 12-1996/$6,251
11-1996/$6,651 9-1996/$7,051 7-1996/$7,451 5-1996/$7,852 3-1996/$8,251 1-1996/$12,651
12-1995/$9,051 11-1995/$9,451 9-1995/$10,251 7-1995/$10,651 5-1995/$11,051

Between 1-1994 and 11-1998 your credit limit was unknown.

7 NATIONAL CREDIT CARD 11-1998/$0 9-1998/$542 7-1998/$300 6-1998/$686 4-1998/$1,400 3-1998/$2,500
420000638... 1-1998/$2,774 12-1997/$599 9-1997/$873 7-1997/$1,413 5-1997/$1,765 4-1997/$2,387
3-1997/$3,400 2-1997/$3,212 1-1997/$4,412 12-1996/$2,453 10-1996/$2,453 10-1996/$1,769
8-1996/$1,200 4-1996/$3,200 2-1996/$4,568 1-1996/$5,582 12-1995/$3,000 10-1995/$3,200
8-1995/$4,500

Between 6-1993 and 11-1998 your credit limit was $8,000.

experian

Prepared for	Report date	Page 6 of 8
JOHN Q CONSUMER	June 01, 1999	
Report number	Questions?	
1687771839	Call 1 888 XXX XXXX	

Page 6 of 8

Others who have requested your credit history.

Listed below are all those who have received information from us in the recent past about your credit history.

Requests initiated by you

You took actions, such as completing a credit application, that allowed the following sources to review your information. Please note that the following information is part of your credit history and is included in our reports to others.

Source	Date	Comments
ABC MORTGAGE 64 MAPLE ROSEVILLE MD 02849	10-18-1998	Real estate loan of $214,000 on behalf of State Bank with 30 year repayment terms. This inquiry is scheduled to continue on record until 10-2000.

Other requests

You may not have initiated the following requests for your credit history, so you may not recognize each source. We offer credit information about you to those with a permissible purposed, for example, to:

- other creditors who want to offer you preapproved credit; an employer who wishes to extend an offer of employment;
- a potential investor in assessing the risk of a current obligation;
- Experian Consumer Assistance to process a report for you
- your current creditors to monitor your accounts (date listed may reflect only the most recent request).

We report these requests only to you as a record of activities, and we do not include any of these requests on credit reports to others.

Source	Date
EXPERIAN PO BOX 949 ALLEN TX 75013	3-99
WORLD BANK 4578 DRIVE NORTH YORKVILLE NY 03939	3-99, 12-98, 9-98, 6-98, 3-98, 12-97, 9-97, 6-97, 3-97
FIDELITY BK NA 300 FIDELITY PLAZA NORTHSHORE NJ 08902	1-99, 7-98, 1-98, 7-97, 1-97
NATIONAL CREDIT CARD 100 THE PLAZA LANEVILLE NJ 08905	7-97, 2-97

experían

Prepared for
JOHN Q CONSUMER
Report number
1687771839

Report date
June 01, 1999
Questions?
Call 1 888 XXX XXXX

Page 7 of 8

Page 7 of 8

Personal information about you

The following information associated with your records has **been reported** to us **by you, your creditors and other sources.** As part of our fraud-prevention program, a notice with additional information may appear in your report.

Names
John Q. Consumer
John Consumer
Jack Q. Consumer

Date of birth
9/27/1959

Driver's license number
CA X123456

Telephone numbers
999 999 9999 home
999 999 9009
999 999 8888

Spouse's Name
Jane

Employers
ABC Corporation
456 Main Street
Anytown, CA 90001

City of Newton

Residences

Our records show you currently are a homeowner. The geographical code shown with each address identifies the state, country, census tract, block group and Metropolitan Statistical Area associated with each address.

Address	Type of address	Geographical code
123 Main Street Anytown, CA 90001	NA	23-914-629331-1-1234
7 Buckingham Drive Southwick, MA 01077	Single family	14-167-353800-6-6464
125 Main Street, Apt. 305 Westfield, MA 01085	Apartment complex	75-344-896002-9-7436
86 Avenue B Belchertown, MA 01007	Single family	73-334-9921145-4-4747

Social Security number variations

As a security precaution, we did not list the Social Security number that you gave us when you contacted us.
018-38-6414
020-44-3032

Notices

The Social Security number that you gave us when you contacted us has been reported by the Social Security Administration as deceased.

The Social Security number that you gave us when you contacted us has not been issued by the Social Security Administration.

The Social Security number that you gave us when you contacted us shows that credit was established before the number was issued.

The Social Security number that you gave us when you contacted us does not match the formal requirements of the Social Security Administration.

D. Dispute Incomplete and Inaccurate Information in Your Credit File

Under the Fair Credit Reporting Act, you have the right to dispute all incomplete and inaccurate information in your credit file. Once the credit bureau receives your letter, it must reinvestigate the items you dispute and get back in touch with you within 30 days. Some states require that credit bureaus complete the reinvestigation more quickly.

These requirements are not hard for a credit bureau to meet. Credit bureaus and more than 6,000 of the nation's creditors are linked by computer, which speeds up the verification process. Furthermore, if you let a credit bureau know that you're trying to obtain a mortgage or car loan, the employees can do a "rush" verification.

If the credit bureau cannot verify the information in dispute, it must remove it. Credit bureaus might remove an item on request without an investigation if rechecking the item is more bother than it's worth. Requesting a reinvestigation won't cost you anything.

Once you've compiled a list of all incomplete and inaccurate information you want corrected or removed, complete the "request for reinvestigation" form which was enclosed with your credit report. If the bureau did not enclose such a form, use *Form F-23: Request Reinvestigation* in Appendix 3 or on the CD-ROM. Don't simply handwrite a letter. Handwritten letters on plain paper often are given minimal attention.

Incorrect information does not have to be negative to be challenged. It is enough that the information is wrong.

Below are some examples of the types of responses you might include on Form F-23:

X The following personal information about me is incorrect:

Erroneous Information	Correct Information
Spouse: Morton Lyle	I divorced Morton Lyle on
	8/23/00. I'm now married to
	Brian Jones.

X The following accounts are not mine:

Creditor's Name	Account Number	Explanation
Dept. of Education	123456789	Pre-marital debt of my
		husband, Brian Jones.
Strong's Dept. Store	0987654321	I've never had a
		Strong's account.

X The account status is incorrect for the following accounts:

Creditor's Name	Account Number	Correct Status
Big Bank	1234 5678 9012	Discharged in
MasterCard		bankruptcy; balance
		owed is $0.

[X] The following inquiries were not authorized:

Creditor's Name	Date of Inquiry	Explanation
Wowza Bank Visa	2/14/01	I did not apply for credit with Wowza Bank nor authorize them to conduct a credit check of me.

[X] Other incorrect information:

Explanation

(1) My credit report states that I filed a Chapter 13 bankruptcy on July 23, 20xx. That is not correct. In fact, I filed a Chapter 7 case and received a discharge of my debts on October 19, 2000.

(2) American Express account is listed twice—one listing indicates the account was discharged in bankruptcy (this is correct); the other listing shows the account with Tenacious Collection Services (incorrect). Furthermore this account is missing the date of delinquency.

Send your letter to the address provided by the credit bureau for disputing information. Also, enclose copies of any documents you have that support your claim.

It is also a good idea to send a copy of your letter to the creditor who furnished the incorrect or incomplete information to the credit bureau. These "furnishing" creditors have a duty to correct and update the information that they send to credit bureaus.

If you don't hear from the credit bureau within 30 days, send a follow-up letter using *Form F-24: Request Follow-Up After Reinvestigation* in Appendix 3 or on the CD-ROM. Send a copy of Form F-24 to the Federal Trade Commission (addresses are listed below), the agency that oversees credit bureaus. Again, keep a copy for your records.

Once the credit bureau receives your request for reinvestigation, it must:

- complete its investigation within 30 days of receiving your complaint (extended to 45 if the bureau receives relevant information from you during the 30-day period)

- contact the creditor reporting the information you dispute within five days of receiving your dispute
- review and consider all relevant information submitted by you, and
- provide you with the results of its reinvestigation within five days of completion, including a new credit report if any changes were made.

If the credit bureau agrees that the information is incorrect or outdated, it must remove or modify the information from the report. You can also ask the bureau to notify past users of the corrected information. But, the credit bureau will only do this if you ask. And, even then, it is only required to send notice to anyone who requested your report within the previous six months, or two years if requested for employment purposes.

Even if the credit bureau agrees that the information is incorrect and fixes it, don't assume that the negative information will be permanently eliminated from your report. The bureaus are required to have procedures to keep incorrect information from reappearing, but unfortunately those procedures often fail. To make sure the errors stay out of your report, you should do the following:

- Obtain another copy of your credit report 3 to 6 months later to confirm that the corrections were made
- Check to see whether your credit reports at the other main credit bureaus contain the same error, and if so, send the results of your successful investigation from the first credit bureau to the others, and
- After three to six months, get another copy of your report from the first credit bureau and check to see if the information has reappeared.

If the credit bureau responds that the creditor reporting the information verified its accuracy and completeness, and that therefore the information will remain in your file, you will need to take more aggressive action in cleaning up your credit report. This may be frustrating and time-consuming.

In your efforts to fix your credit file, here are some ideas to help you:

1. Contact the creditor associated with the incorrect information and demand that it tell the credit

bureau to remove the information. Write to the customer service department, vice president of marketing, and president or CEO. If the information was reported by a collection agency, send the agency a copy of your letter too. Use *Form F-25: Request Removal of Incorrect Information by Creditor* in Appendix 3 or on the CD-ROM to make your request. Be sure to keep a copy of your letter. If the creditor is locally based, pay a visit. Sit down in the office of the customer service department, vice president of marketing, or president or CEO. Do not leave until someone agrees to meet with you and hear your problem. *Remember: You have the right to demand attention; this creditor has verified incorrect information and it should be removed from your credit report.*

Under the Fair Credit Reporting Act (FCRA), creditors who report information to credit bureaus must do the following:

- refrain from reporting information they know is incorrect
- refrain from ignoring information they know contradicts what they have on file
- refrain from reporting incorrect information when they learn that the information is, in fact, incorrect
- provide credit bureaus with correct information when they learn that the information they have been reporting is incorrect
- notify credit bureaus when you dispute information
- note when accounts are "closed by the consumer"
- provide credit bureaus with the month and year of the delinquency of all accounts placed for collection, charged off or similarly treated, and
- finish their investigation of your dispute within the 30-day or 45-day periods the credit bureau must complete its investigation.

(The full text of the FCRA is included in Appendix 2.)

2. If you get a letter from the creditor that agrees that the information is incorrect and should be re-moved from your credit file, send a copy of the creditor's letter to the credit bureau reporting the information. Use *Form F-26: Creditor Verification* found in Appendix 3 or on the CD-ROM.

3. If a creditor cannot or will not assist you in removing the incorrect information, you will have to call the credit bureau directly. Credit bureaus have toll-free numbers to handle consumer disputes about incorrect items in their credit files that are not removed via the normal reinvestigation process. Use the credit bureau's toll-free number as follows:

> Experian 888-397-3742
> Trans Union 800-916-8800
> Equifax .... 800-685-1111 (this is the number to get a copy of your credit report —Equifax requires you to get a copy of your report before it will discuss removal of information)

4. If you were seriously harmed by the credit bureau—for example, it continued to give out incomplete or inaccurate information after you requested corrections—you may be able to sue. The FCRA lets you sue a credit bureau for negligent or willful noncompliance with the law within two years after the bureau's harmful behavior first occurred. In some very limited circumstances, you may have more than two years to sue. You can sue for actual damages, such as court costs, attorney's fees, lost wages and, if applicable, defamation and intentional infliction of emotional distress. In the case of truly outrageous behavior, you can recover punitive damages—damages meant to punish for malicious or willful conduct. Under the FCRA, the court decides the amount of the punitive damages.

You can also sue the creditor that supplied the inaccurate information. However, these types of lawsuits are complicated and the FCRA provides creditors with many ways to avoid liability. You will need to consult a lawyer if you want to pursue this type of lawsuit.

5. If all else fails, consider calling your congressional representative or senator. That person can call the FTC and demand some action.

Federal Trade Commission

Contact the FTC to file a complaint against a credit bureau.

National Office

Consumer Response Center
CRC-240
600 Pennsylvania Ave, NW
Washington, DC 20580
877-382-4357
www.ftc.gov/ftc/bcppriv.htm

Regional Offices

Southeast Region
Suite 1500
225 Peachtree St., NE
Atlanta, GA 30303-2322
(Alabama, Florida, Georgia, Mississippi, North Carolina, South Carolina, Tennessee)

Midwest Region
55 East Monroe Street, Suite 1860
Chicago, IL 60603-5701
(Illinois, Indiana, Iowa, Kansas, Kentucky, Nebraska, North Dakota, Minnesota, Missouri, South Dakota, Wisconsin)

East Central Region
1111 Superior Avenue, Suite 200
Cleveland, OH 44114-2507
(Delaware, Maryland, Michigan, Ohio, Pennsylvania, Virginia, Washington D.C., West Virginia)

Southwest Region
1999 Bryan Street, Suite 2150
Dallas, TX 75201-6808
(Arkansas, Louisiana, New Mexico, Oklahoma, Texas)

Northeast Region
1 Bowling Green
New York, NY 10004
(Connecticut, Maine, Massachusetts, New Hampshire, New Jersey, New York, Puerto Rico, Rhode Island, U.S. Virgin Islands)

Western Region
901 Market Street, Suite 570
San Francisco, CA 94103
[or]
10877 Wilshire Boulevard, Suite 700
Los Angeles, CA 90024
(Arizona, California, Colorado, Hawaii, Nevada, Utah)

Northwest Region
2896 Federal Building
915 Second Avenue
Seattle, WA 98174
(Alaska, Idaho, Montana, Oregon, Washington, Wyoming)

E. Consider Adding a Brief Statement to Your Credit File

If you feel a credit bureau is wrongfully including information in your report, or you want to explain a particular entry, you have the right to put a brief statement in your report. If the reporting agency helps you write the summary, the statement will be limited to one hundred words. Otherwise, there is no word limit, but it is a good idea to keep the statement very brief.

The credit bureau is only required to provide a summary of your statement (not your actual statement) to anyone who requests your file. If your statement is short, the credit bureau is more likely to pass on your statement, unedited. If your statement is long, the credit bureau will probably condense your explanation to just a few sentences. To avoid this problem, keep your statement clear and concise.

Sample Brief Statements

As mentioned, be judicious in your use of consumer statements. But if a particular item in your file is clearly wrong and can be simply explained, consider adding a statement. Here are a few samples:

"I am not unemployed. Since 2002, I have worked as a freelance technical writer, and have earned an average of $50,000 per year."

"Although I was sued by Randy Roofer, I did not pay her because the roof she put on my house is not sealed and she refuses to fix it. I refuse to pay Randy until she repairs the roof. I filed a complaint with the state contractor's board, which is pending."

"I am disputing the debt I owe to Country Electronics. I purchased a CD player which does not work correctly. The store refuses to take the merchandise back, refund my money or give me a replacement CD player. I am trying to resolve the problem with the manufacturer."

"It is technically accurate that I was sued by Jones and Jones Department Store on June 11, 2002. Jones and Jones dismissed the lawsuit, however, when they realized that they had confused my account with another customer's. My account with Jones and Jones has never been delinquent."

"I was hospitalized following a car accident. I sent the medical bills to my insurance company, but the company took over six months to pay the bills. In the meantime, the hospital began collection efforts against me. Those efforts ended when the insurance company paid the bill."

"The late payment notations for NorthBank should not be on my file. I moved and sent NorthBank a change of address, which it did not process correctly. It took NorthBank nearly three months to catch up with me. All that time, I received no bills from the bank."

"The late payment notation for SouthBank should not be on my file. SouthBank moved and did not send me a change of address in a timely manner. I made my payment early, but it went to SouthBank's old address. By the time SouthBank received it at its new address, it was nearly a month late."

If you request it, the bureau must also give the statement or summary to anyone who received a copy of your file within the past six months—or two years if your file was given out for employment purposes.

This is not an unlimited right. Credit bureaus are only required to include a statement in your file if you are disputing the completeness or accuracy of a particular item. If that is the case, they must do it for free. The bureau does not have to include a statement if you are only explaining extenuating circumstances or other reasons why you haven't been able to pay your debts. If the bureau does allow you to add such a statement, it can charge you a fee.

Don't assume that adding a brief statement is the best approach. It's often wiser to simply explain the negative mark to subsequent creditors in person than to try to explain it in such a short statement. Many statements or summaries are simply ineffective. Few creditors who receive credit files read them. In any David (consumer) vs. Goliath (credit bureau) dispute, creditors tend to believe Goliath. To make matters worse, your statement might stay in your file even longer than the disputed information.

F. Add Positive Account Histories to Your Credit File

Often, credit reports don't include accounts that you might expect to find. Some major commercial lenders don't report mortgages or car loans. Local banks or credit unions often don't provide information to credit bureaus.

If your credit file is missing credit histories for accounts you pay on time, send the credit bureaus a copy of a recent account statement and copies of canceled checks (never originals) showing your payment history. Ask the credit bureaus to add the information to your file. While the bureaus aren't required to add account histories, they often do—but may charge you a fee for doing so. Use *Form F-27: Request Addition of Account Histories* from Appendix 3 or on the CD-ROM to make your request.

It may be that credit histories for accounts you pay on time are missing from only one or two credit reports—the third report may have included all accounts when you received it, or you may have focused on cleaning up that report first. In this situation, a simple way to request that the bureaus not reporting the information add it to your file is to send them a copy of the credit report that includes all your accounts.

G. Add Information Showing Stability to Your Credit File

Creditors like to see evidence of stability in your file. If any of the items listed below are missing from your file, you may want to send a letter to the credit bureaus asking that the information be added. Use *Form F-28: Request Addition of Information Showing Stability* in Appendix 3 or on the CD-ROM to make your request.

You may want to add:

- **Your current employment**—employer's name, employer's address and your job title. You may wisely decide not to add this if you think a creditor may sue you or a creditor has a judgment against you. Current employment information may be a green light for a wage garnishment.
- **Your previous employment,** especially if you've had your current job fewer than two years. Include your former employer's name and address and your job title.
- **Your current residence,** and if you own it, say so. (Not all mortgage lenders report their accounts to credit bureaus.) Again, don't do this if you've been sued or you think a creditor may sue you. Real estate is an excellent collection source.
- **Your previous residence,** especially if you've lived at your current address fewer than two years.
- **Your telephone number,** especially if it's unlisted. If you haven't yet given the credit bureaus your phone number, consider doing so now. A creditor who cannot verify a telephone number is often reluctant to grant credit.
- **Your date of birth.** A creditor will probably not grant you credit if it does not know your age. However, creditors also cannot discriminate against you based on your age. (See Chapter 6, Section H.)
- **Your Social Security number.**
- **Bank checking or savings account number**—it's an excellent sign of stability. Again, however, you won't want to add this information if you've been sued or you think a creditor may sue you. A creditor with a judgment against you will likely use this information to try to collect.

Credit bureaus aren't required to add any of this information, but they often do. They are most likely to add information on jobs and residences, as that information is used by creditors in evaluating applications for credit. They will also add your telephone number, date of birth and Social Security number because those items help identify you and lessen the chances of "mixed" credit files—that is, getting other people's credit histories in your file. (Expect to pay a small fee when a credit bureau adds information to your file.)

Enclose any documentation that verifies information you're providing, such as copies of your driver's license, a canceled check, a bill addressed to you, a pay stub showing your employer's name and address or anything else similar. Remember to keep photocopies of all correspondence.

H. Avoid Identity Theft

Identity theft is a growing national epidemic. Estimates by government and consumer affairs organizations place the number of victims of identity theft in the U.S. alone at 900,000 per year—and climbing. The sad truth is that the Internet and its vast collections of easily accessible personal data make identity theft a simple and tantalizing endeavor for the criminally inclined. Contributing to the problem are businesses that lack stringent privacy policies and corporate mistakes in handling sensitive customer information. Incidents of information-rich files being left unsecured in garbage bins and credit slips left unshredded are common—and even the unsavvy thieves know it.

Unfortunately, local police agencies are ill-equipped to handle these sophisticated crimes which often cross state borders. From a police perspective, identity theft is a silent crime. It just doesn't merit the priority of crimes like murder, robbery and other violent crimes more easily reported and televised. District attorneys are in a similar bind. Re-election is secured by winning big verdicts in publicity-generating cases.

But times are changing. Federal and state law enforcement agencies are beginning to take the problem more seriously, especially now that the FBI has declared identity theft as the fastest growing white collar crime in the country.

1. What's in a Stolen Name?

A lot. A thief can obtain a loan, open credit accounts and charge them to their maximum, rent an apartment, buy a car, purchase a cell phone, talk to someone in China all day, and worse, commit a serious crime—all using your name.

Financially, if a credit card in your name is used in a credit scam, you'll likely be responsible for only $50, or possibly nothing because of federal laws capping your liability for unauthorized use of your card. (See Chapter 3, Section A9.) But the financial burdens may be the least of your worries. You may spend months hassling with credit agencies, financial institutions and police departments trying to clear your name and repair the lingering damage. You may have to take time off from work to write letters, make calls, collect evidence and demand action.

And who knows what it will take to repair the anxiety and mental suffering you'll endure. Typically, victims of identity theft report that police agencies are often dismissive or even abusive, credit reporting agencies unresponsive, collection agencies hostile and creditors disbelieving. Psychological scarring can be severe. Some victims liken the experience to feeling physically assaulted; continued sleep disturbances, paranoia and other post-traumatic stress symptoms are not uncommon.

2. How Can an Identity Be Stolen?

In a word—easily. Here are some typical ways in which thieves gather information about you:

- stealing wallets or mail
- former friend, lover, roommate or co-worker with a grudge gathers sensitive information and uses it in an attempt to extract revenge (a more common occurrence than most people realize)
- filling out a change of address form using your name and collecting your mail
- snatching pre-approved credit offers from the trash or recycling bin
- ordering unauthorized credit reports on you by posing as a potential employer, landlord or even you
- illegal computer tapping by a dishonest employee at a business where you have provided information or been granted credit
- looking over your shoulder at phones and ATMs to gather PIN numbers, sometimes with binoculars or listening devices
- breaking into computer systems and searching for people with good credit
- using phony telemarketing schemes to con you into giving them your personal data, and
- using personal information you shared on the Internet.

Perhaps the most frightening—and most thorough—way to steal your identity is by purchasing your Social Security number, mother's maiden name, home and employment address, previous addresses, credit history and more for just a few dollars from one of the new identity search companies spawning on the Internet.

3. How to Protect Yourself

You must guard your personal information assiduously. Here are some tips for keeping your private information secure:

- Don't leave outgoing bill payments in your mailbox for the postman to pick up.
- Keep changing your passwords and PIN numbers. Don't use obvious codes such as birthdays or spouse's, children's or pet's names. Memorize them and shred any piece of paper where they are written.
- Diligently review credit card statements and phone and utility bills. Get a copy of all of your credit reports at least once a year. Promptly respond to any inaccurate information.
- Always take your credit card receipts, and don't throw them away in public.
- Tear up or shred item with personal information on it, as well as any offers of preapproved credit cards you don't intend to use. Also, beware of offers from companies you don't recognize. It's easy to create an official-looking and completely phony credit application offering you pre-approved credit if you provide your Social Security number, mother's maiden name and a signature.
- Don't give personal information over the phone unless absolutely necessary, and never give it unless you initiated the phone call.
- Beware of anyone asking for your Social Security number. If a company refuses to complete a transaction without it, consider taking your business elsewhere. (See Section H4 below)
- Pick up your new checks from the bank instead of having them sent to your home.
- Don't put your personal information on any computer homepage or personal computer profile.
- If you find your personal information somewhere on the Internet, demand that it be removed.
- Buy a shredder and use it religiously.

It is also important to learn more about what happens to the personal information you provide to companies, marketers and government agencies. These organizations may use your personal information to promote their own products and services or they may share it with others.

Many companies and organizations now allow you to "opt out" of having your information shared with others or used for promotional purposes. Opting out will help keep some of your information private and less vulnerable to identity theft. You can find out more about your "opt out" choices from the Federal Trade Commission. (See Section D for FTC addresses and websites).

4. Protecting Your Social Security Number

One good way to minimize the risk of identity theft is to be very careful about giving out your Social Security number (SSN). Many people think they have to provide their SSN to creditors or government entities that ask for it. But this isn't always true—in some cases, you don't have to reveal it.

All government agencies that request your SSN must give you a form explaining whether the information is mandatory or optional. For many government agencies, including tax authorities, welfare offices and state Departments of Motor Vehicles, your SSN is mandatory. But it isn't always mandatory. If it isn't, the government cannot deny you a benefit or service due to your refusal to disclose your SSN.

Employers, as well as most banks, can require that you disclose your SSN. But you are usually not required to give your SSN to private businesses. Sometimes businesses have a legitimate reason to ask for your number, but in other cases, they simply want it for general record keeping. You don't have to give a business your SSN just because they request it. Ask these questions before deciding whether to give out your number:

- Why do you need my number?
- How will my number be used?
- What law requires me to give you my number?
- What will happen if I don't give you my number?

If you're filling out a form and decide not to provide your SSN, you can leave the space blank or write "refused."

But understand that a business can refuse to serve you if you don't disclose your SSN. In some situations, you may want to disclose the number to avoid hassles down the road. In other situations, you may want to take your business elsewhere.

If you're already a victim of identity theft, consider getting a new SSN. This isn't always easy though—the Social Security Administration will only change your number if you fit their definition of "fraud victim." Even if you do fit within the definition, think carefully before you apply for a new SSN. A new SSN will not ensure a clean credit report because credit bureaus may combine the credit records from your old SSN with your new records. For more information, check out the Federal Trade Commission's website at www.ftc.gov and the Social Security Administration's website at www.ssa.gov. At the very least, you should contact the Social Security Administration to report any fraudulent use of your SSN.

5. If Your Identity Is Stolen

Minimizing the disaster of identity theft depends primarily on your vigilant efforts to guard your personal identification privacy, and thus be aware as quickly as possible that you've been the victim of an intrusion. As soon as you are aware of the problem, do the following:

- File a police report and obtain a copy. You may need to send a copy to creditors, collection agencies, credit bureaus, banks and the like.
- Contact your creditors, phone companies, utilities and banks to find out if any of your accounts have been tampered with or if any new accounts have been opened in your name. Ask to speak with someone in the security or fraud department and follow up with a letter. Immediately close any accounts that have been tampered with. Some advocate also closing accounts that haven't yet been affected—the theory being that it's just a matter of time before the thief gets to those too.

But before you do so, think carefully. You may have trouble getting new credit until the problems related to the identity theft are cleared. Instead, you could notify the creditors of unaffected accounts that you have been a victim of identity theft, set up a new password and place a Fraud Alert on the accounts.

- Close unused existing accounts.
- Fill out an FTC identity theft affidavit (www.ftc.gov).
- Call Equifax (800-525-6285), Experian (888-397-3742) and Trans Union (800-680-7289). Request that they place a "fraud alert" statement in your file and a victim's statement asking that creditors call you before opening any new accounts or changing your existing accounts.
- Report stolen checks to Telecheck (800-710-9898), National Processing Company (800-949-7379), International Check Service (800-631-9656) or Equifax (800-437-5120).
- Alert the post office if you suspect the thief may have filed a change of address form. That form will be an important piece of evidence for the police to use.
- Alert all of your utility and phone companies. If you're having trouble getting fraudulent phone charges removed from your account, contact your state Public Utility Commission for local service providers. For long-distance service and cellular providers, contact the Federal Communications Commission at www.fcc.gov or 888-CALL-FCC.
- Keep dated, concise records of your conversations and interactions with everyone you notify of the theft. Make copies of all correspondence you send and receive relating to the theft.
- Contact your local Social Security office to see if your Social Security number has been used fraudulently. (A free Social Security benefits statement is sent every year to anyone age 25 or older.) You'd notice this if your earnings record lists earnings for jobs you've never held. You can get a copy of your earnings report by calling 800-772-1213. If you notice fraudulent use of your Social Security number, call the SSA's fraud hotline at 800-269-0271.
- If your driver's license number is being used fraudulently, you can receive a new number but be prepared to show proof of theft and damage.
- File a complaint with the FTC. The FTC can't bring criminal cases but it can give you information about how to resolve problems that result from identity theft. Contact the FTC by calling the Identity Theft Hotline (877-IDTHEFT), visiting its website (www.consumer.gov/idtheft) or by writing to: Identity Theft Clearinghouse, Federal Trade Commission, 600 Pennsylvania Ave., NW, Washington, DC 20580.

You need to take control of the situation and not waste time waiting for someone else to step up and help you. Do not pay bills that you did not incur. Be persistent with police, credit bureaus, credit card companies and banks. Continue to call, write letters and keep track of your efforts to stop the theft and reverse the damage.

The California state Department of Consumer Affairs (www.dca.ca.gov) distributes a legal guide called "Credit Identity Theft: Tips to Avoid and Resolve Problems." The nonprofit Identity Theft Resource Center lists state-by-state resources for victims of identity theft at www.idtheftcenter.org/local.shtml. You can write them directly at PO Box 26833, San Diego, CA 92196; telephone 858-693-7935; or send an email to itrc@idtheftcenter.org. Remember to let them know which state you live in. Another good list of resources (state and federal agencies and laws) can be found at the LLRX.com website, www.llrx.com/features/idtheft.htm.

The Federal Trade Commission's website, www.ftc.gov, has useful materials on identity theft. From the home page, click on "Consumer Protection," then "Identity Theft."

6. Identity Theft Protection Products and Insurance

If you want to protect yourself from, or at least minimize, the financial losses that occur when your identity is stolen, consider buying special identity theft protection.

Many private companies (often security agencies) now sell products or packages designed to insure against identity theft damages or to protect you from becoming a victim. You can also find products on the Internet. Before you buy these services or products, however, check them out carefully. Some are scams designed to get your personal information and take advantage of you. One cheap product to consider—a paper shredder.

Also, a number of insurance companies sell identity theft protection—either as a separate insurance policy or as an option that comes with your homeowner's insurance policy. These policies provide compensation for common expenses associated with identity theft including lost wages, mailing costs and attorneys' fees.

Identity Theft Resources

www.ftc.gov
www.identitytheft.org
www.privacyrights.org

Law Against ID Theft

In 1998, Congress passed and President Clinton signed the Identity Theft and Assumption Deterrence Act (18 USC 1028). This law makes the use of another person's identity with the intent to commit any unlawful activity under either state or federal law a federal felony. Violations of the Act are investigated by federal agencies, including the Secret Service, FBI and Postal Inspection Service, and prosecuted by the Department of Justice. The law allows for restitution to victims.

Additionally, many states have passed or are considering laws related to identify theft. For a list of state identity theft laws, visit the Federal Consumer Information Center's website at www.consumer.gov.idtheft. Even if your state does not have a law specifically identified as an identity theft law, the issue is likely covered under other state laws.

How Creditors and Employers Use Your Credit Report

I f you've read and followed the advice in Chapter 4, you should feel confident that you've done everything you can to clean up your credit report. If you are back in good financial shape, now is the time to start thinking about rebuilding your credit. But before you do that, it helps to understand who has access to your credit report and how creditors and employers use it to evaluate your credit.

A. Who Can Look at Your Credit Report?

The federal Fair Credit Reporting Act (FCRA) (15 U.S.C. §1681 and following) and state credit reporting laws restrict who can access your credit report and how it can be used. (Appendix 2 contains the text of the FCRA.)

The people and entities that can request your credit report include:

- **Employers**

  Employers often use credit reports to conduct background checks of job applicants and to assess current employees for promotions or job reassignments. Before ordering your credit report, employers must first get your written authorization and provide certain disclosures. Many employers never look at credit reports. And those that do often will not be concerned about your financial problems. If you do have some negative information on your report, you might want to discuss it with the employer before he or she sees the report.

- **Government Agencies**

  Government agencies can request your credit report to determine whether you are eligible for public assistance. They do this to look for any hidden income or assets you might have, not to see if you have unpaid bills. The law also allows state and local government officials to get reports to help determine whether you can make child support payments.

But not all government agencies can look at your credit report. For example, district attorneys cannot look at reports to investigate criminal or civil cases and the Immigration and Naturalization Service (INS) cannot get a report for an immigration proceeding or for reviewing citizenship applications.

- **Insurance Companies**

  Insurance companies can look at your credit report. Usually, they are not interested in your credit history, but instead may ask about your medical history or about any insurance claims you have filed.

- **Collection Agencies**

  Collection agencies can look at your report when trying to collect an overdue debt from you. They mainly do this to try to locate you or find out more about your assets.

- **Judgment Creditors**

  Judgment creditors are allowed to look at credit reports in order to decide whether to begin collection efforts against you. They can also use reports for skip tracing (hiring someone to locate you or your assets).

- **Potential Creditors**

  Creditors are allowed to review your report when you apply for credit. Although this is a broad category, there are some restrictions. For a new transaction, you must have made an offer or otherwise initiated a credit transaction before the creditor can look at your report. It is important to be careful when you are shopping around, especially for cars. Dealers will try to get you to sign an authorization so that they can look at your report and size up your financial situation before beginning their sales pitch. This request will then appear on your credit report and may negatively affect your credit. (See Chapter 4, Section A, for more information about credit inquiries.)

- **Landlords and Mortgage Lenders**

  Landlords and mortgage lenders are also allowed to review your report. You can expect mortgage lenders to scrutinize your report very carefully before offering to lend you money to buy a home.

- **Utility Companies**

  Utility companies can request your credit report. However, there are special rules that prevent utility companies from denying you service in many circumstances, even if you have bad credit. Negative marks will only matter if you owe money to the particular utility company from which you seek service. Even then, most utility companies are required to offer special payment plans and programs for people with low income that allow you to get utility service by making payments that are affordable for you.

- **Student Loans and Grants**

  Most lenders offering federal student loans cannot deny your application because of poor credit. However, there are a few exceptions. For example, lenders are required to check the credit of parents applying for PLUS loans. Also, you cannot get a new federal loan if you are in default on another federal loan. For more on student loans and how to get out of default, see *Take Control of Your Student Loan Debt*, by Robin Leonard and Deanne Loonin (Nolo).

Apart from the entities listed above, most other people and businesses cannot legally request a copy of your credit report. Notably, your credit report cannot be used in divorce, child custody, immigration and other legal proceedings. Government agencies are allowed to look at your report in these cases only if they get a special court order.

It's not always easy to find out if someone who should not have access to your credit report has requested, and received, one anyway. One way to detect unauthorized users is to order your credit report and look for unfamiliar names or businesses in the list of inquiries. (See Chapter 4 for information on how to order your credit report.) If someone has requested your report illegally, you may be able to sue for violation of the Fair Credit Reporting Act—you'll probably need the help of a lawyer to do this. You should also complain to state and federal government agencies. A list of state agencies regulating credit bureaus is contained in Appendix 1. The Federal Trade Commission (at www.ftc.gov) is the primary federal enforcer of the Fair Credit Reporting Act.

B. How Credit Applications Are Evaluated

When you apply for credit, creditors use two primary methods to evaluate your request:

- Weigh your three "Cs"—capacity, collateral and character, and
- Create a "risk score" based on the information in your credit report.

1. Your Three "Cs"

A creditor needs information to determine the likelihood that you will repay a loan or pay charges you incur on a line of revolving credit. This is done by evaluating the three "Cs."

Capacity. This refers to the amount of debts you can realistically pay given your income. Creditors look at how long you've been on your job, your income level and the likelihood that it will increase over time. They also look to see that you're in a stable job or at least a stable job industry. It's important when you fill out a credit application to make your job sound stable, high-level and even "professional." Are you a secretary or are you an executive secretary or the office manager?

Finally, creditors examine your existing credit relationships, such as credit cards, bank loans and mortgages. They want to know your credit limits (you may be denied additional credit if you already have a lot of open credit lines), your current credit balances, how long you've had each account and your payment history—whether you pay late or on time.

Collateral. Creditors like to see that you have assets that they can take from you if you don't pay your debt. Owning a home or liquid assets such as a mutual fund may offer considerable comfort to a creditor reviewing an application. This is especially true if your credit report has negative notations in it, such as late payments.

Character. Creditors develop a feeling of your financial character through objective factors that show stability. These include the length of your residency, the length of your employment, whether you rent or own your home (you're more likely to stay put if you own) and whether you have checking and savings accounts.

2. Your Credit Score

Most credit reports include a credit score. Credit scores are numerical calculations that are supposed to indicate the risk that you will default on your payments. High credit scores indicate less risk and low scores indicate potential problems. Most credit scores range from lows of 300–400 to highs of 800–900. The biggest credit scoring company, Fair, Isaac and Company, estimates that about 40% of Americans have scores over 750. Anything over 750 is considered to be a very good score by most lenders.

Lenders use credit scores to help them decide whether you are a good credit risk for new credit, whether to increase or decrease an existing line of credit, to determine how easy it will be to collect on an account and even to project the likelihood that you will file for bankruptcy. Credit scores are used in about 80% of all mortgages as well as in car loans, credit cards and insurance policies. And your credit score not only determines whether you get a loan, but also what interest rate will be applied. If you get your Fair, Isaac credit score (see below), you can visit its website (at www.myfico.com), plug in your score and find out the prevailing mortgage interest rate that most lenders charge to people with that credit score.

Even though your score may determine whether you can get a loan, credit bureaus are not required to disclose your score to you (therefore, they won't appear on a credit report that you order). However, change is on the horizon. A new California law re-quires that mortgage lenders disclose credit scores to consumers shopping for a mortgage. Other states or the federal government may enact similar laws in the future.

Another big improvement recently came from Fair, Isaac and Company—they have voluntarily made credit scores available for a fee of $12.95. To get your Fair, Isaac credit score, visit www.equifax.com, www.myfico.com or www.scorepower.com.

A few other companies that create credit scores have followed suit. Trans Union now provides your credit score (at no extra charge) when you order a Trans Union credit report. Experian also offers a credit score product for $12.95. (For information on ordering a Trans Union credit report or Experian credit score, see Chapter 4, Section B.)

Although being able to view your credit score is a significant improvement, the jury is still out on how helpful the score will actually be. It is likely that you will get different scores from different companies. And consumer experts are not certain that the score you order from the Internet will be the same one that lenders use to determine whether they will extend credit to you.

Credit scoring companies most likely use the three "Cs" as guidelines for creating scores. Recently, Fair, Isaac and Company disclosed slightly more detailed factors that it uses in generating credit scores. Those factors include:

- Your payment history (about 35% of the score).
- Amounts you owe on credit accounts (about 30% of the score).
  Fair, Isaac looks at the amount you owe on all accounts and whether there is a balance. They are looking to see whether you manage credit responsibly. It may view a large number of accounts with balances as a sign that you are over-extended, and count it against you.
- Length of your credit history (about 15% of the score). In general, a longer credit history increases the score.

- Your new credit (about 10% of the score). Fair, Isaac likes to see that you have an established credit history and that you don't have too many new accounts. Opening several accounts in a short period of time can represent greater risk.
- Types of credit (about 10% of the score). Fair, Isaac is looking for a "healthy mix" of different types of credit. This factor is usually important only if there is not a lot of other information upon which to base your score.

If you do get your credit score, and it seems lower than it should be, there may be a mistake on your credit report. (See Chapter 4 for information on how to clean up your credit report, including getting rid of errors.)

To keep up on credit scoring developments, visit www.creditscoring.com, a private website devoted to credit scoring.

■

CHAPTER 6

Building and Maintaining Good Credit

Establishing and keeping a good credit record is the final step in repairing your credit. This chapter covers the many ways you can build a positive credit history, from getting credit in your own name if you're married or divorced, applying for credit cards, getting a secured card and obtaining bank loans. It also provides tips on how to maintain good credit, from using credit cards wisely to avoiding credit repair clinics.

If you take the steps suggested in this chapter, you will probably be able to get a major credit card or loan in approximately two years. And, in about four years, you may be able to qualify for a mortgage.

But before you start this process, make sure you are financially ready to get more credit. If you get new credit too soon, while you're still in financial trouble, you're likely to dig yourself into deeper debt. First focus on stabilizing your employment, income and debt situation. Get your high priority debts, such as rent, mortgage or car payments, under control. Once you're in decent financial shape, start following the strategies in this chapter to build good credit.

Should You Repair Your Credit?

Habitual overspending can be just as hard to overcome as excessive gambling or drinking. If you think you may be a compulsive spender, one of the worst things you can do is repair your credit and then get more. Instead, you need to get a handle on your spending habits.

Debtors Anonymous, a 12-step support program similar to Alcoholics Anonymous, has programs nationwide. If a Debtors Anonymous group or a therapist recommends that you stay out of the credit system for a while, follow that advice. Even if you don't feel you're a compulsive spender, paying as you spend may still be the way to go—because of finance charges, transaction fees and other charges, buying on credit costs between 20% and 25% more than paying with cash.

Debtors Anonymous groups meet all over the country. If you can't find one in your area, send a self-addressed, stamped envelope to Debtors Anonymous, General Services Board, P.O. Box 920888, Needham, MA 02492-0009. Or call their office and speak to a volunteer or leave your name, address and a request for information. The number is 781-453-2743. You can also visit their website at www.debtorsanonymous.org.

Concern about habitual overspending isn't the only reason to stay outside the credit system. Followers of a movement known as "voluntary simplicity" suggest that reliance on credit is one of the reasons people are overworked, overstressed and have trouble slowing down. Credit gives us the chance to consume—and often we consume far more than we need to live comfortably and at an easy pace.

Much has been written about voluntarily downshifting. Advocates are not suggesting that we all move to the wilderness, quit our jobs and live without electricity and running water. But they do suggest that we take a hard look at our reliance on money—and credit—to bring us happiness.

For more information on voluntary simplicity, take a look at any of these resources:

- *Simplify Your Life: 100 Ways to Slow Down and Enjoy the Things That Really Matter*, by Elaine St. James (Hyperion).
- *Get a Life: You Don't Need a Million to Retire Well*, by Ralph Warner (Nolo).
- *Your Money or Your Life*, by Joe Dominguez and Vicki Robin (Penguin Books).

➡ If you've never been married, skip ahead to Section C.

A. Build Credit in Your Own Name

If you are married, separated or divorced, and most of the credit you obtained is in your spouse's or ex-spouse's name only, you should start to get credit in your name too.

Getting credit in your own name is also an excellent strategy for repairing your credit if:

- All or most of your financial problems can be attributed to your spouse, or
- You and your spouse have gone through financial difficulties together, but most credit was in your spouse's name only.

In order to understand how this works, you first must learn about which of your spouse's accounts can appear on your report. Here are the rules:

- Credit bureaus must include information about your spouse's account on your credit report in two situations: (1) you and your spouse have a joint account (that is, you both can use it), or (2) you are obligated (responsible for paying) on an account belonging to your spouse, even if your spouse is the primary signer or obligor on the account.
- Credit bureaus cannot include information about your spouse's account on your credit report if the account is not joint and you are not responsible for paying the account.

This is usually good news if you are worried that your spouse's negative credit history may reflect badly on you—delinquent accounts in your spouse's name only should not appear on your credit report. However, if you are now divorced or separated and had relied primarily on your spouse to obtain credit, so that most loans and credit cards were in your spouse's name only, you won't have a lengthy history of good credit in your report. You now need to start building good credit in your own name. If you are still married, you can start by mak-

ing sure that all joint accounts and accounts that you are obligated to pay appear on your credit report too. Then, follow the steps outlined in the rest of this chapter for building credit.

B. Ask Creditors to Consider Your Spouse's Credit History

Although a credit bureau cannot include information about your spouse's positive credit accounts on your credit report (unless the account meets one of the two criteria listed in Section A, above), if you are applying for a loan, credit card or other type of credit, you can always ask the creditor to consider any of your spouse's accounts that reflect on your creditworthiness too. For example, if you and your spouse make payments on your spouse's account with joint checks, bring this to the creditor's attention. A creditor doesn't have to consider this information, but it may.

C. Get Credit Cards and Use Them Wisely

If you survived your financial disaster and managed to hold onto one of your credit cards or a department store or gasoline card, use it and pay your bills on time. Your credit history will improve quickly. Most credit reports show payment histories for 24–36 months. If you charge something every month, no matter how small, and pay at least the minimum required every month, your credit report will show steady and proper use of revolving credit.

⚠ **Charge only a small amount each month and pay it in full.** By paying in full, you will avoid incurring interest, as long as you have a card with a grace period. Consumer groups point out that the average consumer who makes only the minimum payment each month ends up paying hundreds of dollars in interest charges alone. For example, if you charge $1,000 on a 19.8% credit card and pay it off by making the minimum payments each month, you'll take over eight years to pay off the loan and will pay almost $850 in interest.

1. Applying for Credit Cards

If you don't currently have a credit card, apply for one. Keep in mind the general guidelines under the three "Cs" discussion in Chapter 5, Section B.2, when completing your credit application. Don't lie, but present yourself in the best possible light.

⚠ Don't plunge in until you're ready.
Getting new credit cards before your finances are in order is a bad idea. Wait until you're out of financial hot water before you apply for credit.

It's often easiest to obtain a card from a department store or gasoline company. These companies usually open your account with a very low credit line. If you start with one credit card, charge items and pay the bill on time, other companies will issue you a card. When you use department store and gasoline cards, try not to carry a balance from one month to the next. The interest rate on these cards can be very high.

Next, apply for a regular credit card from a bank, such as a Visa, MasterCard or Discover card. Competition for customers is fierce, and you may be able to find a card with relatively low initial rates. Depending on how bad your credit history is, however, you may be eligible only for a low credit line or a card with a high interest rate. If you use the card and make your payments, after a year or so you can apply to increase your line of credit or reduce the interest rate.

In fact, no matter what your situation, it makes sense to call your credit card company and ask for a lower interest rate. A study conducted by the United States Public Interest Research Group in 2002 found that more than half of the consumers who complained to their credit card company were able to reduce their interest rate, usually by as much as one third. (To find out more, contact U.S. PIRG at www.uspirg.org.)

It's Raining Credit Cards

If you've been through bankruptcy or other tough financial times but your problems are behind you, or you've never had credit, you may be considered an excellent candidate for a credit card. Your creditors won't tell you this. It's an industry secret they'd like to keep that way.

Credit card issuers send out approximately three billion solicitations each year to American consumers. This number represents an enormous growth since the early 1990s. While the number of American adults hasn't risen that dramatically, the number of American people now considered creditworthy has.

Credit card issuers operate in a fiercely competitive environment. People who have been through bankruptcy are now considered great credit risks—their debt is gone, they have a history of using credit and *they can't file for bankruptcy again for another six years*. In fact, a Texas bankruptcy judge asked a couple who filed for bankruptcy to keep track of how many credit card solicitations they received during the two-year period after they filed their case. The total: 53, with credit limits ranging from $100 to $20,000.

And people who have been through bankruptcy aren't the only people with stuffed mailboxes. New immigrants, low-wage earners and others traditionally kept out of the credit world are being invited to participate at astronomical rates.

Beware of all these offers. They are not meant to be flattering nor are they a sign that you can afford more credit. Credit card issuers are looking for consumers who will run up big balances and pay a lot of interest.

Many people who have had serious financial problems misused or overused their credit cards. The following tips will help you when you apply for credit cards or an increased credit limit:

Be consistent with the name you use. Use your middle initial always or never. Always use your generation (Jr., Sr., II, III, etc.).

Take advantage of preapproved credit for department store, gasoline and bank cards. If your credit is shot, you may not have the luxury of shopping around.

Be honest, but appear sympathetic. Lenders are especially apt to ignore past credit problems that were out of your control—such as a job layoff or illness.

Bolster your credit application. Don't lie, but don't denigrate yourself, either. For example, if you're an administrative assistant, don't put "clerk/ typist" for your job title. Also, if you are married and your spouse has excellent credit, apply jointly or at least indicate on the credit application that you are married.

Apply for credit when you are most likely to get it. For example, apply when you are working, when you've lived at the same address for at least a year and when you don't have an unusually high number of inquiries on your credit report.

Apply for credit from creditors with whom you've done business. For example, if you had a Sears charge card from a store in New Jersey and you moved to California, apply for a Sears card from a store near your new home.

Don't get swept up by credit card gimmicks. Before applying for a credit card that gives you rebates, credit for future purchases or other perks, make sure you will benefit by the offer. Some are good deals, especially cards that give you cash back. But in general, a card with no annual fee and/or low interest rate usually beats the cards with "deals."

Scrutinize any preapproval solicitations for nonbank cards. A "gold" or "platinum" card with a high credit limit may be nothing more than a card that lets you purchase items through catalogues provided by the company itself. No other merchant accepts these cards and the company won't report your charges and payments to the credit bureaus. Also, the items in the catalogues are usually high priced and of low quality.

When it comes to obtaining a new credit card, you may not have as many choices as people who already have good credit. But you should still do some comparison shopping to make sure you are getting the best deal available to you. Credit card terms and interest rates vary—and some of those variations can make a huge difference to your wallet. Always shop for the card with the best interest rate and terms. Here's what you should look for in a credit card:

- **Avoid high interest rates.** Credit card companies disclose the interest rate in several ways, but you want to look at the Annual Percentage Rate (APR). This is the amount of interest, transaction fees and other charges that you will pay per year, expressed as a percentage. It is the best indicator of the actual interest you will pay.

- **Avoid low introductory rates.** Some cards have a low "introductory rate" (also called a "teaser rate.") After a few months, the interest rate will skyrocket. Also, sometimes the advertised rate only applies to certain people, such as those earning a high income. The card company charges a much higher rate to those who don't qualify—which could mean an unpleasant surprise when your first bill arrives.

- **Beware of unfair interest calculations.** Most banks charge interest on the balance owed. A growing number, however, charge interest based on the average daily balance. This is how it works: Say you charge $1,500 on your credit card and pay $1,200 on the due date. When your next bill arrives, a bank using the average daily balance will charge interest on the $1,500 average daily balance from the previous month, not on the $300 you still owe.

- **Review the grace period.** This is the interest-free period of time between the purchase date and the bill due date. It is usually available only to those who do not carry a balance. If you pay your bill in full each month, make sure you have a grace period. Otherwise, you'll pay interest from the date of your purchase. If you carry a balance, a grace period is not important.

- **Avoid high annual fees.** Some credit card companies charge you a flat fee (in addition to interest and other charges) for using their card. Some do not. If you pay off your balance each month, you want a card without an annual fee. If you carry a balance, a card with an annual fee but a low interest rate may be better than a card with no annual fee but a high interest rate.

- **Find out if you'll be charged higher interest rates for cash advances and late payments.** Virtually all credit cards charge higher interest rates for cash advances. And with almost all cards, if you make late payments, the company imposes a new, much higher interest rate. If you think you might pay late once in a while (be realistic), check out these interest rates. Some are as high as 20%.

- **Watch out for extra fees.** Many, if not most, credit card companies charge a hefty fee (upward of $35) if your payment is late or you exceed your credit limit.

- **Evaluate rebates, free miles and other perks.** Many credit cards now allow you to earn cash back, free airline miles, discounts on goods and services, funds for charity or other bonuses by using the card. Don't sign up for a card based on these perks alone—be sure to consider the other card terms as well. If you will pay high interest and high annual

fees, you might be better off without the perks. You can use the money you save to buy airline tickets or contribute to your favorite charity.

Many websites will help you shop for a credit card by surveying large numbers of credit card deals. You can compare and contrast terms and find the best card for you. A few to try are: www.cardtrack.com, www.bankrate.com and www.consumer-action.org (click on the "2001-2002 Credit Card Survey"). For more information on credit cards and how to shop for them, see the Federal Reserve Board's website at http://federalreserve.gov/pubs/shop.

Once you receive a credit card, protect yourself and your efforts to repair your credit by following these suggestions:

Send your creditors a change of address when you move. Many creditors provide change of address boxes on their monthly bills. For your other creditors, you can send a letter, call the customer service phone number or use a post office change of address postcard.

If you need an increase in your credit limit, ask for it. Many creditors will close accounts or charge late fees on customers who exceed their credit limits. But pay close attention; if you're charging to the limit on your credit card, you may be heading for financial trouble.

Take steps to protect your cards. Sign your cards as soon as they arrive. If you have a personal identification number (PIN) that allows you take cash advances, keep the number in your head and never write it down near your credit card. Make a list of your credit card issuers, the account numbers and the issuer's phone numbers so you can quickly call if you need to report a lost or stolen card.

Don't give your credit card number to anyone over the phone unless you placed the call and are certain of the company's reputation. Never, never, never give your credit card number to someone who calls you and tries to sell you something or claims to need your credit card number to send you a "prize." *These are scam artists.*

Read the Fine Print: Beware of Creditors Trying to Collect Discharged Debts

If you've been through bankruptcy, you're no longer liable to pay the debts discharged in your case. It's too bad many creditors don't see it that way.

Read all credit card solicitations carefully, particularly ones that promise to restore your credit. The fine print might tell you that by signing up for the card, you voluntarily agree to repay debts you discharged in your bankruptcy case. The solicitation won't necessarily come from the original creditor whose debt you wiped out. Often the creditor sells the debt to another, so you won't recognize the new creditor (who is now the current owner of your old debt).

Attempts to have you voluntarily repay discharged debts don't come only in the form of credit card solicitations. You might also receive phone calls or dunning letters threatening legal action—"intent to file suit"—if you don't pay up.

Remind any creditor that attempts to collect discharged debts are illegal under the Bankruptcy Code (11 U.S.C. § 524(a)) and prohibited by the Fair Debt Collection Practices Act (15 U.S.C. § 1692e).

2. Cosigners and Guarantors

If you can't get a credit card or loan on your own, consider asking a friend or relative to cosign or serve as guarantor on an account. A cosigner is someone who promises to repay a loan or credit card charges if the primary debtor defaults. Similarly, a guarantor promises the credit grantor that he will pay if the primary debtor does not. Usually, neither the cosigner's nor the guarantor's name appears on the credit account.

Although getting a cosigner or guarantor will help you get credit, it may not help you build credit in all situations. On some cosigned accounts, the creditor will report the information on the cosigner's credit report only, not on yours. The best option is to ask if you can use a guarantor instead of a cosigner. It should make no difference to the creditor.

⚠ **Cosigners and guarantors should fully understand their obligations before they sign on.** For example, if the primary debtor doesn't pay and erases the debt in bankruptcy, the cosigner or guarantor remains fully liable. The Federal Trade Commission's Credit Practices Rule requires that cosigners of credit issued by a financial institution be given the following notice:

> You are being asked to guarantee this debt. Think carefully before you do so. If the borrower doesn't pay the debt, you will have to. Be sure you can afford to pay if you have to, and that you want to accept this responsibility.
>
> You may have to pay up to the full amount of the debt if the borrower does not pay. You may also have to pay late fees or collection costs, which increase this amount.
>
> The creditor can collect this debt from you without first trying to collect from the borrower. The creditor can use the same collection methods against you that can be used against the borrower, such as suing you, garnishing your wages, etc. If this debt is ever in default, that fact may become a part of your credit record.

3. Authorized User Accounts

Another way to repair your credit using a credit card relies on the generosity of a friend or relative you trust.

If you can find someone who is willing to add you to an account as an "authorized user," you can use the credit line but you are not responsible for repaying the charges. The account holder must request that your name be added to the account and can ask that a card be issued in your name. Once your name is on the account, information about the account will probably be added to your file—and you'll be listed as an authorized user.

Of course, because the information concerning the account is reported in your credit file, this technique requires that the account holder not default. If she does, that information will appear in your credit report—exactly what you don't want.

4. Secured Credit Cards

Many people with poor credit histories are denied regular credit cards. If your application is rejected, consider whether you truly need a credit card. Millions of people get along just fine without them. If you decide that you really need a card—for example, you travel quite a bit and need a card to reserve hotel rooms and rent cars—then you can apply for a secured credit card. With a secured credit card, you deposit a sum of money with a bank and are given a credit card with a credit limit for a percentage of the amount you deposit—as low as 50% and as high as 120%. Depending on the bank, you'll be required to deposit as little as a few hundred dollars or as much as a few thousand.

Unfortunately, secured credit cards can be expensive. Many banks charge application and processing fees in addition to an annual fee. Also the interest rate on secured credit cards is often close to 22%, while you earn only 2% or 3% on the money you deposit. And some banks have eliminated the grace period—that is, interest on your balance begins to accrue on the date you charge, not 25 days later. If you find a card with a grace period and pay your bill in full each month, you can avoid the interest charges.

Many secured credit cards have a conversion option. This lets you convert the card into a regular credit card after several months or a year if you use the secured card responsibly. Because regular credit cards typically have lower interest rates and annual fees than secured credit cards, it's usually preferable to obtain a card with a conversion option.

To find a bank offering a secured credit card, call some local banks or do some surfing on the Internet. Two sources of information are Bank Rate Monitor (www.bankrate.com) and BHA Customer Service, 540-389-5445.

Avoid 900-number advertisements for "instant credit" or other come-ons. Obtaining a secured credit card through one of these programs will probably cost you a lot—in application fees, processing fees and phone charges. Sometimes you call one 900 number and are told you must call a second or third number. These ads also frequently mislead consumers into thinking their line of credit will be higher than it actually will be.

Don't use your home as collateral. If you do opt for a secured credit card, make sure it isn't secured by your home. If it is, and you get behind on your card payments, you could lose your home.

How Many Credit Cards Should You Carry?

Once you succeed in getting a credit card, you might be hungry to apply for many more cards. Not so fast. Having too much credit probably contributed to your debt problems in the first place. Ideally, you should carry one bank credit card, one department store card and one gasoline card. Your inclination may be to charge everything on your bank card and not bother using a department store or gasoline card. When creditors look in your credit file, however, they want to see that you can handle more than one credit account at a time. Don't build up interest charges on these cards—just use them and pay the bill in full.

Creditors frown on applicants who have a lot of open credit. So keeping many cards may mean that you'll be turned down for other credit—perhaps credit you really need. And if your credit applications are turned down, your file will contain inquiries from the companies that rejected you. Your credit file will look like you were desperately trying to get credit, something creditors never like to see.

5. Closing Credit Card Accounts

If you want to close some accounts, here are some rules to follow:

- Close accounts you don't need. You can close an account even if you haven't paid off the balance. The card issuer will close your account, cancel your privileges and send you monthly statements until you pay off your balance. Or contact the bank whose card you are keeping and ask it to transfer your remaining balance on the account you are closing to the account you are keeping.

- Close accounts on which you are delinquent—otherwise the credit card issuer may close them for you. If you're delinquent on all your accounts, keep open the most current account.

- If you pay your bill in full each month—that is, you don't carry a balance—close the accounts with the highest annual fees. Make sure that the accounts you keep open have a grace period—a 20-25 day period each month in which you can pay off your bill and not incur any interest.

- If you carry a balance, close the accounts with the highest interest rates and shortest grace periods. Also, read your contract to understand the credit card company's billing practice. Interest may be calculated on the previous two months' balance, the average daily balance for the month or your balance at the end of the billing cycle. Keep the cards that charge interest on the balance at the end of the billing cycle.

How to Close a Credit Card Account

If you want to close a credit card account, make sure you do it the right way.

- Write a letter to the company and request a "hard close." If you don't do this, the company may give you a "soft close," which means new charges can go through, even though you asked that the account be closed. With a soft close, you are susceptible to credit card fraud.

- Also request, in writing, that the credit card company report to the credit bureaus that your account was "closed by consumer request." Accounts that are erroneously reported as "closed by creditor" will hurt your credit rating.

- After 30 days, check your credit report to ensure that it reflects that the account in question was "closed by consumer request."

D. Open Deposit Accounts

Creditors look for bank accounts as a sign of stability. Quite frankly, they also look for bank accounts as a source of how you will pay your bills. If you fill out a credit application and cannot provide a checking account number, you probably won't be given credit.

A savings or money market account, too, will improve your standing with creditors. Even if you never deposit additional money into the account, creditors assume that people who have savings or money market accounts use them. Having an account reassures creditors of two things: You are making an effort to build up savings, and if you don't pay your bill and the creditor must sue you to collect, it has a source to collect its judgment.

Just because you've had poor credit history, you shouldn't be denied an account. Shop around and compare fees, such as check writing fees, ATM fees, monthly service charges, the minimum balance to waive the monthly charge, interest rates on savings and the like.

To learn more about ATM and other bank fees, visit the following websites: www.uspirg.org (U.S. Public Interest Research Group), www.consumersunion.org (Consumers Union), www.consumer-action.org (Consumer Action) and www.ftc.gov (Federal Trade Commission).

E. Work With Local Merchants

Another way to repair your credit is to approach a local merchant (such as an electronics or furniture store) and arrange to purchase an item on credit. Many local stores will work with you in setting up a payment schedule, but be prepared to put down a deposit of up to 30% or to pay a high rate of interest. If you still don't qualify, the merchant might agree to give you credit if you get someone to cosign or guarantee the loan. (See Section C.2, above.) Or you may be able to get credit by first buying an item on layaway.

Even if a local merchant won't extend you credit, it may very well let you make a purchase on a layaway plan. When you purchase an item on layaway, the seller keeps the merchandise until you fully pay for it. Only then are you entitled to pick it up. One advantage of layaway is that you don't pay interest. One disadvantage is that it may be months before you actually get the item. This might be fine if you're buying a dress for your cousin's wedding that is eight months away. This isn't so fine if your mattress is so shot that you wake up with a backache every morning.

Layaway purchases are not reported to credit bureaus. If you purchase an item on layaway and make all the payments on time, however, the store may be willing to issue you a store credit card or store credit privileges.

F. Obtain a Bank Loan

One way to repair your credit is to take some money you've saved and open a savings account. You ask the bank to give you a loan against the money in your account. In exchange, you have no access to your money—you give your passbook to the bank and the bank won't give you an ATM card for the account—so there's no risk to the bank if you fail to make the payments. If the bank doesn't offer these types of loans, apply for a personal loan and offer either a cosigner or to secure it against some collateral you own.

No matter what kind of loan you get, be sure you know the following:

- **Does the bank report these loan payments to credit bureaus?** This is key; the whole reason you take out the loan is to repair your credit. If a bank doesn't report your payments to a credit bureau, there's no reason to take out a loan.
- **What is the minimum deposit amount required for loans?** Some banks won't give you a loan unless you have $3,000 in an account; others will lend you money on $50. Find a bank that fits your budget.

- **What is the interest rate?** The interest rate on the loan is usually much higher than what people with good credit pay. You will probably pay between 8% and 12% interest on the loan. Yes, this means you'll lose a little money on the transaction, but it can be worth it if you're determined to repair your credit.

- **What is the maximum amount you can borrow?** On passbook loans, banks won't lend you 100% of what's in your account; most will lend you between 80% and 90%.

- **What is the repayment schedule?** Banks usually give you one to three years to repay the loan. Some banks have no minimum monthly repayment amount on passbook loans; you could pay nothing for nearly the entire loan period and then pay the entire balance in the last month. Although you can pay the loan back in only one or two payments, don't. Pay it off over at least 12 months so that monthly installment payments appear in your credit file.

G. Avoid Credit Repair Clinics

You've probably seen ads for companies that claim they can fix your credit, qualify you for a loan or get you a credit card. Their pitches are tempting, especially if your credit is bad and you desperately want to buy a new car or house.

Avoid these outfits. They are a bad idea, for two reasons: First, they charge you for doing what you can do yourself, or with the help of a nonprofit debt counselor. Some of them are more interested in helping themselves to your money than in doing you any good—they'll take your fee and disappear, paying just a few of your creditors or none. Second, some of them are extremely shady or outright criminal. Many of their practices are fraudulent, deceptive and even illegal. Some suggest that you create a new identity by applying for an IRS Employer Identification number (EIN), a nine-digit number that resembles a Social Security number, and use it instead of your Social Security number. Not only is this illegal, but by using an EIN, you won't earn Social Security benefits—and, it doesn't work.

Credit repair clinics devise new schemes as often as consumer protection agencies catch onto their previous ones.

Even assuming that a credit repair company is legitimate, don't listen to its come-ons. These companies can't do anything for you that you can't do yourself. What they will do, however, is charge you between $250 and $5,000 for their unnecessary services. Here's what credit repair clinics claim to be able to do for you:

Remove incorrect information from your credit file. You can do that yourself under the Fair Credit Reporting Act. See Chapter 4.

Remove correct, but negative, information from your credit file. Negative items in your credit file can legally stay there for seven or ten years, as long as they are correct. No one can wave a wand and make them go away. One tactic of credit repair services is to try to take advantage of the law requiring credit bureaus to verify information if the customer disputes it. Credit repair clinics do this by challenging every item in a credit file—negative, positive or neutral—with the hope of overwhelming the credit bureau into removing information without verifying it. Credit bureaus are aware of this tactic and often dismiss these challenges on the ground that they are frivolous, a right credit bureaus have under the Fair Credit Reporting Act. You are better off getting your file and selectively challenging the incomplete and inaccurate items.

Even if the credit bureau removes information that a credit bureau had the right to include in your file, it's no doubt only a temporary removal. Most correct information reappears after 30–60 days, when the creditor that first reported the information to the credit bureaus re-reports it.

Get outstanding debt balances and court judgments removed from your credit file. Credit repair clinics often advise debtors to pay outstanding debts if the creditor agrees to remove the negative information from your credit file. This is certainly a negotiation tactic you want to consider (see Chapter 3, Section C), but you don't need to pay a credit repair clinic for this advice.

Get a major credit card. Credit repair clinics can give you a list of banks that offer secured credit cards. While this information is helpful in rebuilding credit, it's not worth hundreds or thousands of dollars—you can get a list yourself for little or nothing. (See Section C.4, above.)

The federal Credit Repair Organizations Act (15 U.S.C. §§1679–1679j) regulates for-profit credit repair clinics (the text is included in Appendix 2). Some dubious credit repair clinics have tried to get around these regulations by setting themselves up as nonprofits, but they still take your money and provide poor results—or do nothing for you that you couldn't do for yourself.

Under the federal law, a credit repair clinic must:

- inform you of your rights under the Fair Credit Reporting Act
- accurately represent what it can and cannot do
- not collect any money until all promised services are performed
- provide a written contract, and
- let you cancel the contract within three days of signing.

Any lawsuit you bring against a credit repair clinic for violation of this law must be filed within five years of the violation. A court may award actual damages, punitive damages (meant to punish) and attorneys' fees.

A few states provide additional protections to consumers who use credit repair clinics. For example, some states give you more than three days to cancel the credit repair contract, require the credit repair clinic to perform the promised services within a specific amount of time and require that the credit repair clinic inform you about available nonprofit credit counseling services. The chart below lists the states that provide these additional protections.

The chart below lists the states that provide these additional protections and the code section where you can find the text of these provisions. To find your state law, visit your public library or local law library. Or, visit Nolo's website, at www.nolo.com and click on the "State Law" tab of the Law Center.

If you're still tempted to use a credit repair organization (whether or not it claims to be a nonprofit), do the following:

- Ask whether or not the company is bonded. A company that is bonded has posted money in the event it goes out of business or goes bankrupt and dissatisfied consumers seek a refund. A legitimate company should be willing to give you the name of the company through which it is bonded. Call the bonding company for verification.
- Ask to see a copy of the contract before you sign. Carefully check the company's fees, claims of what it can do and your right to a refund. Avoid any company that won't give you a written agreement or a right to cancel if you change your mind.
- Call your local Better Business Bureau and your state consumer affairs office (a list is in Appendix 1) to see if either has complaints on file for the company.
- Ask for the names and phone numbers of satisfied customers. Be wary of any satisfied customers you speak to whose claims sound nearly verbatim like the claims of the company. These people are probably phonies—people who pose as satisfied customers, but who never used the company's service and are simply paid to say good things about the company.

H. Avoid Becoming the Victim of Credit Discrimination

When you're trying to build good credit, the last thing you need is to be denied credit for a reason other than poor creditworthiness. Unfortunately, some people are denied credit for reasons entirely unrelated to their ability to pay, such as their race, gender or age.

Fortunately, several powerful federal laws and some state laws prohibit discrimination in credit transactions. This section discusses the laws prohibiting credit discrimination and provides information on what to do if you think a creditor has violated one of these laws.

State Laws Providing Additional Protections Concerning Credit Repair Clinics

Arizona

Ariz. Rev. Stat. Ann. §§ 44-1701 to 44-1712

Credit repair service may not charge or collect a fee for referring consumer to a retail seller who will or may extend credit that is on substantially the same terms as those available to the general public.

Arkansas

Ark. Code Ann. §§ 4-91-101 to 4-91-109

Credit repair service may not charge or collect a fee for referring consumer to a retail seller who will or may extend credit that is on substantially the same terms as those available to the general public.

Cancellation rights. May cancel contract within 5 days of signing. Any payment must be returned within 10 days of receipt of cancellation notice.

California

Cal. Civ. Code §§ 1789.10 to 1789.22

Credit repair service may not: charge or collect a fee for referring consumer to a retail seller who will or may extend credit that is on substantially the same terms as those available to the general public or on the same terms that would have been extended without the assistance of the credit repair organization; submit a debtor's dispute to a consumer credit reporting agency without the debtor's knowledge; or use a consumer credit reporting agency's telephone system or toll-free number to represent the caller as the debtor without the debtor's authorization.

Cancellation rights. May cancel contract within 5 working days of signing.

Time limit for performing services. 6 months.

Colorado

Colo. Rev. Stat. §§ 12-14.5-101 to 12-14.5-113

Cancellation rights. May cancel contract within 5 working days of signing.

Connecticut

Conn. Gen. Stat. Ann. § 36a-700

State protections do not exceed federal laws.

Delaware

Del. Code Ann. tit. 6, §§ 2401 to 2414

Credit repair service may not charge or collect a fee for referring consumer to a retail seller who will or may extend credit that is on substantially the same terms as those available to the general public.

Credit repair service must disclose a complete and accurate statement of the availability of nonprofit credit counseling services.

Time limit for performing services. 180 days.

District of Columbia

D.C. Code Ann. §§ 28-4601 to 28-4608

Credit repair service may not charge or collect a fee for referring consumer to a retail seller who will or may extend credit that is on substantially the same terms as those available to the general public.

Cancellation rights. May cancel contract within 5 calendar days of signing. Must be reimbursed within 10 days of receipt of cancellation notice.

Florida

Fla. Stat. Ann. §§ 817.701 to 817.706

Cancellation rights. May cancel contract within 5 days of signing. Any payment must be returned within 10 days of receipt of cancellation notice.

Georgia

Ga. Code Ann. §§ 16-9-59; 18-5-1 to 18-5-3

Who may provide service. Only nonprofit organizations or federally regulated banks may offer credit repair services; attorneys and real estate brokers may provide credit repair services incidental to their regular business practice.

Hawaii

Haw. Rev. Stat. § 481B-12

State protections do not exceed federal laws.

Idaho

Idaho Code §§ 26-2222, 26-2223

Who may provide service. Only nonprofit organizations may provide credit counseling or other debt management services.

Illinois

815 Ill. Comp. Stat. §§ 605/1 to 605/16

Credit repair service may not charge or collect a fee for referring consumer to a retail seller who will or may extend credit that is on substantially the same terms as those available to the general public.

State Laws Providing Additional Protections Concerning Credit Repair Clinics (continued)

Cancellation rights. Any payment must be returned within 10 days of receipt of cancellation notice.

Indiana

Ind. Code Ann. §§ 24-5-15-1 to 24-5-15-11

Credit repair service may not charge or collect a fee for referring consumer to a retail seller who will or may extend credit that is on substantially the same terms as those available to the general public.

Credit repair service must disclose a complete and accurate statement of the availability of nonprofit credit counseling services.

Cancellation rights. Any payment must be returned within 10 days of receipt of cancellation notice, or any other written notice.

Iowa

Iowa Code §§ 538A.1 to 538A.14

Credit repair service may not charge or collect a fee for referring consumer to a retail seller who will or may extend credit that is on substantially the same terms as those available to the general public.

Cancellation rights. Any payment must be returned within 10 days of receipt of cancellation notice.

Kansas

Kan. Stat. Ann. §§ 50-1101 to 50-1115

Credit repair service may not charge or collect a fee for referring consumer to a retail seller who will or may extend credit that is on substantially the same terms as those available to the general public.

Credit repair service must disclose a complete and accurate statement of the availability of nonprofit credit counseling services.

Kentucky

Ky. Rev. Stat. Ann. §§ 380.010 to 390.990

Who may provide service. Debt adjustment services may be provided only by a nonprofit organization, attorney, debtor's regular full-time employee, creditor providing service at no cost or lender who, at the debtor's request, adjusts debts at no additional cost as part of disbursing the loan funds.

Louisiana

La. Rev. Stat. Ann. §§ 9:3573.1 to 9:3573.16

Credit repair service may not make nonessential requests for debtor's credit information from a credit reporting organization.

Credit repair service must disclose a complete and accurate statement of the availability of nonprofit credit counseling services.

Cancellation rights. May cancel contract within 5 days of signing. Any payment must be returned within 10 days of receipt of cancellation notice.

Maine

Me. Rev. Stat. Ann. tit. 9-A, §§ 10-101 to 10-401

Credit repair service is required to keep consumer fees in an escrow account separate from any operating accounts of the business, pending completion of services offered.

Maryland

Md. Code Ann. [Com. Law] §§ 14-1901 to 14-1916

Credit repair service may not: charge or collect a fee for referring consumer to a retail seller who will or may extend credit that is on substantially the same terms as those available to the general public; or assist a consumer to obtain credit at a rate of interest which is in violation of federal or state maximum rate.

Cancellation rights. Any payment must be returned within 10 days of receipt of cancellation notice.

Massachusetts

Mass. Gen. Laws ch. 93, §§ 68A to 68E

Credit repair service may not charge or collect a fee for referring consumer to a retail seller who will or may extend credit that is on substantially the same terms as those available to the general public.

Cancellation rights. Any payment must be returned within 10 days of receipt of cancellation notice.

Michigan

Mich. Comp. Laws § 445.1821 to 445.1825

Credit repair service may not: charge or collect a fee for referring consumer to a retail seller who will or may extend credit that is on substantially the same terms as those available to the general public; submit a debtor's dispute to a consumer credit reporting agency without the debtor's knowledge; or provide a service that is not pursuant to a written contract.

State Laws Providing Additional Protections Concerning Credit Repair Clinics (continued)

Time limit for performing services. 90 days.

Minnesota

Minn. Stat. Ann. §§ 332.52 to 332.60

Credit repair service may not charge or collect a fee for referring consumer to a retail seller who will or may extend credit that is on substantially the same terms as those available to the general public.

Credit repair service must disclose: the name and address of any person who directly or indirectly owns or controls a 10% or greater interest in the credit services organization; any litigation or unresolved complaint filed within the preceding 5 years with the state, any other state or the U.S., or a notarized statement that there has been no such litigation or complaint; and the percentage of customers during the past year for whom the credit services organization fully and completely performed the services it agreed to provide.

Cancellation rights. May cancel contract within 5 days of signing. Any payment must be returned within 10 days of receipt of cancellation notice.

Mississippi

Mississippi passed the Nonprofit Debt Management Services Act in 2003. It has not yet been codified.

Who may provide service. Only a nonprofit organization may operate as a licensed Debt Management Service.

Credit repair service may not purchase any debt, lend money or provide credit, operate as a debt collector or structure a negative amortization agreement for the consumer.

Credit repair service is required to maintain separate account records for each consumer. May not commingle trust accounts with any business operating accounts

Fees. May not charge more than: a one-time fee of $75.00 for setting up a debt management plan; $25.00 per month to maintain plan; $15.00 for obtaining an individual credit report or $25.00 for a joint report. Educational courses and products may be offered for a fee, but consumer must be informed that purchasing them is not mandatory for receiving debt management services.

Missouri

Mo. Rev. Stat. §§ 407.635 to 407.644

Credit repair service may not charge or collect a fee for referring consumer to a retail seller who will or may extend credit that is on substantially the same terms as those available to the general public.

Credit repair service must disclose a complete and accurate statement of the availability of nonprofit credit counseling services.

Cancellation rights. Any payment must be returned within 10 days of receipt of cancellation notice.

Time limit for performing services. 180 days.

Montana

Mont. Code Ann. §§ 31-3-201 to 31-3-203

Who may provide service. Nonprofit or charitable corporations or associations may provide debt adjustment or debt management services. Exceptions: business or person who provides a $10,000 bond, and who charges no more than $75 for processing and documentation and 15% of the total amount owed for debt adjusting; attorneys, CPAs, banks and title companies as part of regular practice or business; persons acting under court orders; trade and sales associations who adjust debts with business establishments; employers for their employees; and lender who, at the debtor's request, adjusts debts at no additional cost as part of disbursing the loan funds.

Collection agencies may not provide debt management services.

Nebraska

Neb. Rev. Stat. §§ 45-801 to 45-815

Credit repair service may not charge or collect a fee for referring consumer to a retail seller who will or may extend credit that is on substantially the same terms as those available to the general public.

Cancellation rights. Any payment must be returned within 10 days of receipt of cancellation notice.

Nevada

Nev. Rev. Stat. Ann. §§ 598.741 to 598.787

Credit repair service may not: charge or collect a fee for referring consumer to a retail seller who will or may extend credit that is on substantially the same terms as

State Laws Providing Additional Protections Concerning Credit Repair Clinics (continued)

those available to the general public; submit a debtor's dispute to a consumer credit reporting agency without the debtor's knowledge; or call a consumer credit reporting agency and represent the caller as the debtor.

Credit repair service must disclose a complete and accurate statement of the availability of nonprofit credit counseling services, including toll-free numbers if available.

Cancellation rights. May cancel contract within 5 days of signing.

New Hampshire
N.H. Rev. Stat. Ann. §§ 359-D:1 to 359-D:11

Credit repair service may not charge or collect a fee for referring consumer to a retail seller who will or may extend credit that is on substantially the same terms as those available to the general public.

Cancellation rights. May cancel contract within 5 days of signing. Any payment must be returned within 5 days of receipt of cancellation notice.

New Jersey
N.J. Stat. Ann. §§ 17:16G-1 to 17:16G-6; N.J. Admin. Code tit. 3, § 25-1.2

Who may provide service. Only nonprofit organizations may provide credit counseling or debt adjustment services. No more than 40% of the board of directors can be employed by a corporation or institution which offers credit to the general public.

Fees. Monthly debt adjustment fee cannot exceed one percent of the debtor's gross monthly income or $25.00, whichever is less. Credit counseling services fee cannot exceed $60.00 per month.

New Mexico
N.M. Stat. Ann. §§ 56-2-1 to 56-2-4

Who may provide service. Nonprofit corporations organized as a community effort to assist debtors may provide debt adjustment services. Exceptions: attorney; regular, full-time employee of a debtor who does it as part of job; person authorized by court or state or federal law; creditor who provides debt adjustment without cost; and lender who, at the debtor's request, adjusts debts at no additional cost as part of disbursing the loan funds.

New York
N.Y. Gen. Bus. Law §§ 458-a to 458-k

Credit repair service is required to annex a copy of the consumer's current credit report to the contract and clearly mark the adverse entries proposed to be modified.

North Carolina
N.C. Gen. Stat. §§ 66-220 to 66-226

Credit repair service may not charge or collect a fee for referring consumer to a retail seller who will or may extend credit that is on substantially the same terms as those available to the general public.

Cancellation rights. Any payment must be returned within 10 days of receipt of cancellation notice.

North Dakota
N.D. Cent. Code §§ 13-06-01 to 13-06-03; 13-07-01 to 13-07-07

Credit repair service may not enter into an agreement with a debtor unless a thorough written budget analysis indicates that the debtor can reasonably meet the requirements of the financial adjustment plan and will benefit from it.

Credit repair service is required to credit any interest accrued as a result of payments deposited in a trust account to debt management education programs.

Fees. May charge an origination fee of up to $50; may take up to 15% of any sum deposited by the debtor for distribution as partial payment of the service's total fee.

Ohio
Ohio Rev. Code Ann. §§ 4712.01 to 4712.99

Credit repair service may not charge or collect a fee for referring consumer to a person that extends credit, except when credit has actually been extended as a result of the referral; submit the debtor' disputes to a consumer reporting agency without the debtor's signed, written authorization and positive identification; or contact a consumer reporting agency to submit or obtain information about a debtor, stating or implying to be the debtor or debtor's attorney, guardian or other legal representative.

Credit repair service must disclose a complete and accurate statement of the availability of nonprofit budget and debt counseling services; the percentage of custom-

State Laws Providing Additional Protections Concerning Credit Repair Clinics (continued)

ers during the past year for whom the credit services organization fully and completely performed the services it agreed to provide.

Time limit for performing service. 60 days.

Oklahoma

Okla. Stat. Ann. tit. 24, §§ 131 to 139

Credit repair service may not charge or collect a fee for referring consumer to a retail seller who will or may extend credit that is on substantially the same terms as those available to the general public.

Cancellation rights. May cancel contract within 5 days of signing. Any payment must be returned within 10 days of receipt of cancellation notice.

Oregon

Or. Rev. Stat. §§ 646.380 to 646.396

Credit repair service may not charge or collect a fee for referring consumer to a retail seller who will or may extend credit that is on substantially the same terms as those available to the general public.

Credit repair service is required to print all contracts in at least 10-point type.

Pennsylvania

73 Pa. Cons. Stat. Ann. §§ 2181 to 2192

Credit repair service may not charge or collect a fee for referring consumer to a retail seller who will or may extend credit that is on substantially the same terms as those available to the general public.

Cancellation rights. May cancel contract within 5 days of signing. Any payment must be returned within 15 days of receipt of cancellation notice.

Rhode Island

R.I. Gen. Laws §§ 5-66-1 to 5-66-9

Who may provide service. Only the Rhode Island Consumers' Council and other bona fide nonprofit organizations may conduct the business of debt consolidation and management. (Rhode Island uses the term "debt pooling.")

Credit repair service is required to provide a written statement of account within a reasonable time after debtor's request and within 90 days after completion of service; a verbal accounting at any time during normal business hours.

Tennessee

Tenn. Code Ann. §§ 47-18-1001 to 47-18-1011

Credit repair service may not charge or collect a fee for referring consumer to a retail seller who will or may extend credit that is on substantially the same terms as those available to the general public; use a program or plan which charges installment payments directly to a credit card prior to full and complete performance of the services it has agreed to perform.

Credit repair service must disclose a complete and accurate statement of the availability of nonprofit budget and debt counseling services.

Cancellation rights. May cancel contract within 5 business days of signing. Any payment must be returned within 10 days of receipt of cancellation notice.

Texas

Tex. Fin. Code Ann. §§ 393.001 to 393.505

Credit repair service may not charge or collect a fee for referring consumer to a retail seller who will or may extend credit that is on substantially the same terms as those available to the general public.

Credit repair service must disclose a complete and accurate statement of the availability of nonprofit budget and debt counseling services.

Cancellation rights. Any payment must be returned within 10 days of receipt of cancellation notice.

Time limit for performing service. 180 days.

Utah

Utah Code Ann. §§ 13-21-1 to 13-21-7

Credit repair service may not charge or collect a fee for referring consumer to a retail seller who will or may extend credit that is on substantially the same terms as those available to the general public.

Cancellation rights. May cancel contract within 5 days of signing. Any payment must be returned within 10 days of receipt of cancellation notice.

Vermont

Vt. Stat. Ann. tit. 8, §§ 4861 to 4874

Who may provide service. Debt adjustment may be provided only by bona fide nonprofit religious, fraternal or cooperative organizations that offer services exclusively for members; attorneys as part of regular practice; finan-

State Laws Providing Additional Protections Concerning Credit Repair Clinics (continued)

cial or trust institutions in the regular course of business; persons authorized by court order or state or federal law.

Fees. May charge no more than a 10% overall fee and a one-time $25 service charge.

Virginia
Va. Code Ann. §§ 59.1-335.1 to 59.1-335.12

Credit repair service may not charge or collect a fee for referring consumer to a retail seller who will or may extend credit that is on substantially the same terms as those available to the general public.

Credit repair service must disclose. Information statement must include the following notice in at least 10-point bold type: "You have no obligation to pay any fees or charges until all services have been performed completely for you." The notice must also be conspicuously posted on a sign in the repair service's place of business, so that it is noticeable and readable when consumers are being interviewed.

Cancellation rights. Any payment must be returned within 10 days of receipt of cancellation notice.

Washington
Wash. Rev. Code Ann. §§ 19.134.010 to 19.134.900

Credit repair service may not charge or collect a fee for referring consumer to a retail seller who will or may extend credit that is on substantially the same terms as those available to the general public.

Cancellation rights. May cancel contract within 5 days of signing. Any payment must be returned within 10 days of receipt of cancellation notice.

West Virginia
W. Va. Code §§ 46A-6C-1 to 46A-6C-12

Credit repair service may not charge or collect a fee for referring consumer to a retail seller who will or may extend credit that is on substantially the same terms as those available to the general public.

Credit repair service must disclose a complete and accurate statement of the availability of nonprofit budget and debt counseling services.

Cancellation rights. Any payment must be returned within 10 days of receipt of cancellation notice.

Time limit for performing service. 180 days.

Wisconsin
Wis. Stat. Ann. §§ 422.501 to 422.506

Credit repair service may not charge or collect a fee for referring consumer to a retail seller who will or may extend credit that is on substantially the same terms as those available to the general public.

Cancellation rights. May cancel contract within 5 days of signing. Any payment must be returned within 15 days of receipt of cancellation notice.

Wyoming

Who may provide service. Only nonprofits and attorneys may offer debt adjustment services.

Current as of May 2003

1. Laws Prohibiting Credit Discrimination

Two federal laws, the Equal Credit Opportunity Act (ECOA) and the Fair Housing Act (FHA), cover most situations in the credit area.

The ECOA (15 U.S.C. §§ 1691 et seq.) is quite broad in scope. It prohibits discrimination in any part of a credit transaction, including:

- applications for credit
- credit evaluation
- restrictions in granting credit such as requiring collateral or security deposits
- credit terms
- loan servicing
- treatment upon default, and
- collection procedures.

The ECOA requires a creditor to give you notice when it denies your credit application or changes the terms. In a denial of credit, it also must provide you with a written explanation.

The ECOA prohibits a creditor from refusing to grant credit because of your:

- race or color
- national origin
- sex
- marital status
- religion
- age, or
- public assistance status.

The federal Fair Housing Act (FHA) (42 U.S.C. §§ 3601 et seq.) prohibits discrimination in residential real estate transactions. It covers loans to purchase, improve or maintain your house or loans in which your home is used as collateral. The FHA also prohibits discrimination in the rental housing market. Like the ECOA, the FHA prohibits discrimination based on race, color, religion, national origin and sex. In addition, the FHA prohibits discrimination based on:

- familial status, and
- disability.

In addition to the ECOA and FHA, other federal laws are useful. For example, the Community Reinvestment Act (12 U.S.C. §§ 2901 et seq.) can be used to combat discrimination by banks and lenders. And often, state antidiscrimination laws provide even more protection than do federal laws. Below, we discuss in detail some of the important categories in which credit discrimination is prohibited.

a. Race Discrimination

In general, lenders are prohibited from asking a person's race on a credit application or ascertaining it from any means other than the personal observation of a loan officer (such as a credit file). There is one important exception to this law. A mortgage lender must request a person's race for the sole purpose of monitoring home mortgage applications. Other creditors may ask for this information, but only to monitor their own practices for discrimination. Creditors may not use the information to make a credit decision.

Unfortunately, prohibiting race discrimination doesn't mean it has disappeared. In fact, lenders are accused of getting around race discrimination prohibitions by redlining—that is, denying credit to residents of predominantly nonwhite neighborhoods. More recently, consumer advocates have charged lenders with reverse redlining, which involves aggressively marketing their highest priced loan products to communities of color.

b. National Origin Discrimination

Discrimination based on national origin is prohibited under the ECOA, the FHA and most state credit discrimination laws. The exact definition of "national origin" is often unclear, but it generally refers to an individual's ancestry. A creditor might be discriminating based on national origin if it treats people with Latino or Asian surnames differently than people with European names. This category has also been interpreted to include discrimination against non-English speakers. However, it does not necessarily include non-citizens. A creditor is allowed to consider an applicant's residency status in the United States in certain circumstances.

c. Sex Discrimination

The ECOA, FHA and many state laws prohibit credit discrimination based on sex. This category often overlaps with the "marital status" category.

Specific examples of prohibited sex discrimination include:

- Rating female-specific jobs (such as waitress) lower than male-specific jobs (such as waiter) for purpose of obtaining credit
- Denying credit because an applicant's income comes from sources historically associated with women—for example, part-time jobs, alimony or child support
- Requiring married women who apply for credit alone to provide information about their husbands while not requiring married men to provide information about their wives, and
- Denying credit to a pregnant woman who anticipates taking a maternity leave.

However, a creditor is allowed to ask your sex when you apply for a real estate loan. The federal government collects this information for statistical purposes. Other creditors may ask for this information as well, although you can refuse to give the information.

d. Marital Status Discrimination

The ECOA and many state laws prohibit discrimination based on marital status. The FHA has a similar provision which prohibits discrimination based on familial status.

These laws require that a married person be allowed to apply for credit in her name only. A creditor cannot require an applicant's spouse to cosign when the applicant requests an individual account as long as no jointly held or community property is involved and the applicant can meet the creditor's standards on her own.

Creditors can only ask about your spouse or former spouse when you apply for your own credit if:

- Your spouse will be permitted to use the account
- Your spouse will be liable on the account
- You are relying on your spouse's income to repay the credit
- You live in a community property state (Arizona, California, Idaho, Louisiana, Nevada, New Mexico, Texas, Washington or Wisconsin) or you are relying on property located in a community property state to establish your credit worthiness, or
- You are relying on alimony, child support or other maintenance payments from a spouse to repay the creditor. (You are not required to reveal this income if you don't want the creditor to consider it in evaluating your application.)

e. Sexual Orientation Discrimination

No federal law specifically prohibits credit discrimination based on sexual orientation. However, a few states prohibit this type of discrimination.

f.   Age Discrimination

The ECOA and many state laws prohibit credit discrimination based on age. This is mostly meant to protect the elderly (defined in the ECOA as people aged 62 or over). Creditors are allowed to consider age in order to give more favorable treatment to an older person (for example, considering an older person's long payment history that a younger person hasn't had time to build yet). However, age cannot be used to an older person's detriment. For example, a creditor cannot automatically refuse to consider income often associated with the elderly such as part-time employment or retirement benefits.

g.   Other Discrimination Prohibited by State Law

A few states have enacted laws barring credit discrimination on grounds other than those covered by the federal laws. Check with your state consumer protection office or do some research on your own to see if there are additional grounds in your state.

Legal Research Help. For tips on doing your own legal research, see *Legal Research: How to Find & Understand the Law*, by Stephen Elias and Susan Levinkind (Nolo).

h.   Postbankruptcy Discrimination

If you're considering filing for bankruptcy or you've been through bankruptcy, you may be worried that you'll suffer discrimination. There are two categories of legal protection against this kind of discrimination, depending on whether you are dealing with a private person or a governmental entity.

Private employers may not fire you or otherwise discriminate against you solely because you filed for bankruptcy. (11 U.S.C. § 525(b).) It is unclear whether or not the act prohibits employers from not hiring you because you went through bankruptcy.

Unfortunately, however, other forms of discrimination in the private sector aren't necessarily illegal. If you seek to rent an apartment and the landlord does a credit check and refuses to rent to you because you filed for bankruptcy, there's not much you can do other than try to show that you'll pay your rent and be a responsible tenant. If a bank refuses to give you a loan because it perceives you as a poor credit risk, you may have little recourse.

All federal, state and local governmental entities are prohibited from denying, revoking, suspending or refusing to renew a license, permit, charter, franchise or other similar grant solely because you filed for bankruptcy. (11 U.S.C. § 525(a).) Judges interpreting this law have ruled that the government cannot:

- deny you a job or fire you
- deny or terminate your public benefits
- deny or refuse to renew your state liquor license
- withhold your college transcript
- deny you a driver's license, or
- deny you a contract, such as a contract for a construction project.

In general, courts have ruled that the intent of the statute is to prohibit a government entity from standing in your way of pursuing a livelihood involving a license, permit, charter or franchise, but that it does not mean that a government agency must extend you credit, such as a government-backed home loan. (See, for example, *Watts v. Pennsylvania Housing Finance Co.,* 876 F.2d 1090 (3rd Cir. 1989) and *Toth v. Michigan State Housing Development Authority,* 136 F.3d 477 (6th Cir. 1998).) However, a government agency cannot exclude you from a student loan program if you have filed for bankruptcy. (11 USC § 525(c).)

In addition, once any government-related debt has been canceled in bankruptcy, all acts against you that arise out of that debt also must end. For example, if a state university has withheld your transcript because you haven't paid back your student loan, once the loan is discharged, you must be given your transcript.

Keep in mind that only government denials based on your bankruptcy are prohibited. You may be denied a loan, job or apartment for reasons unrelated to the bankruptcy (for example, you earn too much to qualify for public housing), or for reasons related to your future credit worthiness (for instance, the government concludes you won't be able to repay a student loan).

2. What to Do If a Creditor Discriminates Against You

If you think that a creditor has discriminated against you on a prohibited basis, you should complain to the Federal Trade Commission (www.ftc.gov) and the federal agency that regulates the particular creditor. If the discrimination is related to housing, contact the Department of Housing and Urban Development (www.hud.gov). You may also want to contact an attorney for help.

You can learn more from these websites:

- www.innercitypress.org
- www.aclu.org (American Civil Liberties Union)
- www.communitychange.org (Nonprofit Center for Community Change), and
- www.usdoj.gov (U.S. Department of Justice). ■

Resources

Below are organizations, agencies and publications that can provide valuable help in your efforts to repair your credit.

A. Credit and Debt Counseling Agencies

Credit and debt counseling agencies are organizations funded primarily by major creditors, such as department stores, credit card companies and banks, who can work with you to help you repay your debts and improve your financial picture. Many are nonprofit companies, but some are not.

To use a credit or debt counseling agency to help you pay your debts, you must have some disposable income. A counselor contacts your creditors to let them know that you've sought assistance and need more time to pay. Based on your income and debts, the counselor, with your creditors, decides on how much you pay. You then make one payment each month to the counseling agency, which in turn pays your creditors. The agency asks the creditors to return a small percentage of the money to fund its work. This arrangement is generally referred to as a debt management program.

Some creditors will make overtures to help you when you're on a debt management program. But few creditors will make interest concessions, such as waiving a portion of the accumulated interest to help you repay the principal. More likely, you'll get late fees dropped and the opportunity to reinstate your credit if you successfully complete a debt management program.

Participating in a credit or debt counseling agency's debt management program is a little bit like filing for Chapter 13 bankruptcy. (See Chapter 1, Section C.5.) Working with a credit or debt counseling agency has one advantage: no bankruptcy will appear on your credit record.

But a debt management program also has two disadvantages when compared to Chapter 13 bankruptcy. First, if you miss a payment, Chapter 13 protects you from creditors who would otherwise start collection actions. A debt management program has no such protection and any one creditor can pull the plug on your plan. Also, a debt management program plan usually requires that your debts be paid in full. In Chapter 13 bankruptcy, you're required to pay the value of your nonexempt property, which can mean that you pay only a small fraction of your unsecured debts.

The combination of high consumer debt and easy access to information (the Internet) has led to an explosion in the number of credit and debt counseling agencies ready to offer you help. Some provide limited services, such as budgeting and debt repayment, while others offer a range of services, from debt counseling to financial planning.

When choosing a credit and debt counseling agency, look for a company that is truly a nonprofit. Many for-profit outfits use names that sound like a nonprofit, such as "foundation," to confuse you. And your inquiry shouldn't stop there. Many of the unscrupulous credit and debt counseling companies have nonprofit status. These companies often try to get you to pay "voluntary contributions" up front or pay other fees. At a minimum, always ask about fees before agreeing to give your business to a particular counselor. And review the "Questions to Ask a Credit or Debt Counseling Agency," below.

Some experts caution against using even the legitimate nonprofit credit and debt counseling agencies companies. Critics of these companies point out that they get most of their funding from creditors. (Some offices also receive grants from private agencies such as the United Way and federal agencies including the Department of Housing and Urban Development.) Therefore, say critics, counselors cannot be objective in counseling debtors to file for bankruptcy if they know the office won't receive any funds.

In response to this and other consumer concerns, credit and debt counseling agencies accredited by the National Foundation for Consumer Credit (the majority of agencies are) reached an agreement with the Federal Trade Commission to disclose the following to consumers:

Questions to Ask a Credit or Debt Counseling Agency

Myvesta.org (formerly Debt Counselors of America) suggests that you ask the following questions before using any counseling agency.

1. Will you send me information on your agency and programs? There is no reason you should be required to provide account numbers and balances or any information other than a name and mailing address before an agency will agree to send you information about itself. Some agencies require account numbers and balances to see if you have enough debt for them to be interested in helping you. If an agency won't provide you with information about its programs, consider that a warning sign.

2. Do you pay referral fees? No agency should pay referral fees to outside parties or pay agents to enroll consumers into a debt management program. This may be a warning signal that the agency is simply interested in placing as many consumers as possible into a repayment program, rather than providing educational assistance.

3. What should I do if I cannot afford the minimum payment? A good agency will not quickly dismiss you or tell you to file bankruptcy simply because you cannot meet the minimum debt management program payment. Ask about hardship programs.

4. What kind of training do you have that makes you qualified to assist me? A home study course or a few hours of class are not sufficient training. A good counseling agency provides its counselors with regular training from lawyers, Certified Financial Planners and other experts.

5. What kind of security measures do you take to protect my information? It is important that the agency you select has sufficient security in place to protect your confidential information.

6. Can I get up-to-date, regular reports of the status of my accounts? If access is by telephone only, will a knowledgeable person be available when you call to give you the information you need?

7. Will you answer my general questions, even if I am not in your repayment program? Ask any agency you are considering for advice if it can assist you with information even if you are not going to enroll in its debt management program.

8. What kinds of educational programs and services do you provide? Educational seminars are great but you might need some hard and fast answers about your situation without having to wait for the next seminar.

9. Is there a minimum amount of debt I have to have in order to work with you? The answer should always be "no." If an agency is there to help, it should not turn you away because you do not have enough debt.

10. Will you help me with all my debts? Some agencies offer little assistance for secured debts like car payments or mortgages, or government debts like taxes and student loans. Make sure you'll receive full service.

11. Is there a mandatory up-front fee? Some agencies charge a mandatory up-front fee for their debt management program—as much as $250 or more. These fees may be so high that they prevent you from getting assistance.

12. Will you sell my name or address to outside parties? Be sure you know the agency's privacy policy. Ask before your name and address appears on a mailing list sold to outside organizations.

13. How often do you pay creditors? Although your creditors will be paid only once a month, make sure the agency sends payments out at least weekly. Your payment should not sit at the agency for a month waiting for the next payment cycle.

- that creditors fund a large portion of the cost of their operations
- that the credit agency must balance the ability of the debtor to make payments with the requirements of the creditors that fund the office, and
- a reliable estimate of how long it will take a debtor to repay his or her debts under a debt management program.

⚠ If you sign up for a debt management plan, keep paying your bills directly until you know that your creditors have approved the plan. Make sure the agency's schedule means it will pay your debts before they are due each month. Call each of your creditors the first month to make sure the agency paid them on time.

1. Consumer Credit Counseling Service

Consumer Credit Counseling Service (CCCS) is the oldest credit or debt counseling agency in the country. Actually, CCCS isn't one agency. CCCS is the primary operating name of many credit and debt counseling agencies affiliated with the National Foundation for Consumer Credit (NFCC).

CCCS may charge you a small start-up fee of about $20 and a monthly fee (an average of about $11) for setting up a repayment plan. CCCS also helps people make monthly budgets, for a small fee of about $12, or sometimes free. If you can't afford the fee, CCCS will waive it. In most CCCS offices, the primary service offered is a debt management program. A few offices have additional services, such as helping you save money toward buying a house or reviewing your credit report.

CCCS has more than 1,100 offices, located in every state. Look in the phone book to find the one nearest you or contact the main office at 801 Roeder Road, Suite 900, Silver Spring, MD 20910, 800-388-2227 (voice) or at www.nfcc.org.

2. Myvesta.org

Myvesta.org (formerly called Debt Counselors of America) offers budgeting and debt management programs, like other debt and credit counseling agencies. But unlike most other agencies, Myvesta.org has a financial planning department with Certified Financial Planners and a Crisis Relief Team to assist consumers who are turned away by other credit or debt counseling agencies or who have very complex problems. Myvesta.org is also the first credit or debt counseling agency that is a registered investment advisor.

Myvesta offers services that other counseling agencies don't, helping people to manage their money by doing everything from balancing their checkbook and paying bills to evaluating purchases and loans. It also offers a lifestyle makeover program called the Comprehensive Bankruptcy Alternative. Although Myvesta offers some free services, including educational material on its website, the average client pays about $500 for Myvesta's service. The average comprehensive client pays $5,500 and has $52,000 in credit card debt.

Myvesta.org has only one office. That's because Myvesta.org offers its services via phone, fax, e-mail and the Internet. You can contact Myvesta.org at P.O. Box 8587, Gaithersburg, MD 20898-8587, 301-762-5270 (voice), info@myvesta.org (email) or www.myvesta.org (Internet).

3. Other Credit and Debt Counseling Agencies

Surf the Internet and you'll find many other credit and debt counseling agencies offering a variety of services. Be sure to ask questions about their services before signing up.

B. Debtors Anonymous

Debtors Anonymous is a 12-step support program which uses many of the guidelines of Alcoholics Anonymous. Debtors Anonymous groups meet all over the country. If you can't find one in your area, send a self-addressed, stamped envelope to Debtors Anonymous, General Services Board, P.O. Box 920888, Needham, MA 02492-0009. Or call their office and speak to a volunteer or leave your name and address and a request for information. Their number is 781-453-2743. You can also visit their website at www.debtorsanonymous.org.

C. Nolo Publications

Several Nolo publications can provide you with information to supplement what is in this book.

Money Troubles: Legal Strategies to Cope With Your Debts, by Robin Leonard, provides extensive information on prioritizing your debts, negotiating with creditors and deciding whether or not bankruptcy is for you.

How to File for Chapter 7 Bankruptcy, by Stephen Elias, Albin Renauer, Robin Leonard, and Kathleen Michon, is a detailed, thorough how-to guide for filing for Chapter 7 bankruptcy. Recommended for readers who are certain they want to file for Chapter 7.

Chapter 13 Bankruptcy: Repay Your Debts, by Robin Leonard, explains Chapter 13 bankruptcy and includes the forms and instructions necessary to file a Chapter 13 bankruptcy case.

Bankruptcy: Is It the Right Solution to Your Debt Problems?, by Robin Leonard, answers the most common—and not so common—questions about Chapter 7 bankruptcy and Chapter 13 bankruptcy, to help you decide if bankruptcy is right for you.

Take Control of Your Student Loan Debt, by Robin Leonard and Deanne Loonin, contains extensive information on student loans, including understanding payment options, applying for a deferment or cancelation, getting out of default and determining if you can eliminate the loans in bankruptcy.

Stand Up to the IRS, by Frederick W. Daily, guides taxpayers through the ins and outs of an audit, self-representation in tax court, challenging tax bills and setting up repayment plans for tax bills they do owe. Named one of top three personal finance books by *Money* Magazine.

Everybody's Guide to Small Claims Court, by Ralph Warner, is an indispensable guide for anyone wanting to sue a credit bureau or collection agency in small claims court, or to defend against a small claims court action filed by a collector.

Divorce and Money: How to Make the Best Financial Decisions During Divorce, by Violet Woodhouse and Dale Fetherling, is a thorough workbook for people making financial decisions while ending their marriage. Divorce is a time when you are at risk of damaging your credit. This book gives tips on dividing the assets and allocating the debts while protecting your precious credit rating.

D. Other Publishers

A number of publications from non-Nolo publishers have a wealth of information beyond what is in this book.

The Ultimate Credit Handbook, by Gerri Detweiler (Plume Books), covers everything you'd want to know about credit ratings, credit cards, completing credit applications, protecting your credit privacy and many other topics.

Surviving Debt: A Guide for Consumers in Financial Stress, by National Consumer Law Center. NCLC is a nonprofit organization that normally publishes books to assist lawyers. NCLC uses its years of experience in counseling low-income debtors across the country to offer tips on all kinds of debts and income sources, including government benefits, defenses to collection lawsuits and strategies when your house is in foreclosure. Order from NCLC, 77 Summer Street, 10th Floor, Boston, MA 02110, 617-542-9595 or consumerlaw@nclc.org (email).

What Every Credit Card User Needs to Know, by Howard Strong (Owl Books), includes almost everything you need to know about selecting and using credit cards. It also contains many useful sample letters.

E. Online Resources

If you have access to the Internet, there is a good deal of information you can find using your computer. But you can't do it all—not every court decision or state statute is available online. Furthermore, unless you know what you are looking for—the case name and citation or the code section—you may have difficulty finding it.

Still, there are a number of useful sites:

- **Nolo.com's Legal Research Center [www.nolo.com].**

  This center has links to each state's online legal information, including state statutes, as well as links to federal statues and United States Supreme Court cases.

Specific debt, credit, finance, consumer protection and bankruptcy information is available at a few sites, including the following:

- **www.nolo.com**

  Nolo's online site includes a vast amount of legal information for consumers. This includes sets of FAQs (frequently asked questions), Ask Auntie Nolo legal questions on a wide variety of legal topics and articles on legal issues.

- **www.myvesta.org**

  Myvesta.org, a nonprofit online resource dedicated to helping people get out of debt, maintains a website designed to help you deal with your financial problems. Their advice covers budgeting, financial recovery, debt management and debt payoff. The site is updated daily, is free, lists software, publications and information, contains special programs to help you get out of debt, and has a debt forum where you can post your specific

questions for myvesta.org's counselors to answer. More information on myvesta.org is in Section A, above.

- **http://ftc.gov**

  The Federal Trade Commission's website provides free publications on many consumer topics, including credit repair. It also provides links to the full text of numerous consumer protection laws (click on "Rules & Acts" in any of the consumer topics).

- **www.pueblo.gsa.gov**

  The Consumer Information Center provides the latest in consumer news as well as many publications of interest to consumers, including the Consumer Information Catalog.

- **www.fdic.gov www.federalreserve.gov**

  The Federal Deposit Insurance Corporation and Federal Reserve Board websites have consumer information and resources for understanding and researching banks and financial institutions.

- **www.irs.gov**

  The Internal Revenue Service provides tax information, forms and publications.

- **www.fraud.org**

  The National Fraud Information Center's website provides lots of information on how to protect yourself from telemarketing and Internet scams and how to report fraud.

F. State Consumer Protection Agencies

The state agencies listed below enforce consumer protection laws and provide consumer protection information. Many of these agencies regulate credit bureaus, accept complaints about credit bureaus in their state and provide free information about your rights as they relate to collection bureaus.

If your state can't or won't help you, contact the Federal Trade Commission. (See Chapter 4, Section D, for addresses and telephone numbers of the FTC regional offices.)

State Consumer Protection Agencies

Alabama

Consumer Affairs Division
Office of Attorney General
Alabama State House
11 South Union Street, Third Floor
Montgomery, AL 36130
334-242-7335
800-392-5658
www.ago.state.al.us

Alaska

Consumer Protection Unit
Fair Business Practices Section
Attorney General's Office
1031 West 4th Ave., Suite 200
Anchorage AK 99501
907-269-5100
www.law.state.ak.us/consumer

Arizona

Consumer Information and Complaints
Office of Attorney General
1275 West Washington Street
Phoenix, AZ 85007-2026
602-542-5763
800-352-8431
602-542-5002 (TTY)
www.ag.state.az.us

Arkansas

Consumer Protection Division
Office of the Attorney General
323 Center Street, Suite 200
Little Rock, AR 72201
501-682-2341
800-482-8982
501-682-6073 (TTY)
www.ag.state.ar.us/consumer/
home.htm

California

Public Inquiry Unit
Office of the Attorney General
Department of Justice
P.O. Box 944255
Sacramento, CA 94244-2550
916 322-3360
800 952-5225
http://caag.state.ca.us/consumers/
index.htm

Colorado

Consumer Protection Section
Office of Attorney General
1525 Sherman Street, Seventh Floor
Denver, CO 80203
303-866-5189
800-222-4444
www.state.colorado.gov

Connecticut

Consumer Credit Division
Department of Banking
260 Constitution Plaza
Hartford, CT 06103-1800
860-240-8200
800-831-7225
www.state.ct.us/dob/pages/
ccdiv.htm

Delaware

Consumer Protection Unit
Office of the Attorney General
820 North French Street, Fourth Fl.
Wilmington, DE 19801
302-577-8600
800-220-5424
www.state.de.us/attgen/
consumer.htm

District of Columbia

Department of Consumer and
   Regulatory Affairs
941 North Capitol Street, N.E.
Washington, DC 20002
202-442-4400
www.dcra.dc.gov

Florida

Division of Consumer Services
Department of Agriculture and
   Consumer Services
407 South Calhoun St., Mayo Building
Tallahassee, FL 32399-0800
850-488-2221
800-435-7352
http://doacs.state.fl.us/consumer

Georgia

Governor's Office of Consumer
   Affairs
2 Martin Luther King, Jr. Drive, Suite
   356
Atlanta, GA 30334
404-651-8600
800-869-1123
www2.state.ga.us/gaoca

Hawaii

Office of Consumer Protection
235 S. Beretonia St., Suite 801
Leiopapa A Kamehameha Building
Honolulu, HI 96813
808-587-3222
www.state.hi.us/dcca/ocp

Idaho

Consumer Protection Unit
Office of Attorney General
P.O. Box 83720
Boise, ID 83720-0010
208-334-2424
800-432-3545
www.state.id.us/ag

State Consumer Protection Agencies (cont'd)

Illinois
Consumer Protection Division
Office of Attorney General
100 W. Randolph Street
Chicago, IL 60601
312-814-3000
800-386-5438
800-964-3013 (TTY)
www.ag.state.il.us/consumer/
  consumer.htm

Indiana
Consumer Credit Division
Department of Financial Institutions
402 West Washington St., Room
  W066
Indianapolis, IN 46204
317-232-3955
800-382-4880
www.dfi.state.in.us/conscredit

Iowa
Consumer Protection Division
Office of Attorney General
1305 E. Walnut Street
Des Moines, IA 50319
515-281-5926
www.state.ia.us/government/ag/
  consumer.html

Kansas
Consumer Protection Division
Office of Attorney General
120 S.W. Tenth Street, 2nd Floor
Topeka, KS 66612=1597
785-296-3751
800-432-2310
785-291-3767 (TTY)
www.ink.org/public/ksag/
contents/consumer/main.htm

Kentucky
Consumer Protection Division
Office of Attorney General
1024 Capitol Center Drive
Frankfort, KY 40601
502-696-5389
888-423-8257
www.law.state.ky.us/cp

Louisiana
Consumer Protection Section
Office of Attorney General
P.O. Box 94005
Baton Rouge, LA 70804-9005
225-342-9638
800-351-4889
www.ag.state.la.us/consumer.shtml

Maine
Consumer Information and Mediation
  Service
Public Protection Division
Office of the Attorney General
State House, Station No. 6
Augusta, ME 04333-0006
207-626-8849
207-626-8865 (TTY)
www.state.me.us./ag/consumer.htm

Maryland
Consumer Protection Division
Office of Attorney General
200 St. Paul Pl., 6th Floor
Baltimore, MD 21202-2022
410-576-6550
888-743-0023
www.oag.state.md.us/
  consumer

Massachusetts
Office of Consumer Affairs and Business Regulation
10 Park Plaza, Suite 5170
Boston, MA 02116
617-727-7780 (hotline)
617-727-7755
888-288-3757
www.state.ma.us/consumer

Michigan
Consumer Protection Division
Office of Attorney General
P.O. Box 30213
Lansing, MI 48909
517-373-1140
877-765-8388
www.ag.state.mi.us/cp

Minnesota
Consumer Connection
Office of Attorney General
1400 NCL Tower
445 Minnesota Street
St. Paul, MN 55101-2130
651-296-3353
800-657-3787
651-297-7206 (TTY)
800-366-4812 (TTY)
www.ag.state.mn.us/consumer

Mississippi
Consumer Protection Division
Office of Attorney General
P.O. Box 22947
Jackson, MS 39225-2947
601-359-4230
800-281-4418
www.ago.state.ms.us/divisions/
  consumer/consumer-protection.html

State Consumer Protection Agencies (cont'd)

Missouri
Consumer Protection Division
Office of Attorney General
P.O. Box 899
Jefferson City, MO 65102
573-751-3321
800-392-8222
www.ago.state.mo.us/fraud.htm

Montana
Legal and Consumer Affairs
Department of Commerce
1424 Ninth Ave.
P.O. Box 200501
Helena, MT 59690
406-841-2700
www.mtfinanceonline.com

Nebraska
Consumer Protection Division
Office of Attorney General
2115 State Capitol Building
P.O. Box 98920
Lincoln, NE 68509-8920
402-471-2682
800-727-6432
www.nol.org/home/ago

Nevada
Consumer Affairs Division
Department of Business and Industry
1850 E. Sahara Ave., Suite 101
Las Vegas, NV 89104
702-486-7355
  [or]
4600 Kietzke Lane
Building B, Suite #3
Reno, NV 89502
775-688-1800
www.fyiconsumer.org

New Hampshire
Consumer Protection and Antitrust
  Bureau
Department of Justice
33 Capitol Street
Concord, NH 03301-6397
603-271-3641
www.state.nh.us/nhdoj/
  consumer/cpb.html

New Jersey
Division of Consumer Affairs
Department of Law and Public Safety
124 Halsey Street
Newark, NJ 07102
973-504-6200
900-242-5846
973-504-6588 (TDD)
www.state.nj.us/lps/ca

New Mexico
Consumer Protection Division
Office of Attorney General
P.O. Drawer 1508
Santa Fe, NM 87504-1508
505-827-6060
800-678-1508
www.ago.state.nm.us/protection/
  consumer_protection.html

New York
Consumer Protection Board
5 Empire State Plaza, Suite 2101
Albany, NY 12223-1556
518-474-1471
518-474-8583 (Complaint Unit)
800-697-1220
800-788-9898 (TTY)
www.consumer.state.ny.us

North Carolina
Consumer Protection Section
Department of Justice
P.O. Box 629
Raleigh, NC 27602-0629
919-716-6000
www.jus.state.nc.us/cpframe.htm

North Dakota
Consumer Protection Division
Office of Attorney General
600 East Boulevard
Bismarck, ND 58505-0040
701-328-3404
800-472-2600
www.ag.state.nd.us/ndag

Ohio
Consumer Protection Section
Office of Attorney General
State Office Tower
30 East Broad Street, 17th Floor
Columbus, OH 43215-3428
614-466-4320
800-282-0515
www.ag.state.oh.us

Oklahoma
Consumer Protection Unit
Office of Attorney General
4545 N. Lincoln Blvd., Suite 112
Oklahoma City, OK 73105-3498
405-521-3921
www.oag.state.ok.us

State Consumer Protection Agencies (cont'd)

Oregon

Financial Fraud/Consumer Protection
Section
1162 Court Street, NE
Salem, OR 97310
503-378-4320
503-229-5576 (Portland toll-free)
877-877-9392
www.doj.state.or.us/FinFraud/
welcome3.htm

Pennsylvania

Bureau of Consumer Protection
Office of Attorney General
Strawberry Square, 14th Floor
Harrisburg, PA 17120
717-787-9707
800-441-2555
www.attorneygeneral.gov/ppd/bcp

Rhode Island

Consumer Protection Unit
Department of Attorney General
150 S. Main Street
Providence, RI 02903
401-274-4400
800-852-7776
401-453-0410 (TTY)
www.riag.state.ri.us/consumer

South Carolina

Department of Consumer Affairs
P.O. Box 5757
3600 Forest Drive, 3rd Floor
Columbia, SC 29250
803-734-4200
800-922-1594
www.state.sc.us/consumer

South Dakota

Division of Consumer Affairs
Office of Attorney General
500 East Capitol Ave.
Pierre, SD 57501-5070
605-773-4400
800-300-1986
www.state.sd.us/attorney

Tennessee

Division of Consumer Affairs
Department of Commerce and
Insurance
500 James Robertson Parkway,
Fifth Floor
Nashville, TN 37243-0600
615-741-4737
800-342-8385
www.state.tn.us/consumer

Texas

Consumer Protection Division
Office of Attorney General
P.O. Box 12548
Austin, TX 78711-2548
512-463-2185
800-621-0508
www.oag.state.tx.us/
consumer/consumer.shtml

Utah

Division of Consumer Protection
Department of Commerce
160 E. 300 South
Box 146704
Salt Lake City, UT 84114-6704
801-530-6601
800-721-7233
www.commerce.utah.gov/dcp/
index.html

Vermont

Consumer Assistance
Office of Attorney General
104 Morrill Hall-UVM
Burlington, VT 05405
802-656-3183
800-649-2424
www.state.vt.us/atg/consumer.htm

Virginia

Office of Consumer Affairs
Department of Agriculture and Consumer Services
1100 Bank St.
Richmond, VA 23219
804-786-2042
800-552-9963
www.vdacs.state.va.us/consumers/
index.html

Washington

Consumer Resource Center
Office of Attorney General
P.O. Box 40100
112 Washington St. SE
Olympia, WA 98504-0118
360-733-6210
800-551-4636
800-276-9883 (TDD)
www.wa.gov/ago/consumer

West Virginia

Consumer Protection Division
Office of Attorney General
1900 Kanawha Blvd., Room 26E
Charleston, WV 25305-9924
304-558-8986
800-368-8808
www.state.wv.us/wvag

State Consumer Protection Agencies (cont'd)

Wisconsin

Bureau of Consumer Protection
Department of Agriculture, Trade
  and Consumer Protection
2811 Agriculture Drive
P.O. Box 8911
Madison, WI 53708-8911
608-224-4949
800-422-7128
608-224-5058 (TTY)
http://datcp.state.wi.us/core/
  consumerinfo

Wyoming

Consumer Affairs Section
Office of Attorney General
Herschler Building, East
122 West 5th Street
Cheyenne, WY 82002
307-777-7874
800-438-5799
www.attorneygeneral.state.wy.us/
  consumer.htm

■

Federal Credit Reporting and Credit Repair Laws

This Appendix contains many of the rules regulating credit bureaus. You'll find the federal government's rules in the Fair Credit Reporting Act (FCRA). In addition, most states have enacted laws related to credit reporting and credit bureaus. To get your state law, contact your state consumer protection agency (listed in Appendix 1, Section F). This appendix also includes the text of the Federal Credit Repair Organizations Act—the law that regulates credit repair clinics. A summary of state laws that govern credit repair clinics is found in Chapter 6, Section G.

The text of these statutes was current as of May, 2003. To check for changes in the law, see Nolo's legal research center (www.nolo.com) and obtain a copy of the statute in question. Or visit your local law library.

If a credit bureau violates the federal FCRA, you can register a complaint with the Federal Trade Commission (addresses and phone numbers are in Chapter 4, Section D). You can also sue for negligent or willful noncompliance with the federal FCRA within two years of the bureau's violation. You can sue for actual damages, such as court costs, attorneys' fees, lost wages, and if applicable, infliction of emotional distress. In cases of truly outrageous behavior, you can ask for punitive damages—damages meant to punish for malicious or willful conduct.

If a credit bureau violates a state law, you can register a complaint with the appropriate state agency (addresses and phone numbers are in Appendix 1, Section F). You can probably also sue for noncompliance with the state law. If you are thinking about suing, however, you'll need to find the full state law and read it carefully. (Look for the law at a local law library, a large public library or on the Internet.)

These lawsuits can probably be filed in small claims court without the help of an attorney. (See *Everybody's Guide to Small Claims Court*, by Ralph Warner (Nolo) for definitive information on suing in small claims court.) If you plan to ask for punitive damages, you'll probably need a lawyer's help to file in a regular court.

Text of the Federal Fair Credit Reporting Act

Short Title

This title may be cited as the Fair Credit Reporting Act.

15 U.S.C. § 1681. Congressional findings and statement of purpose

(a) Accuracy and fairness of credit reporting. The Congress makes the following findings:

(1) The banking system is dependent upon fair and accurate credit reporting. Inaccurate credit reports directly impair the efficiency of the banking system, and unfair credit reporting methods undermine the public confidence which is essential to the continued functioning of the banking system.

(2) An elaborate mechanism has been developed for investigating and evaluating the credit worthiness, credit standing, credit capacity, character, and general reputation of consumers.

(3) Consumer reporting agencies have assumed a vital role in assembling and evaluating consumer credit and other information on consumers.

(4) There is a need to insure that consumer reporting agencies exercise their grave responsibilities with fairness, impartiality, and a respect for the consumer's right to privacy.

(b) Reasonable procedures. It is the purpose of this subchapter to require that consumer reporting agencies adopt reasonable procedures for meeting the needs of commerce for consumer credit, personnel, insurance, and other information in a manner which is fair and equitable to the consumer, with regard to the confidentiality, accuracy, relevancy, and proper utilization of such information in accordance with the requirements of this subchapter.

15 U.S.C. § 1681a. Definitions; rules of construction

(a) Definitions and rules of construction set forth in this section are applicable for the purposes of this subchapter.

(b) The term "person" means any individual, partnership, corporation, trust, estate, cooperative, association, government or governmental subdivision or agency, or other entity.

(c) The term "consumer" means an individual.

(d) Consumer report.

    (1) In general. The term "consumer report" means any written, oral, or other communication of any information by a consumer reporting agency bearing on a consumer's credit worthiness, credit standing, credit capacity, character, general reputation, personal characteristics, or mode of living which is used or expected to be used or collected in whole or in part for the purpose of serving as a factor in establishing the consumer's eligibility for:

        (A) credit or insurance to be used primarily for personal, family, or household purposes;

        (B) employment purposes; or

        (C) any other purpose authorized under section 1681b of this title.

    (2) Exclusions. The term 'consumer report' does not include:

        (A) any:

            (i) report containing information solely as to transactions or experiences between the consumer and the person making the report;

            (ii) communication of that information among persons related by common ownership or affiliated by corporate control; or

            (iii) communication of other information among persons related by common ownership or affiliated by corporate control, if it is clearly and conspicuously disclosed to the consumer that the information may be communicated among such persons and the consumer is given the opportunity, before the time that the information is initially communicated, to direct that such information not be communicated among such persons;

        (B) any authorization or approval of a specific extension of credit directly or indirectly by the issuer of a credit card or similar device;

        (C) any report in which a person who has been requested by a third party to make a specific extension of credit directly or indirectly to a consumer conveys his or her decision with respect to such request, if the third party advises the consumer of the name and address of the person to whom the request was made, and such person makes the disclosures to the consumer required under section 1681m; or

        (D) a communication described in subsection (o) of this section.

(e) The term "investigative consumer report" means a consumer report or portion thereof in which information on a consumer's character, general reputation, personal characteristics, or mode of living is obtained through personal interviews with neighbors, friends, or associates of the consumer reported on or with others with whom he is acquainted or who may have knowledge concerning any such items of information. However, such information shall not include specific factual information on a consumer's credit record obtained directly from a creditor of the consumer or from a consumer reporting agency when such information was obtained directly from a creditor of the consumer or from the consumer.

(f) The term "consumer reporting agency" means any person which, for monetary fees, dues, or on a cooperative nonprofit basis, regularly engages in whole or in part in the practice of assembling or evaluating consumer credit information or other information on consumers for the purpose of furnishing consumer reports to third parties, and which uses any means or facility of interstate commerce for the purpose of preparing or furnishing consumer reports.

(g) The term "file," when used in connection with information on any consumer, means all of the information on that consumer recorded and retained by a consumer reporting agency regardless of how the information is stored.

(h) The term "employment purposes" when used in connection with a consumer report means a report used for the purpose of evaluating a consumer for employment, promotion, reassignment or retention as an employee.

(i) The term "medical information" means information or records obtained, with the consent of the individual to whom it relates, from licensed physicians or medical practitioners, hospitals, clinics, or other medical or medically related facilities.

(j) Definitions relating to child support obligations.

(1) Overdue support. The term "overdue support" has the meaning given to such term in Section 666(e) of Title 42.

(2) State or local child support enforcement agency. The term "State or local child support enforcement agency" means a State or local agency which administers a State or local program for establishing and enforcing child support obligations.

(k) Adverse action.

(1) Actions included. The term "adverse action":

(A) has the same meaning as in section 1691(d)(6) of this title; and

(B) means:

(i) a denial or cancellation of, an increase in any charge for, or a reduction or other adverse or unfavorable change in the terms of coverage or amount of, any insurance, existing or applied for, in connection with the underwriting of insurance;

(ii) a denial of employment or any other decision for employment purposes

that adversely affects any current or prospective employee;

(iii) a denial or cancellation of, an increase in any charge for, or any other adverse or unfavorable change in the terms of, any license or benefit described in section 1681b(a)(3)(D) of this title; and

(iv) an action taken or determination that is:

(I) made in connection with an application that was made by, or a transaction that was initiated by, any consumer, or in connection with a review of an account under section 1681(a)(3)(F)(ii) of this title; and

(II) adverse to the interests of the consumer.

(2) Applicable findings, decisions, commentary, and orders. For purposes of any determination of whether an action is an adverse action under paragraph (1)(A), all appropriate final findings, decisions, commentary, and orders issued under section 1691(d)(6) of this title by the Board of Governors of the Federal Reserve System or any court shall apply.

(l) Firm offer of credit or insurance. The term "firm offer of credit or insurance" means any offer of credit or insurance to a consumer that will be honored if the consumer is determined, based on information in a consumer report on the consumer, to meet the specific criteria used to select the consumer for the offer, except that the offer may be further conditioned on one or more of the following:

(1) The consumer being determined, based on information in the consumer's application for the credit or insurance, to meet specific criteria bearing on credit worthiness or insurability, as applicable, that are established:

(A) before selection of the consumer for the offer; and

(B) for the purpose of determining whether to extend credit or insurance pursuant to the offer.

(2) Verification:

    (A) that the consumer continues to meet the specific criteria used to select the consumer for the offer, by using information in a consumer report on the consumer, information in the consumer's application for the credit or insurance, or other information bearing on the credit worthiness or insurability of the consumer; or

    (B) of the information in the consumer's application for the credit or insurance, to determine that the consumer meets the specific criteria bearing on credit worthiness or insurability.

(3) The consumer furnishing any collateral that is a requirement for the extension of the credit or insurance that was:

    (A) established before selection of the consumer for the offer of credit or insurance; and

    (B) disclosed to the consumer in the offer of credit or insurance.

(m) Credit or insurance transaction that is not initiated by the consumer. The term "credit or insurance transaction that is not initiated by the consumer" does not include the use of a consumer report by a person with which the consumer has an account or insurance policy, for purposes of:

(1) reviewing the account or insurance policy; or

(2) collecting the account.

(n) State. The term "State" means any State, the Commonwealth of Puerto Rico, the District of Columbia, and any territory or possession of the United States.

(o) Excluded communications. A communication is described in this subsection if it is a communication:

(1) that, but for subsection (d)(2)(D), would be an investigative consumer report;

(2) that is made to a prospective employer for the purpose of:

    (A) procuring an employee for the employer; or

    (B) procuring an opportunity for a natural person to work for the employer;

(3) that is made by a person who regularly performs such procurement;

(4) that is not used by any person for any purpose other than a purpose described in subparagraph (A) or (B) of paragraph (2); and

(5) with respect to which:

    (A) the consumer who is the subject of the communication:

        (i) consents orally or in writing to the nature and scope of the communication, before the collection of any information for the purpose of making the communication;

        (ii) consents orally or in writing to the making of the communication to a prospective employer, before the making of the communication; and

        (iii) in the case of consent under clause (i) or (ii) given orally, is provided written confirmation of that consent by the person making the communication, not later than three business days after the receipt of the consent by that person;

    (B) the person who makes the communication does not, for the purpose of making the communication, make any inquiry that if made by a prospective employer of the consumer who is the subject of the communication would violate any applicable Federal or State equal employment opportunity law or regulation; and

    (C) the person who makes the communication:

        (i) discloses in writing to the consumer who is the subject of the communication, not later than five business days after receiving any request from the consumer for such disclosure, the nature and substance of all information in the consumer's file at the time of the request, except that the sources of any information that is acquired solely for use in making the communication and is actually used for no other purpose, need not be disclosed other than under appropriate discovery procedures in any court of competent jurisdiction in which an action is brought; and

  (ii) notifies the consumer who is the subject of the communication, in writing, of the consumer's right to request the information described in clause (i).

(p) Consumer reporting agency that compiles and maintains files on consumers on a nationwide basis. The term "consumer reporting agency that compiles and maintains files on consumers on a nationwide basis" means a consumer reporting agency that regularly engages in the practice of assembling or evaluating, and maintaining, for the purpose of furnishing consumer reports to third parties bearing on a consumer's credit worthiness, credit standing, or credit capacity, each of the following regarding consumers residing nationwide:

  (1) Public record information.

  (2) Credit account information from persons who furnish that information regularly and in the ordinary course of business.

15 U.S.C. § 1681b. Permissible purposes of consumer reports

(a) In general. Subject to subsection (c), any consumer reporting agency may furnish a consumer report under the following circumstances and no other:

  (1) In response to the order of a court having jurisdiction to issue such an order, or a subpoena issued in connection with proceedings before a Federal grand jury.

  (2) In accordance with the written instructions of the consumer to whom it relates.

  (3) To a person which it has reason to believe:

    (A) intends to use the information in connection with a credit transaction involving the consumer on whom the information is to be furnished and involving the extension of credit to, or review or collection of an account of, the consumer; or

    (B) intends to use the information for employment purposes; or

    (C) intends to use the information in connection with the underwriting of insurance involving the consumer; or

    (D) intends to use the information in connection with a determination of the consumer's eligibility for a license or other benefit granted by a governmental instrumentality required by law to consider an applicant's financial responsibility or status; or

    (E) intends to use the information, as a potential investor or servicer, or current insurer, in connection with a valuation of, or an assessment of the credit or prepayment risks associated with, an existing credit obligation; or

    (F) otherwise has a legitimate business need for the information:

      (i) in connection with a business transaction that is initiated by the consumer; or

      (ii) to review an account to determine whether the consumer continues to meet the terms of the account.

(b) Conditions for furnishing and using consumer reports for employment purposes.

  (1) Certification from user. A consumer reporting agency may furnish a consumer report for employment purposes only if:

    (A) the person who obtains such report from the agency certifies to the agency that:

      (i) the person has complied with paragraph (2) with respect to the consumer report, and the person will comply with paragraph (3) with respect to the consumer report if paragraph (3) becomes applicable; and

    (ii) information from the consumer report will not be used in violation of any applicable Federal or State equal employment opportunity law or regulation; and

(B) the consumer reporting agency provides with the report, or has previously provided, a summary of the consumer's rights under this title, as prescribed by the Federal Trade Commission under section 1681g(c)(3) of this title.

(2) Disclosure to consumer

    (A) In general. Except as provided in subparagraph (B), a person may not procure a consumer report, or cause a consumer report to be procured, for employment purposes with respect to any consumer, unless:

        (i) a clear and conspicuous disclosure has been made in writing to the consumer at any time before the report is procured or caused to be procured, in a document that consists solely of the disclosure, that a consumer report may be obtained for employment purposes; and

        (ii) the consumer has authorized in writing (which authorization may be made on the document referred to in clause (i)) the procurement of the report by that person.

    (B) Application by mail, telephone, computer, or other similar means. If a consumer described in subparagraph (C) applies for employment by mail, telephone, computer, or other similar means, at any time before a consumer report is procured or caused to be procured in connection with that application—

        (i) the person who procures the consumer report on the consumer for employment purposes shall provide to the consumer, by oral, written, or electronic means, notice that a consumer report may be obtained for employment purposes, and a summary of the consumer's rights under section 1681m(a)(3) of this title; and

        (ii) the consumer shall have consented, orally, in writing, or electronically to the procurement of the report by that person.

    (C) Scope

    Subparagraph (B) shall apply to a person procuring a consumer report on a consumer in connection with the consumer's application for employment only if:

        (i) the consumer is applying for a position over which the Secretary of Transportation has the power to establish qualifications and maximum hours of service pursuant to the provisions of section 31502 of title 49, or a position subject to safety regulation by a State transportation agency; and

        (ii) as of the time at which the person procures the report or causes the report to be procured the only interaction between the consumer and the person in connection with that employment application has been by mail, telephone, computer, or other similar means.

(3) Conditions on use for adverse actions

    (A) In general. Except as provided in subparagraph (B), in using a consumer report for employment purposes, before taking any adverse action based in whole or in part on the report, the person intending to take such adverse action shall provide to the consumer to whom the report relates:

(i)   a copy of the report; and

(ii) a description in writing of the rights of the consumer under this subchapter, as prescribed by the Federal Trade Commission under section 1681g(c)(3) of this title.

(B) Application by mail, telephone, computer, or other similar means.

(i)   If a consumer described in subparagraph (C) applies for employment by mail, telephone, computer, or other similar means, and if a person who has procured a consumer report on the consumer for employment purposes takes adverse action on the employment application based in whole or in part on the report, then the person must provide to the consumer to whom the report relates, in lieu of the notices required under subparagraph (A) of this section and under section 1681m(a) of this title, within 3 business days of taking such action, an oral, written or electronic notification—

(I)   that adverse action has been taken based in whole or in part on a consumer report received from a consumer reporting agency;

(II) of the name, address and telephone number of the consumer reporting agency that furnished the consumer report (including a toll-free telephone number established by the agency if the agency compiles and maintains files on consumers on a nationwide basis);

(III) that the consumer reporting agency did not make the decision to take the adverse action and is unable to provide to the consumer the specific reasons

why the adverse action was taken; and

(IV) that the consumer may, upon providing proper identification, request a free copy of a report and may dispute with the consumer reporting agency the accuracy or completeness of any information in a report.

(ii) If, under clause (B)(i)(IV), the consumer requests a copy of a consumer report from the person who procured the report, then, within 3 business days of receiving the consumer's request, together with proper identification, the person must send or provide to the consumer a copy of a report and a copy of the consumer's rights as prescribed by the Federal Trade Commission under section 1681g(c)(3) of this title.

(C) Scope

Subparagraph (B) shall apply to a person procuring a consumer report on a consumer in connection with the consumer's application for employment only if:

(i)   the consumer is applying for a position over which the Secretary of Transportation has the power to establish qualifications and maximum hours of service pursuant to the provisions of section 31502 of title 49, or a position subject to safety regulation by a State transportation agency; and

(ii) as of the time at which the person procures the report or causes the report to be procured the only interaction between the consumer and the person in connection with that employment application has been by mail, telephone, computer, or other similar means.

(4) Exception for national security investigations

(A) In general.

In the case of an agency or department of the United States Government which seeks to obtain and use a consumer report for employment purposes, paragraph (3) shall not apply to any adverse action by such agency or department which is based in part on such consumer report, if the head of such agency or department makes a written finding that:

  (i) the consumer report is relevant to a national security investigation of such agency or department;

  (ii) the investigation is within the jurisdiction of such agency or department;

  (iii) there is reason to believe that compliance with paragraph (3) will:

    (I) endanger the life or physical safety of any person;

    (II) result in flight from prosecution;

    (III) result in the destruction of, or tampering with, evidence relevant to the investigation;

    (IV) result in the intimidation of a potential witness relevant to the investigation;

    (V) result in the compromise of classified information; or

    (VI) otherwise seriously jeopardize or unduly delay the investigation or another official proceeding.

(B) Notification of consumer upon conclusion of investigation. Upon the conclusion of a national security investigation described in subparagraph (A), or upon the determination that the exception under subparagraph (A) is no longer required for the reasons set forth in such subparagraph, the official exercising the authority in such subparagraph shall provide to the consumer who is the subject of the consumer report with regard to which such finding was made:

  (i) a copy of such consumer report with any classified information redacted as necessary;

  (ii) notice of any adverse action which is based, in part, on the consumer report; and

  (iii) the identification with reasonable specificity of the nature of the investigation for which the consumer report was sought.

(C) Delegation by head of agency or department.

For purposes of subparagraphs (A) and (B), the head of any agency or department of the United States Government may delegate his or her authorities under this paragraph to an official of such agency or department who has personnel security responsibilities and is a member of the Senior Executive Service or equivalent civilian or military rank.

(D) Report to the Congress

Except as provided in subparagraph E, not later than January 31 of each year, the head of each agency and department of the United States Government that exercised authority under this paragraph during the preceding year shall submit a report to the Congress on the number of times the department or agency exercised such authority during the year.

(E) Reports to Congressional intelligence committees

In the case of a report to be submitted under subparagraph (D) to the congressional intelligence committees (as defined in section 401a of Title 50), the submittal date for such report shall be as provided in section 415b of Title 50.

(F) Definitions

For purposes of this paragraph, the following definitions shall apply:

  (i) Classified information

    The term "classified information"

means information that is protected from unauthorized disclosure under Executive Order No. 12958 or successor orders.

      (ii) National security investigation The term "national security investigation" means any official inquiry by an agency or department of the United States Government to determine the eligibility of a consumer to receive access or continued access to classified information or to determine whether classified information has been lost or compromised.

(c) Furnishing reports in connection with credit or insurance transactions that are not initiated by the consumer.

    (1) In general. A consumer reporting agency may furnish a consumer report relating to any consumer pursuant to subparagraph (A) or (C) of subsection (a)(3) in connection with any credit or insurance transaction that is not initiated by the consumer only if:

      (A) the consumer authorizes the agency to provide such report to such person; or

      (B)

        (i) the transaction consists of a firm offer of credit or insurance;

        (ii) the consumer reporting agency has complied with subsection (e); and

        (iii) there is not in effect an election by the consumer, made in accordance with subsection (e), to have the consumer's name and address excluded from lists of names provided by the agency pursuant to this paragraph.

    (2) Limits on information received under paragraph (1)(b). A person may receive pursuant to paragraph (1)(B) only:

      (A) the name and address of a consumer;

      (B) an identifier that is not unique to the consumer and that is used by the person solely for the purpose of verifying the identity of the consumer; and

      (C) other information pertaining to a consumer that does not identify the relationship or experience of the consumer with respect to a particular creditor or other entity.

    (3) Information regarding inquiries. Except as provided in section 1681g(a)(5) of this title, a consumer reporting agency shall not furnish to any person a record of inquiries in connection with a credit or insurance transaction that is not initiated by a consumer.

(d) Reserved.

(e) Election of consumer to be excluded from lists.

    (1) In general. A consumer may elect to have the consumer's name and address excluded from any list provided by a consumer reporting agency under subsection (c)(1)(B) in connection with a credit or insurance transaction that is not initiated by the consumer by notifying the agency in accordance with paragraph (2) that the consumer does not consent to any use of a consumer report relating to the consumer in connection with any credit or insurance transaction that is not initiated by the consumer.

    (2) Manner of notification. A consumer shall notify a consumer reporting agency under paragraph (1):

      (A) through the notification system maintained by the agency under paragraph (5); or

      (B) by submitting to the agency a signed notice of election form issued by the agency for purposes of this subparagraph.

    (3) Response of agency after notification through system. Upon receipt of notification of the election of a consumer under paragraph (1) through the notification system maintained by the agency under paragraph (5), a consumer reporting agency shall:

      (A) inform the consumer that the election is effective only for the 2-year period following the election if the consumer does not submit to the agency a signed notice of election form issued by the agency for purposes of paragraph (2)(B); and

(B) provide to the consumer a notice of election form, if requested by the consumer, not later than five business days after receipt of the notification of the election through the system established under paragraph (5), in the case of a request made at the time the consumer provides notification through the system.

(4) Effectiveness of election. An election of a consumer under paragraph (1):

(A) shall be effective with respect to a consumer reporting agency beginning five business days after the date on which the consumer notifies the agency in accordance with paragraph (2);

(B) shall be effective with respect to a consumer reporting agency:

   (i) subject to subparagraph (C), during the two-year period beginning five business days after the date on which the consumer notifies the agency of the election, in the case of an election for which a consumer notifies the agency only in accordance with paragraph (2)(A); or

   (ii) until the consumer notifies the agency under subparagraph (C), in the case of an election for which a consumer notifies the agency in accordance with paragraph (2)(B);

(C) shall not be effective after the date on which the consumer notifies the agency, through the notification system established by the agency under paragraph (5), that the election is no longer effective; and

(D) shall be effective with respect to each affiliate of the agency.

(5) Notification system.

(A) In general. Each consumer reporting agency that, under subsection (c)(1)(B),

furnishes a consumer report in connection with a credit or insurance transaction that is not initiated by a consumer shall:

   (i) establish and maintain a notification system, including a toll-free telephone number, which permits any consumer whose consumer report is maintained by the agency to notify the agency, with appropriate identification, of the consumer's election to have the consumer's name and address excluded from any such list of names and addresses provided by the agency for such a transaction; and

   (ii) publish by not later than 365 days after September 30, 1996, and not less than annually thereafter, in a publication of general circulation in the area served by the agency:

      (I) a notification that information in consumer files maintained by the agency may be used in connection with such transactions; and

      (II) the address and toll-free telephone number for consumers to use to notify the agency of the consumer's election under clause (i).

(B) Establishment and maintenance as compliance. Establishment and maintenance of a notification system (including a toll-free telephone number) and publication by a consumer reporting agency on the agency's own behalf and on behalf of any of its affiliates in accordance with this paragraph is deemed to be compliance with this paragraph by each of those affiliates.

(6) Notification system by agencies that operate nationwide. Each consumer reporting agency that compiles and maintains files on consumers on a nationwide basis shall establish and

maintain a notification system for purposes of paragraph (5) jointly with other such consumer reporting agencies.

(f) Certain use or obtaining of information prohibited. A person shall not use or obtain a consumer report for any purpose unless:

(1) the consumer report is obtained for a purpose for which the consumer report is authorized to be furnished under this section; and

(2) the purpose is certified in accordance with section 1681e by a prospective user of the report through a general or specific certification.

(g) Furnishing reports containing medical information. A consumer reporting agency shall not furnish for employment purposes, or in connection with a credit or insurance transaction, a consumer report that contains medical information about a consumer, unless the consumer consents to the furnishing of the report.

15 U.S.C. § 1681c. Reporting of requirements relating to information contained in consumer reports prohibited

(a) Information excluded from consumer reports—prohibited items. Except as authorized under subsection (b) of this section, no consumer reporting agency may make any consumer report containing any of the following items of information:

(1) Cases under title 11 or under the Bankruptcy Act that, from the date of entry of the order for relief or the date of adjudication, as the case may be, antedate the report by more than ten years.

(2) Civil suits, civil judgments, and records of arrests that, from date of entry, antedate the report by more than seven years or until the governing statute of limitations has expired, whichever is the longer period.

(3) Paid tax liens which, from date of payment, antedate the report by more than seven years.

(4) Accounts placed for collection or charged to profit and loss which antedate the report by more than seven years.

(5) Any other adverse item of information, other than records of convictions of crimes which antedates the report by more than seven years.

(b) Exempted cases. The provisions of subsection (a) of this section are not applicable in the case of any consumer credit report to be used in connection with:

(1) a credit transaction involving, or which may reasonably be expected to involve, a principal amount of $150,000 or more;

(2) the underwriting of life insurance involving, or which may reasonably be expected to involve, a face amount of $150,000 or more; or

(3) the employment of any individual at an annual salary which equals, or which may reasonably be expected to equal, $75,000 or more.

(c) Running of reporting period.

(1) In general. The seven-year period referred to in paragraphs (4) and (6) of subsection (a) of this section shall begin, with respect to any delinquent account that is placed for collection (internally or by referral to a third party, whichever is earlier), charged to profit and loss, or subjected to any similar action, upon the expiration of the 180-day period beginning on the date of the commencement of the delinquency which immediately preceded the collection activity, charge to profit and loss, or similar action.

(2) Effective date. Paragraph (1) shall apply only to items of information added to the file of a consumer on or after the date that is 455 days after September 30, 1996.

(d) Information required to be disclosed. Any consumer reporting agency that furnishes a consumer report that contains information regarding any case involving the consumer that arises under title 11, United States Code, shall include in the report an identification of the chapter of such title 11 under which such case arises if provided by the source of the information. If any case arising or filed under title 11, United States Code, is withdrawn by the consumer before a final judgment, the consumer reporting agency shall include in the report that such case or filing was withdrawn upon receipt of documentation certifying such withdrawal.

(e) Indication of closure of account by consumer. If a consumer reporting agency is notified pursuant to section 1681t(a)(4) of this section that a credit account of a consumer was voluntarily closed by the consumer, the agency shall indicate that fact in any consumer report that includes information related to the account.

(f) Indication of dispute by consumer. If a consumer reporting agency is notified pursuant to section 1681s2(a)(3) of this title that information regarding a consumer who was furnished to the agency is disputed by the consumer, the agency shall indicate that fact in each consumer report that includes the disputed information.

15 U.S.C. § 1681d. Disclosure of investigative consumer reports

(a) Disclosure of fact of preparation. A person may not procure or cause to be prepared an investigative consumer report on any consumer unless:

(1) it is clearly and accurately disclosed to the consumer that an investigative consumer report including information as to his character, general reputation, personal characteristics, and mode of living, whichever are applicable, may be made, and such disclosure (A) is made in a writing mailed, or otherwise delivered, to the consumer, not later than three days after the date on which the report was first requested, and (B) includes a statement informing the consumer of his right to request the additional disclosures provided for under subsection (b) of this section and the written summary of the rights of the consumer prepared pursuant to section 1681g of this title; and

(2) the person certifies or has certified to the consumer reporting agency that:

(A) the person has made the disclosures to the consumer required by paragraph (1); and

(B) the person will comply with subsection (b).

(b) Disclosure on request of nature and scope of investigation. Any person who procures or causes to be prepared an investigative consumer report on any consumer shall, upon written request made by the consumer within a reasonable period of time after the receipt by him of the disclosure required by subsection (a)(1) of this section, make a complete and accurate disclosure of the nature and scope of the investigation requested. This disclosure shall be made in a writing mailed, or otherwise delivered, to the consumer not later than five days after the date on which the request for such disclosure was received from the consumer or such report was first requested, whichever is the later.

(c) Limitation on liability upon showing of reasonable procedures for compliance with provisions. No person may be held liable for any violation of subsection (a) or (b) of this section if he shows by a preponderance of the evidence that at the time of the violation he maintained reasonable procedures to assure compliance with subsection (a) or (b) of this section.

(d) Prohibitions.

(1) Certification. A consumer reporting agency shall not prepare or furnish an investigative consumer report unless the agency has received a certification under subsection (a)(2) from the person who requested the report.

(2) Inquiries. A consumer reporting agency shall not make an inquiry for the purpose of preparing an investigative consumer report on a consumer for employment purposes if the making of the inquiry by an employer or prospective employer of the consumer would violate any applicable Federal or State equal employment opportunity law or regulation.

(3) Certain public record information. Except as otherwise provided in section 1681k of this title, a consumer reporting agency shall not furnish an investigative consumer report that includes information that is a matter of public record and that relates to an arrest, indictment, conviction, civil judicial action, tax lien, or outstanding judgment, unless the agency has verified the accuracy of the information during the 30-day period ending on the date on which the report is furnished.

(4) Certain adverse information. A consumer reporting agency shall not prepare or furnish an investigative consumer report on a consumer that contains information that is adverse to the interest of the consumer and that is obtained through a personal interview with a neighbor, friend, or associate of the consumer or with another person with whom the consumer is acquainted or who has knowledge of such item of information, unless:

(A) the agency has followed reasonable procedures to obtain confirmation of the information, from an additional source that has independent and direct knowledge of the information; or

(B) the person interviewed is the best possible source of the information.

15 U.S.C. § 1681e. Compliance procedures

(a) Identity and purposes of credit users. Every consumer reporting agency shall maintain reasonable procedures designed to avoid violations of section 1681c of this title and to limit the furnishing of consumer reports to the purposes listed under section 1681b of this title. These procedures shall require that prospective users of the information identify themselves, certify the purposes for which the information is sought, and certify that the information will be used for no other purpose. Every consumer reporting agency shall make a reasonable effort to verify the identity of a new prospective user and the uses certified by such prospective user prior to furnishing such user a consumer report. No consumer reporting agency may furnish a consumer report to any person if it has reasonable grounds for believing that the consumer report will not be used for a purpose listed in section 1681b of this title.

(b) Accuracy of report. Whenever a consumer reporting agency prepares a consumer report it shall follow reasonable procedures to assure maximum possible accuracy of the information concerning the individual about whom the report relates.

(c) Disclosure of consumer reports by users allowed. A consumer reporting agency may not prohibit a user of a consumer report furnished by the agency on a consumer from disclosing the contents of the report to the consumer, if adverse action against the consumer has been taken by the user based in whole or in part on the report.

(d) Notice to users and furnishers of information.

(1) Notice requirement. A consumer reporting agency shall provide to any person:

(A) who regularly and in the ordinary course of business furnishes information to the agency with respect to any consumer; or

(B) to whom a consumer report is provided by the agency; a notice of such person's responsibilities under this subchapter.

(2) Content of notice. The Federal Trade Commission shall prescribe the content of notices under paragraph (1), and a consumer reporting agency shall be in compliance with this subsection if it provides a notice under paragraph (1) that is substantially similar to the Federal Trade Commission prescription under this paragraph.

(e) Procurement of consumer report for resale.

(1) Disclosure. A person may not procure a consumer report for purposes of reselling the report (or any information in the report) unless the person discloses to the consumer reporting agency that originally furnishes the report:

(A) the identity of the end-user of the report (or information); and

(B) each permissible purpose under section 1681b for which the report is furnished to the end-user of the report (or information).

(2) Responsibilities of procurers for resale. A person who procures a consumer report for purposes of reselling the report (or any information in the report) shall:

(A) establish and comply with reasonable procedures designed to ensure that the report (or information) is resold by the person only for a purpose for which the report may be furnished under section 1681b of this title, including by requiring that each person to which the report (or information) is resold and that resells or provides the report (or information) to any other person:

(i) identifies each end user of the resold report (or information);

(ii) certifies each purpose for which the report (or information) will be used; and

(iii) certifies that the report (or information) will be used for no other purpose; and

(B) before reselling the report, make reasonable efforts to verify the identifications and certifications made under subparagraph (A).

(3) Resale of consumer report to a Federal agency or department. Notwithstanding paragraph (1) or (2), a person who procures a consumer report for purposes of reselling the report (or any information in the report) shall not disclose the identity of the end-user of the report under paragraph (1) or (2) if:

(A) the end user is an agency or department of the United States Government which procures the report from the person for purposes of determining the eligibility of the consumer concerned to receive access or continued access to classified information (as defined in section 1681b(b)(4)(E)(i) of this title); and

(B) the agency or department certifies in writing to the person reselling the report that nondisclosure is necessary to protect classified information or the safety of persons employed by or contracting with, or undergoing investigation for work or contracting with the agency or department.

15 U.S.C. § 1681f. Disclosures to governmental agencies

Notwithstanding the provisions of section 1681b of this title, a consumer reporting agency may furnish identifying information respecting any consumer, limited to his name, address, former addresses, places of employment, or former places of employment, to a governmental agency.

15 U.S.C. § 1681g. Disclosures to consumers

(a) Information on file; sources; report recipients. Every consumer reporting agency shall, upon request, and subject to section 1681h(a)(1) of this title, clearly and accurately disclose to the consumer:

(1) All information in the consumer's file at the time of the request, except that nothing in this paragraph shall be construed to require a consumer reporting agency to disclose to a consumer any information concerning credit scores or any other risk scores or predictors relating to the consumer.

(2) The sources of the information; except that the sources of information acquired solely for use in preparing an investigative consumer report and actually used for no other purpose need not be disclosed: Provided, That in the event an action is brought under this subchapter, such sources shall be available to the plaintiff under appropriate discovery procedures in the court in which the action is brought.

(3)

   (A) Identification of each person (including each end-user identified under section 1681e(e)(1) of this title) that procured a consumer report:

   (i) for employment purposes, during the two-year period preceding the date on which the request is made; or

   (ii) for any other purpose, during the one-year period preceding the date on which the request is made.

   (B) An identification of a person under subparagraph (A) shall include:

   (i) the name of the person or, if applicable, the trade name (written in full) under which such person conducts business; and

   (ii) upon request of the consumer, the address and telephone number of the person.

   (C) Subparagraph (A) does not apply if: (i) the end user is an agency or department of the United States Government that procures the report from the person for purposes of determining the eligibility of the consumer to whom the report relates to receive access or continued access to classified information (as defined in section 1681b(b)(4)(E)(i) of this title); and

   (ii) the head of the agency or department makes a written finding as prescribed under section 1681b(b)(4)(A) of this title.

(4) The dates, original payees, and amounts of any checks upon which is based any adverse characterization of the consumer, included in the file at the time of the disclosure.

(5) A record of all inquiries received by the agency during the one-year period preceding the request that identified the consumer in connection with a credit or insurance transaction that was not initiated by the consumer.

(b) Exempt information. The requirements of subsection (a) of this section respecting the disclosure of sources of information and the recipients of consumer reports do not apply to information received or consumer reports furnished prior to the effective date of this subchapter except to the extent that the matter involved is contained in the files of the consumer reporting agency on that date.

(c) Summary of rights required to be included with disclosure.

   (1) Summary of rights. A consumer reporting agency shall provide to a consumer, with each written disclosure by the agency to the consumer under this section:

   (A) a written summary of all of the rights that the consumer has under this title; and

   (B) in the case of a consumer reporting agency that compiles and maintains files on consumers on a nationwide basis, a toll-free telephone number established by the agency, at which personnel are accessible to consumers during normal business hours.

   (2) Specific items required to be included. The summary of rights required under paragraph (1) shall include:

   (A) a brief description of this title and all rights of consumers under this title;

   (B) an explanation of how the consumer may exercise the rights of the consumer under this title;

   (C) a list of all Federal agencies responsible for enforcing any provision of this title and the address and any appropriate phone number of each such agency, in a form that will assist the consumer in selecting the appropriate agency;

   (D) a statement that the consumer may have additional rights under State law and that the consumer may wish to contact a State or local consumer protection agency or a State attorney general to learn of those rights; and

    (E) a statement that a consumer reporting agency is not required to remove accurate derogatory information from a consumer's file, unless the information is outdated under section 1681c or cannot be verified.

(3) Form of summary of rights. For purposes of this subsection and any disclosure by a consumer reporting agency required under this title with respect to consumers' rights, the Federal Trade Commission (after consultation with each Federal agency referred to in section 1681s(b)) shall prescribe the form and content of any such disclosure of the rights of consumers required under this title. A consumer reporting agency shall be in compliance with this subsection if it provides disclosures under paragraph (1) that are substantially similar to the Federal Trade Commission prescription under this paragraph.

(4) Effectiveness. No disclosures shall be required under this subsection until the date on which the Federal Trade Commission prescribes the form and content of such disclosures under paragraph (3).

15 U.S.C. § 1681h. Conditions and form of disclosure to consumers

(a) In general.

    (1) Proper identification. A consumer reporting agency shall require, as a condition of making the disclosures required under section 1681g of this title, that the consumer furnish proper identification.

    (2) Disclosure in writing. Except as provided in subsection (b), the disclosures required to be made under section 1681g shall be provided under that section in writing.

(b) Other forms of disclosure.

    (1) In general. If authorized by a consumer, a consumer reporting agency may make the disclosures required under 1681g of this title:

        (A) other than in writing; and

        (B) in such form as may be:

            (i) specified by the consumer in accordance with paragraph (2); and

            (ii) available from the agency.

    (2) Form. A consumer may specify pursuant to paragraph (1) that disclosures under section 1681g shall be made:

        (A) in person, upon the appearance of the consumer at the place of business of the consumer reporting agency where disclosures are regularly provided, during normal business hours, and on reasonable notice;

        (B) by telephone, if the consumer has made a written request for disclosure by telephone;

        (C) by electronic means, if available from the agency; or

        (D) by any other reasonable means that is available from the agency.

(c) Trained personnel. Any consumer reporting agency shall provide trained personnel to explain to the consumer any information furnished to him pursuant to section 1681g of this title.

(d) Persons accompanying consumer. The consumer shall be permitted to be accompanied by one other person of his choosing, who shall furnish reasonable identification. A consumer reporting agency may require the consumer to furnish a written statement granting permission to the consumer reporting agency to discuss the consumer's file in such person's presence.

(e) Limitation of liability. Except as provided in sections 1681n and 1681o of this title, no consumer may bring any action or proceeding in the nature of defamation, invasion of privacy, or negligence with respect to the reporting of information against any consumer reporting agency, any user of information, or any person who furnishes information to a consumer reporting agency, based on information disclosed pursuant to section 1681g, 1681h, or 1681m of this title or based on information disclosed by a user of a consumer report to or for a consumer against whom the user has taken adverse action, based whole or in part on the report, except as to false information furnished with malice or willful intent to injure such consumer.

15 U.S.C. § 1681i. Procedure in case of disputed accuracy

(a) Reinvestigations of disputed information.

  (1) Reinvestigation required.

    (A) In general. If the completeness or accuracy of any item of information contained in a consumer's file at a consumer reporting agency is disputed by the consumer and the consumer notifies the agency directly of such dispute, the agency shall reinvestigate free of charge and record the current status of the disputed information, or delete the item from the file in accordance with paragraph (5), before the end of the 30-day period beginning on the date on which the agency receives the notice of the dispute from the consumer.

    (B) Extension of period to reinvestigate. Except as provided in subparagraph (C), the 30-day period described in subparagraph (A) may be extended for not more than 15 additional days if the consumer reporting agency receives information from the consumer during that 30-day period that is relevant to the reinvestigation.

    (C) Limitations on extension of period to reinvestigate. Subparagraph (B) shall not apply to any reinvestigation in which, during the 30-day period described in subparagraph (A), the information that is the subject of the reinvestigation is found to be inaccurate or incomplete or the consumer reporting agency determines that the information cannot be verified.

  (2) Prompt notice of dispute to furnisher of information.

    (A) In general. Before the expiration of the five-business-day period beginning on the date on which a consumer reporting agency receives notice of a dispute from any consumer in accordance with paragraph (1), the agency shall provide notification of the dispute to any person who provided any item of information in dispute, at the address and in the manner established with the person. The notice shall include all relevant information regarding the dispute that the agency has received from the consumer.

    (B) Provision of other information from consumer. The consumer reporting agency shall promptly provide to the person who provided the information in dispute all relevant information regarding the dispute that is received by the agency from the consumer after the period referred to in subparagraph (A) and before the end of the period referred to in paragraph (1)(A).

  (3) Determination that dispute is frivolous or irrelevant.

    (A) In general. Notwithstanding paragraph (1), a consumer reporting agency may terminate a reinvestigation of information disputed by a consumer under that paragraph if the agency reasonably determines that the dispute by the consumer is frivolous or irrelevant, including by reason of a failure by a consumer to provide sufficient information to investigate the disputed information.

    (B) Notice of determination. Upon making any determination in accordance with subparagraph (A) that a dispute is frivolous or irrelevant, a consumer reporting agency shall notify the consumer of such determination not later than 5 business days after making such determination, by mail or, if authorized by the consumer for that purpose, by any other means available to the agency.

(C) Contents of notice. A notice under subparagraph (B) shall include:

    (i) the reasons for the determination under subparagraph (A); and

    (ii) identification of any information required to investigate the disputed information, which may consist of a standardized form describing the general nature of such information.

(4) Consideration of consumer information. In conducting any reinvestigation under paragraph (1) with respect to disputed information in the file of any consumer, the consumer reporting agency shall review and consider all relevant information submitted by the consumer in the period described in paragraph (1)(A) with respect to such disputed information.

(5) Treatment of inaccurate or unverifiable information.

    (A) In general. If, after any reinvestigation under paragraph (1) of any information disputed by a consumer, an item of the information is found to be inaccurate or incomplete or cannot be verified, the consumer reporting agency shall promptly delete that item of information from the consumer's file or modify that item of information, as appropriate, based on the results of the reinvestigation.

    (B) Requirements relating to reinsertion of previously deleted material.

        (i) Certification of accuracy of information. If any information is deleted from a consumer's file pursuant to subparagraph (A), the information may not be reinserted in the file by the consumer reporting agency unless the person who furnishes the information certifies that the information is complete and accurate.

        (ii) Notice to consumer. If any information that has been deleted from a consumer's file pursuant to subparagraph (A) is reinserted in the file, the consumer reporting agency shall notify the consumer of the reinsertion in writing not later than five business days after the reinsertion or, if authorized by the consumer for that purpose, by any other means available to the agency.

        (iii) Additional information. As part of, or in addition to, the notice under clause (ii), a consumer reporting agency shall provide to a consumer in writing not later than five business days after the date of the reinsertion:

            (I) a statement that the disputed information has been reinserted;

            (II) the business name and address of any furnisher of information contacted and the telephone number of such furnisher, if reasonably available, or of any furnisher of information that contacted the consumer reporting agency, in connection with the reinsertion of such information; and

            (III) a notice that the consumer has the right to add a statement to the consumer's file disputing the accuracy or completeness of the disputed information.

    (C) Procedures to prevent reappearance. A consumer reporting agency shall maintain reasonable procedures designed to prevent the reappearance in a consumer's file, and in consumer reports on the consumer, of information that is deleted pursuant to this paragraph (other than information that is reinserted in accordance with subparagraph (B)(i)).

    (D) Automated reinvestigation system. Any consumer reporting agency that compiles and maintains files on consumers on a nationwide basis shall implement an automated system through which furnishers of information to that consumer reporting agency may report the results of a reinvestigation that finds incomplete or inaccurate information in a consumer's file to other such consumer reporting agencies.

(6) Notice of results of reinvestigation.

   (A) In general. A consumer reporting agency shall provide written notice to a consumer of the results of a reinvestigation under this subsection not later than five business days after the completion of the reinvestigation, by mail or, if authorized by the consumer for that purpose, by other means available to the agency.

   (B) Contents. As part of, or in addition to, the notice under subparagraph (A), a consumer reporting agency shall provide to a consumer in writing before the expiration of the five-day period referred to in subparagraph (A):

      (i) a statement that the reinvestigation is completed;

      (ii) a consumer report that is based upon the consumer's file as that file is revised as a result of the reinvestigation;

      (iii) a notice that, if requested by the consumer, a description of the procedure used to determine the accuracy and completeness of the information shall be provided to the consumer by the agency, including the business name and address of any furnisher of information contacted in connection with such information and the telephone number of such furnisher, if reasonably available;

      (iv) a notice that the consumer has the right to add a statement to the consumer's file disputing the accuracy or completeness of the information; and

      (v) a notice that the consumer has the right to request under subsection (d) that the consumer reporting agency furnish notifications under that subsection.

(7) Description of reinvestigation procedure. A consumer reporting agency shall provide to a consumer a description referred to in paragraph (6)(B)(iii) by not later than 15 days after receiving a request from the consumer for that description.

(8) Expedited dispute resolution. If a dispute regarding an item of information in a consumer's file at a consumer reporting agency is resolved in accordance with paragraph (5)(A) by the deletion of the disputed information by not later than three business days after the date on which the agency receives notice of the dispute from the consumer in accordance with paragraph (1)(A), then the agency shall not be required to comply with paragraphs (2), (6), and (7) with respect to that dispute if the agency:

   (A) provides prompt notice of the deletion to the consumer by telephone;

   (B) includes in that notice, or in a written notice that accompanies a confirmation and consumer report provided in accordance with subparagraph (C), a statement of the consumer's right to request under subsection (d) that the agency furnish notifications under that subsection; and

   (C) provides written confirmation of the deletion and a copy of a consumer report on the consumer that is based on the consumer's file after the deletion, not later than five business days after making the deletion.

(b) Statement of dispute. If the reinvestigation does not resolve the dispute, the consumer may file a brief statement setting forth the nature of the dispute. The consumer reporting agency may limit such statements to not more than one hundred words if it provides the consumer with assistance in writing a clear summary of the dispute.

(c) Notification of consumer dispute in subsequent consumer reports. Whenever a statement of a dispute is filed, unless there is reasonable grounds to believe that it is frivolous or irrelevant, the consumer reporting agency shall, in any subsequent consumer report containing the information in question, clearly note that it is disputed by the consumer and provide either the consumer's statement or a clear and accurate codification or summary thereof.

(d) Notification of deletion of disputed information. Following any deletion of information which is found to be inaccurate or whose accuracy can no longer be verified or any notation as to disputed information, the consumer reporting agency shall, at the request of the consumer, furnish notification that the item has been deleted or the statement, codification or summary pursuant to subsection (b) or (c) of this section to any person specifically designated by the consumer who has within two years prior thereto received a consumer report for employment purposes, or within six months prior thereto received a consumer report for any other purpose, which contained the deleted or disputed information.

15 U.S.C. § 1681j. Charges for disclosures

(a) Reasonable charges allowed for certain disclosures.

(1) In general. Except as provided in subsections (b), (c), and (d), a consumer reporting agency may impose a reasonable charge on a consumer:

(A) for making a disclosure to the consumer pursuant to section 1681g, which charge:
(i) shall not exceed $8;* and
(ii) shall be indicated to the consumer before making the disclosure; and

(B) for furnishing, pursuant to section 1681i(d), following a reinvestigation under section 1681i(a), a statement, codification, or summary to a person designated by the consumer under that section after the 30-day period beginning on the date of notification of the consumer under paragraph (6) or (8) of section 611(a) with respect to the reinvestigation, which charge:
(i) shall not exceed the charge that the agency would impose on each designated recipient for a consumer report; and
(ii) shall be indicated to the consumer before furnishing such information.

(2) Modification of amount. The Federal Trade Commission shall increase the amount referred to in paragraph (1)(A)(i) on January 1 of each year, based proportionally on changes in the Consumer Price Index, with fractional changes rounded to the nearest fifty cents.*

(b) Free disclosure after adverse notice to consumer. Each consumer reporting agency that maintains a file on a consumer shall make all disclosures pursuant to section 1681g without charge to the consumer if, not later than 60 days after receipt by such consumer of a notification pursuant to section 1681m, or of a notification from a debt collection agency affiliated with that consumer reporting agency stating that the consumer's credit rating may be or has been adversely affected, the consumer makes a request under section 1681g of this title.

(c) Free disclosure under certain other circumstances. Upon the request of the consumer, a consumer reporting agency shall make all disclosures pursuant to section 1681g once during any 12-month period without charge to that consumer if the consumer certifies in writing that the consumer:

(1) is unemployed and intends to apply for employment in the 60-day period beginning on the date on which the certification is made;

(2) is a recipient of public welfare assistance; or

---

*The FTC has the authority to change this amount by January 1 of each new year to reflect changes in the Consumer Price Index. As of 2003, the amount is $9.

(3) has reason to believe that the file on the consumer at the agency contains inaccurate information due to fraud.

(d) Other charges prohibited. A consumer reporting agency shall not impose any charge on a consumer for providing any notification required by this title or making any disclosure required by this title, except as authorized by subsection (a).

15 U.S.C. § 1681k. Public record information for employment purposes

(a) In general.

A consumer reporting agency which furnishes a consumer report for employment purposes and which for that purpose compiles and reports items of information on consumers which are matters of public record and are likely to have an adverse effect upon a consumer's ability to obtain employment shall:

(1) at the time such public record information is reported to the user of such consumer report, notify the consumer of the fact that public record information is being reported by the consumer reporting agency, together with the name and address of the person to whom such information is being reported; or

(2) maintain strict procedures designed to insure that whenever public record information which is likely to have an adverse effect on a consumer's ability to obtain employment is reported it is complete and up to date. For purposes of this paragraph, items of public record relating to arrests, indictments, convictions, suits, tax liens, and outstanding judgments shall be considered up to date if the current public record status of the item at the time of the report is reported.

(b) Exemption for national security investigations. Subsection (a) of this section does not apply in the case of an agency or department of the United States Government that seeks to obtain and use a consumer report for employment purposes, if the head of the agency or department makes a written finding as prescribed under section 1681b(b)(4)(A) of this title.

15 U.S.C. § 1681l. Restrictions on investigative consumer reports

Whenever a consumer reporting agency prepares an investigative consumer report, no adverse information in the consumer report (other than information which is a matter of public record) may be included in a subsequent consumer report unless such adverse information has been verified in the process of making such subsequent consumer report, or the adverse information was received within the three-month period preceding the date the subsequent report is furnished.

15 U.S.C. § 1681m. Requirements on users of consumer reports

(a) Duties of users taking adverse actions on the basis of information contained in consumer reports. If any person takes any adverse action with respect to any consumer that is based in whole or in part on any information contained in a consumer report, the person shall:

(1) provide oral, written, or electronic notice of the adverse action to the consumer;

(2) provide to the consumer orally, in writing, or electronically:

(A) the name, address, and telephone number of the consumer reporting agency (including a toll-free telephone number established by the agency if the agency compiles and maintains files on consumers on a nationwide basis) that furnished the report to the person; and

(B) a statement that the consumer reporting agency did not make the decision to take the adverse action and is unable to provide the consumer the specific reasons why the adverse action was taken; and

(3) provide to the consumer an oral, written, or electronic notice of the consumer's right:

(A) to obtain, under section 1681j, a free copy of a consumer report on the consumer from the consumer reporting agency referred to in paragraph (2), which notice shall include an indication of the 60-day period under that section for obtaining such a copy; and

(B) to dispute, under section 1681i, with a consumer reporting agency the accuracy or completeness of any information in a consumer report furnished by the agency.

(b) Adverse action based on reports of persons other than consumer reporting agencies.

(1) In general. Whenever credit for personal, family, or household purposes involving a consumer is denied or the charge for such credit is increased either wholly or partly because of information obtained from a person other than a consumer reporting agency bearing upon the consumer's credit worthiness, credit standing, credit capacity, character, general reputation, personal characteristics, or mode of living, the user of such information shall, within a reasonable period of time, upon the consumer's written request for the reasons for such adverse action received within sixty days after learning of such adverse action, disclose the nature of the information to the consumer. The user of such information shall clearly and accurately disclose to the consumer his right to make such written request at the time such adverse action is communicated to the consumer.

(2) Duties of person taking certain actions based on information provided by affiliate.

(A) Duties, generally. If a person takes an action described in subparagraph (B) with respect to a consumer, based in whole or in part on information described in subparagraph (C), the person shall:

(i) notify the consumer of the action, including a statement that the consumer may obtain the information in accordance with clause (ii); and

(ii) upon a written request from the consumer received within 60 days after transmittal of the notice required by clause (i), disclose to the consumer the nature of the information upon which the action is based by not later than 30 days after receipt of the request.

(B) Action described. An action referred to in subparagraph (A) is an adverse action described in section 1681a(k)(1)(A) of this title, taken in connection with a transaction initiated by the consumer, or any adverse action described in clause (i) or (ii) of section 1681a(k)(1)(B) of this title.

(C) Information described. Information referred to in subparagraph (A):

(i) except as provided in clause (ii), is information that:

(I) is furnished to the person taking the action by a person related by common ownership or affiliated by common corporate control to the person taking the action; and

(II) bears on the credit worthiness, credit standing, credit capacity, character, general reputation, personal characteristics, or mode of living of the consumer; and

(ii) does not include:

(I) information solely as to transactions or experiences between the consumer and the person furnishing the information; or

(II) information in a consumer report.

(c) Reasonable procedures to assure compliance. No person shall be held liable for any violation of this section if he shows by a preponderance of the evidence that at the time of the alleged violation he maintained reasonable procedures to assure compliance with the provisions of this section.

(d) Duties of users making written credit or insurance solicitations on the basis of information contained in consumer files.

(1) In general. Any person who uses a consumer report on any consumer in connection with any credit or insurance transaction that is not initiated by the consumer, that is provided to that person under section 1681b(c)(1)(B) of this title, shall provide with each written solicitation made to the consumer regarding the transaction a clear and conspicuous statement that:

  (A) information contained in the consumer's consumer report was used in connection with the transaction;

  (B) the consumer received the offer of credit or insurance because the consumer satisfied the criteria for credit worthiness or insurability under which the consumer was selected for the offer;

  (C) if applicable, the credit or insurance may not be extended if, after the consumer responds to the offer, the consumer does not meet the criteria used to select the consumer for the offer or any applicable criteria bearing on credit worthiness or insurability or does not furnish any required collateral;

  (D) the consumer has a right to prohibit information contained in the consumer's file with any consumer reporting agency from being used in connection with any credit or insurance transaction that is not initiated by the consumer; and

  (E) the consumer may exercise the right referred to in subparagraph (D) by notifying a notification system established under section 1681b(e).

(2) Disclosure of address and telephone number. A statement under paragraph (1) shall include the address and toll-free telephone number of the appropriate notification system established under section 1681b(e).

(3) Maintaining criteria on file. A person who makes an offer of credit or insurance to a consumer under a credit or insurance transaction described in paragraph (1) shall maintain on file the criteria used to select the consumer to receive the offer, all criteria bearing on credit worthiness or insurability, as applicable, that are the basis for determining whether or not to extend credit or insurance pursuant to the offer, and any requirement for the furnishing of collateral as a condition of the extension of credit or insurance, until the expiration of the three-year period beginning on the date on which the offer is made to the consumer.

(4) Authority of federal agencies regarding unfair or deceptive acts or practices not affected. This section is not intended to affect the authority of any Federal or State agency to enforce a prohibition against unfair or deceptive acts or practices, including the making of false or misleading statements in connection with a credit or insurance transaction that is not initiated by the consumer.

15 U.S.C. § 1681n. Civil liability for willful noncompliance

(a) In general. Any person who willfully fails to comply with any requirement imposed under this subchapter with respect to any consumer is liable to that consumer in an amount equal to the sum of:

(1)

  (A) any actual damages sustained by the consumer as a result of the failure or damages of not less than $100 and not more than $1,000; or

  (B) in the case of liability of a natural person for obtaining a consumer report under false pretenses or knowingly without a permissible purpose, actual damages sustained by the consumer as a result of the failure or $1,000, whichever is greater;

(2) such amount of punitive damages as the court may allow; and

(3) in the case of any successful action to enforce any liability under this section, the

costs of the action together with reasonable attorney's fees as determined by the court.

(b) Civil liability for knowing noncompliance. Any person who obtains a consumer report from a consumer reporting agency under false pretenses or knowingly without a permissible purpose shall be liable to the consumer reporting agency for actual damages sustained by the consumer reporting agency or $1,000, whichever is greater.

(c) Attorney's fees. Upon a finding by the court that an unsuccessful pleading, motion, or other paper filed in connection with an action under this section was filed in bad faith or for purposes of harassment, the court shall award to the prevailing party attorney's fees reasonable in relation to the work expended in responding to the pleading, motion, or other paper.

15 U.S.C. § 1681o. Civil liability for negligent noncompliance

(a) In general. Any person who is negligent in failing to comply with any requirement imposed under this subchapter with respect to any consumer is liable to that consumer in an amount equal to the sum of:

(1) any actual damages sustained by the consumer as a result of the failure;

(2) in the case of any successful action to enforce any liability under this section, the costs of the action together with reasonable attorney's fees as determined by the court.

(b) Attorney's fees. On a finding by the court that an unsuccessful pleading, motion, or other paper filed in connection with an action under this section was filed in bad faith or for purposes of harassment, the court shall award to the prevailing party attorney's fees reasonable in relation to the work expended in responding to the pleading, motion, or other paper.

15 U.S.C. § 1681p. Jurisdiction of courts; limitation of actions

An action to enforce any liability created under this subchapter may be brought in any appropriate United States district court without regard to the amount in controversy, or in any other court of competent jurisdiction, within two years from the date on which the liability arises, except that where a defendant has materially and willfully misrepresented any information required under this subchapter to be disclosed to an individual and the information so misrepresented is material to the establishment of the defendant's liability to that individual under this subchapter, the action may be brought at any time within two years after discovery by the individual of the misrepresentation.

15 U.S.C. § 1681q. Obtaining information under false pretenses

Any person who knowingly and willfully obtains information on a consumer from a consumer reporting agency under false pretenses shall be fined under Title 18, United States Code, imprisoned for not more than two years, or both.

15 U.S.C. § 1681r. Unauthorized disclosures by officers or employees

Any officer or employee of a consumer reporting agency who knowingly and willfully provides information concerning an individual from the agency's files to a person not authorized to receive that information shall be fined under Title 18, United States Code, imprisoned for not more than two years, or both.

15 U.S.C. § 1681s. Administrative enforcement

(a)

(1) Enforcement by Federal Trade Commission. Compliance with the requirements imposed under this subchapter shall be enforced under the Federal Trade Commission Act (15 U.S.C. 41 et seq.) by the Federal Trade Commission with respect to consumer reporting agencies and all other persons subject thereto, except to the extent that enforcement of the requirements imposed under this subchapter is specifically committed to some other government agency under subsection (b) hereof. For the purpose of the

exercise by the Federal Trade Commission of its functions and powers under the Federal Trade Commission Act, a violation of any requirement or prohibition imposed under this subchapter shall constitute an unfair or deceptive act or practice in commerce in violation of section 5(a) of the Federal Trade Commission Act (15 U.S.C. 45(a)) and shall be subject to enforcement by the Federal Trade Commission under section 5(b) thereof (15 U.S.C. 45(b)) with respect to any consumer reporting agency or person subject to enforcement by the Federal Trade Commission pursuant to this subsection, irrespective of whether that person is engaged in commerce or meets any other jurisdictional tests in the Federal Trade Commission Act. The Federal Trade Commission shall have such procedural, investigative, and enforcement powers, including the power to issue procedural rules in enforcing compliance with the requirements imposed under this subchapter and to require the filing of reports, the production of documents, and the appearance of witnesses as though the applicable terms and conditions of the Federal Trade Commission Act were part of this subchapter. Any person violating any of the provisions of this subchapter shall be subject to the penalties and entitled to the privileges and immunities provided in the Federal Trade Commission Act as though the applicable terms and provisions thereof were part of this subchapter.

(2)

    (A) In the event of a knowing violation, which constitutes a pattern or practice of violations of this title, the Commission may commence a civil action to recover a civil penalty in a district court of the United States against any person that violates this title. In such action, such person shall be liable for a civil penalty of not more than $2,500 per violation.

    (B) In determining the amount of a civil penalty under subparagraph (A), the court shall take into account the degree of culpability, any history of prior such conduct, ability to pay, effect on ability to continue to do business, and such other matters as justice may require.

(3) Notwithstanding paragraph (2), a court may not impose any civil penalty on a person for a violation of section 1681u(a)(1) unless the person has been enjoined from committing the violation, or ordered not to commit the violation, in an action or proceeding brought by or on behalf of the Federal Trade Commission, and has violated the injunction or order, and the court may not impose any civil penalty for any violation occurring before the date of the violation of the injunction or order.

(b) Enforcement by other agencies. Compliance with the requirements imposed under this title with respect to consumer reporting agencies, persons who use consumer reports from such agencies, persons who furnish information to such agencies, and users of information that are subject to subsection (d) of section 1681m of this title shall be enforced under:

(1) section 8 of the Federal Deposit Insurance Act (12 U.S.C. 1818), in the case of:

    (A) national banks, and Federal branches and Federal agencies of foreign banks, by the Office of the Comptroller of the Currency;

    (B) member banks of the Federal Reserve System (other than national banks), branches and agencies of foreign banks (other than Federal branches, Federal agencies, and insured State branches of foreign banks), commercial lending companies owned or controlled by foreign banks, and organizations operating under section 25 or 25(a) of the Federal Reserve Act (12 U.S.C. 601 et seq., 611 et seq.), by the Board of Governors of the Federal Reserve System; and

(C) banks insured by the Federal Deposit Insurance Corporation (other than members of the Federal Reserve System) and insured State branches of foreign banks, by the Board of Directors of the Federal Deposit Insurance Corporation.

(2) section 8 of the Federal Deposit Insurance Act (12 U.S.C. 1818), by the Director of the Office of Thrift Supervision, in the case of a savings association the deposits of which are insured by the Federal Deposit Insurance Corporation;

(3) the Federal Credit Union Act (12 U.S.C. 1751 et seq.), by the Administrator of the National Credit Union Administration with respect to any Federal credit union;

(4) subtitle IV of title 49, by the Interstate Commerce Commission with respect to any common carrier subject to such subtitle;

(5) the Federal Aviation Act of 1958 (49 App. U.S.C. 1301 et seq.), by the Secretary of Transportation with respect to any air carrier or foreign air carrier subject to that Act; and

(6) the Packers and Stockyards Act, 1921 (7 U.S.C. 181 et seq.) (except as provided in section 406 of that Act (7 U.S.C. 226, 227)), by the Secretary of Agriculture with respect to any activities subject to that Act. The terms used in paragraph (1) that are not defined in this subchapter or otherwise defined in section 3(s) of the Federal Deposit Insurance Act (12 U.S.C. 1813(s)) shall have the meaning given to them in section 1(b) of the International Banking Act of 1978 (12 U.S.C. 3101).

(c) State action for violations.

(1) Authority of states. In addition to such other remedies as are provided under State law, if the chief law enforcement officer of a State, or an official or agency designated by a State, has reason to believe that any person has violated or is violating this title, the State:

(A) may bring an action to enjoin such violation in any appropriate United States district court or in any other court of competent jurisdiction;

(B) subject to paragraph (5), may bring an action on behalf of the residents of the State to recover:

(i) damages for which the person is liable to such residents under sections 1681n and 1681o as a result of the violation;

(ii) in the case of a violation of section 1681t(a), damages for which the person would, but for section 1681t(c), be liable to such residents as a result of the violation; or

(iii) damages of not more than $1,000 for each willful or negligent violation; and

(C) in the case of any successful action under subparagraph (A) or (B), shall be awarded the costs of the action and reasonable attorney fees as determined by the court.

(2) Rights of federal regulators. The State shall serve prior written notice of any action under paragraph (1) upon the Federal Trade Commission or the appropriate Federal regulator determined under subsection (b) and provide the Commission or appropriate Federal regulator with a copy of its complaint, except in any case in which such prior notice is not feasible, in which case the State shall serve such notice immediately upon instituting such action. The Federal Trade Commission or appropriate Federal regulator shall have the right:

(A) to intervene in the action;

(B) upon so intervening, to be heard on all matters arising therein;

(C) to remove the action to the appropriate United States district court; and

(D) to file petitions for appeal.

(3) Investigatory powers. For purposes of bringing any action under this subsection, nothing in this subsection shall prevent the chief law enforcement officer, or an official or agency

designated by a State, from exercising the powers conferred on the chief law enforcement officer or such official by the laws of such State to conduct investigations or to administer oaths or affirmations or to compel the attendance of witnesses or the production of documentary and other evidence.

(4) Limitation on state action while federal action pending. If the Federal Trade Commission or the appropriate Federal regulator has instituted a civil action or an administrative action under section 8 of the Federal Deposit Insurance Act for a violation of this title, no State may, during the pendency of such action, bring an action under this section against any defendant named in the complaint of the Commission or the appropriate Federal regulator for any violation of this title that is alleged in that complaint.

(5) Limitations on state actions for violation of section 1681t(a)(1).

(A) Violation of injunction required. A State may not bring an action against a person under paragraph (1)(B) for a violation of section 1681t(a)(1), unless:

(i) the person has been enjoined from committing the violation, in an action brought by the State under paragraph (1)(A); and

(ii) the person has violated the injunction.

(B) Limitation on damages recoverable. In an action against a person under paragraph (1)(B) for a violation of section 1681t(a)(1), a State may not recover any damages incurred before the date of the violation of an injunction on which the action is based.

(d) Enforcement under other authority. For the purpose of the exercise by any agency referred to in subsection (b) of this section of its powers under any Act referred to in that subsection, a violation of any requirement imposed under this subchapter shall be deemed to be a violation of a requirement imposed under that Act. In addi-

tion to its powers under any provision of law specifically referred to in subsection (b) of this section, each of the agencies referred to in that subsection may exercise, for the purpose of enforcing compliance with any requirement imposed under this subchapter any other authority conferred on it by law.

(e) Regulatory authority

(1) The Federal banking agencies referred to in paragraphs (1) and (2) of subsection (b) shall jointly prescribe such regulations as necessary to carry out the purposes of this subchapter with respect to any persons identified under paragraphs (1) and (2) of subsection (b), and the Board of Governors of the Federal Reserve System shall have authority to prescribe regulations consistent with such joint regulations with respect to bank holding companies and affiliates (other than depository institutions and consumer reporting agencies) of such holding companies.

(2) The Board of the National Credit Union Administration shall prescribe such regulations as necessary to carry out the purposes of this subchapter with respect to any persons identified under paragraph (3) of subsection (b).

15 U.S.C. § 1681s-1. Information on overdue child support obligations

Notwithstanding any other provision of this subchapter, a consumer reporting agency shall include in any consumer report furnished by the agency in accordance with section 1681b of this title, any information on the failure of the consumer to pay overdue support which:

(1) is provided:

(A) to the consumer reporting agency by a State or local child support enforcement agency; or

(B) to the consumer reporting agency and verified by any local, State, or Federal Government agency; and

(2) antedates the report by 7 years or less.

15 U.S.C. § 1681s-2. Responsibilities of persons who furnish information to consumer reporting agencies

(a) Duty of furnishers of information to provide accurate information.

    (1) Prohibition.

        (A) Reporting information with actual knowledge of errors. A person shall not furnish any information relating to a consumer to any consumer reporting agency if the person knows or consciously avoids knowing that the information is inaccurate.

        (B) Reporting information after notice and confirmation of errors. A person shall not furnish information relating to a consumer to any consumer reporting agency if:

            (i) the person has been notified by the consumer, at the address specified by the person for such notices, that specific information is inaccurate; and

            (ii) the information is, in fact, inaccurate.

        (C) No address requirement. A person who clearly and conspicuously specifies to the consumer an address for notices referred to in subparagraph (B) shall not be subject to subparagraph (A); however, nothing in subparagraph (B) shall require a person to specify such an address.

    (2) Duty to correct and update information. A person who:

        (A) regularly and in the ordinary course of business furnishes information to one or more consumer reporting agencies about the person's transactions or experiences with any consumer; and

        (B) has furnished to a consumer reporting agency information that the person determines is not complete or accurate,

    shall promptly notify the consumer reporting agency of that determination and provide to the agency any corrections to that information, or any additional information, that is necessary to make the information provided by the person to the agency complete and accurate, and shall not thereafter furnish to the agency any of the information that remains not complete or accurate.

    (3) Duty to provide notice of dispute. If the completeness or accuracy of any information furnished by any person to any consumer reporting agency is disputed to such person by a consumer, the person may not furnish the information to any consumer reporting agency without notice that such information is disputed by the consumer.

    (4) Duty to provide notice of closed accounts. A person who regularly and in the ordinary course of business furnishes information to a consumer reporting agency regarding a consumer who has a credit account with that person shall notify the agency of the voluntary closure of the account by the consumer, in information regularly furnished for the period in which the account is closed.

    (5) Duty to provide notice of delinquency of accounts. A person who furnishes information to a consumer reporting agency regarding a delinquent account being placed for collection, charged to profit or loss, or subjected to any similar action shall, not later than 90 days after furnishing the information, notify the agency of the month and year of the commencement of the delinquency that immediately preceded the action.

(b) Duties of furnishers of information upon notice of dispute.

    (1) In general. After receiving notice pursuant to section 1681i(a)(2) of a dispute with regard to the completeness or accuracy of any information provided by a person to a consumer reporting agency, the person shall:

        (A) conduct an investigation with respect to the disputed information;

        (B) review all relevant information provided by the consumer reporting agency pursuant to section 1681i(a)(2);

    (C) report the results of the investigation to the consumer reporting agency; and

    (D) if the investigation finds that the information is incomplete or inaccurate, report those results to all other consumer reporting agencies to which the person furnished the information and that compile and maintain files on consumers on a nationwide basis.

  (2) Deadline. A person shall complete all investigations, reviews, and reports required under paragraph (1) regarding information provided by the person to a consumer reporting agency, before the expiration of the period under section 1681i(a)(1) within which the consumer reporting agency is required to complete actions required by that section regarding that information.

(c) Limitation on liability. Sections 1681n and 1681o of this title do not apply to any failure to comply with subsection (a), except as provided in section 1681s(c)(1)(B) of this title.

(d) Limitation on enforcement. Subsection (a) shall be enforced exclusively under section 1681s of this title by the Federal agencies and officials and the State officials identified in that section.

15 U.S.C. § 1681t. Relation to state laws

(a) In general. Except as provided in subsections (b) and (c), this title does not annul, alter, affect, or exempt any person subject to the provisions of this subchapter from complying with the laws of any State with respect to the collection, distribution, or use of any information on consumers, except to the extent that those laws are inconsistent with any provision of this subchapter, and then only to the extent of the inconsistency.

(b) General exceptions. No requirement or prohibition may be imposed under the laws of any State:

  (1) with respect to any subject matter regulated under:

    (A) subsection (c) or (e) of section 1681b of this title, relating to the prescreening of consumer reports;

    (B) section 1681i, relating to the time by which a consumer reporting agency must take any action, including the provision of notification to a consumer or other person, in any procedure related to the disputed accuracy of information in a consumer's file, except that this subparagraph shall not apply to any State law in effect on September 30, 1996;

    (C) subsections (a) and (b) of section 1681m of this title, relating to the duties of a person who takes any adverse action with respect to a consumer;

    (D) section 1681m(d) of this title, relating to the duties of persons who use a consumer report of a consumer in connection with any credit or insurance transaction that is not initiated by the consumer and that consists of a firm offer of credit or insurance;

    (E) section 1681c of this title, relating to information contained in consumer reports, except that this subparagraph shall not apply to any State law in effect on September 30, 1996; or

    (F) section 1681t of this title, relating to the responsibilities of persons who furnish information to consumer reporting agencies, except that this paragraph shall not apply:

      (i) with respect to section 54A(a) of chapter 93 of the Massachusetts Annotated Laws (as in effect on September 30, 1996); or

      (ii) with respect to section 1785.25(a) of the California Civil Code (as in effect on September 30, 1996);

  (2) with respect to the exchange of information among persons affiliated by common ownership or common corporate control, except that this paragraph shall not apply with respect to subsection (a) or (c)(1) of section 2480e of title 9, Vermont Statutes Annotated (as in effect on September 30, 1996); or

(3) with respect to the form and content of any disclosure required to be made under section 1681g(c).

(c) Definition of firm offer of credit or insurance. Notwithstanding any definition of the term "firm offer of credit or insurance" (or any equivalent term) under the laws of any State, the definition of that term contained in section 1681a(l) shall be construed to apply in the enforcement and interpretation of the laws of any State governing consumer reports.

(d) Limitations. Subsections (b) and (c):

(1) do not affect any settlement, agreement, or consent judgment between any State Attorney General and any consumer reporting agency in effect on September 30, 1996; and

(2) do not apply to any provision of State law (including any provision of a State constitution) that:

(A) is enacted after January 1, 2004;

(B) states explicitly that the provision is intended to supplement this subchapter; and

(C) gives greater protection to consumers than is provided under this subchapter.

15 U.S.C. § 1681u. Disclosures to FBI for counterintelligence purposes

(a) Identity of financial institutions. Notwithstanding section 1681b of this title or any other provision of this subchapter, a consumer reporting agency shall furnish to the Federal Bureau of Investigation the names and addresses of all financial institutions (as that term is defined in section 3401 of Title 12) at which a consumer maintains or has maintained an account, to the extent that information is in the files of the agency, when presented with a written request for that information, signed by the Director of the Federal Bureau of Investigation, or the Director's designee in a position not lower than Deputy Assistant Director at Bureau headquarters or a Special Agent in Charge of a Bureau field office designated by the Director, which certifies compliance with this section. The Director or the Director's designee may make such a certification only if the Director or the Director's designee has determined in writing, that such information is sought for the conduct of an authorized investigation to protect against international terrorism or clandestine intelligence activities, provided that such an investigation of a United States person is not conducted solely upon the basis of activities protected by the first amendment to the Constitution of the United States.

(b) Identifying information. Notwithstanding the provisions of section 1681b of this title or any other provision of this subchapter, a consumer reporting agency shall furnish identifying information respecting a consumer, limited to name, address, former addresses, places of employment, or former places of employment, to the Federal Bureau of Investigation when presented with a written request, signed by the Director or the Director's designee in a position not lower than Deputy Assistant Director at Bureau headquarters or a Special Agent in Charge of a Bureau field office designated by the Director, which certifies compliance with this subsection. The Director or the Director's designee may make such a certification only if the Director or the Director's designee has determined in writing that such information is sought for the conduct of an authorized investigation to protect against international terrorism or clandestine intelligence activities, provided that such an investigation of a United States person is not conducted solely upon the basis of activities protected by the first amendment to the Constitution of the United States.

(c) Court order for disclosure of consumer reports. Notwithstanding section 1681b of this title or any other provision of this subchapter, if requested in writing by the Director of the Federal Bureau of Investigation, or a designee of the Director in a position not lower than Deputy Assistant Director at Bureau headquarters or a Special

Agent in Charge in a Bureau field office designated by the Director, a court may issue an order ex parte directing a consumer reporting agency to furnish a consumer report to the Federal Bureau of Investigation, upon a showing in camera that the consumer report is sought for the conduct of an authorized investigation to protect against international terrorism or clandestine intelligence activities, provided that such an investigation of a United States person is not conducted solely upon the basis of activities protected by the first amendment to the Constitution of the United States.

The terms of an order issued under this subsection shall not disclose that the order is issued for purposes of a counterintelligence investigation.

(d) Confidentiality. No consumer reporting agency or officer, employee, or agent of a consumer reporting agency shall disclose to any person, other than those officers, employees, or agents of a consumer reporting agency necessary to fulfill the requirement to disclose information to the Federal Bureau of Investigation under this section, that the Federal Bureau of Investigation has sought or obtained the identity of financial institutions or a consumer report respecting any consumer under subsection (a), (b), or (c) of this section, and no consumer reporting agency or officer, employee, or agent of a consumer reporting agency shall include in any consumer report any information that would indicate that the Federal Bureau of Investigation has sought or obtained such information or a consumer report.

(e) Payment of fees. The Federal Bureau of Investigation shall, subject to the availability of appropriations, pay to the consumer reporting agency assembling or providing report or information in accordance with procedures established under this section a fee for reimbursement for such costs as are reasonably necessary and which have been directly incurred in searching, reproducing, or transporting books, papers, records, or other data required or requested to be produced under this section.

(f) Limit on dissemination. The Federal Bureau of Investigation may not disseminate information obtained pursuant to this section outside of the Federal Bureau of Investigation, except to other Federal agencies as may be necessary for the approval or conduct of a foreign counterintelligence investigation, or, where the information concerns a person subject to the Uniform Code of Military Justice, to appropriate investigative authorities within the military department concerned as may be necessary for the conduct of a joint foreign counterintelligence investigation.

(g) Rules of construction. Nothing in this section shall be construed to prohibit information from being furnished by the Federal Bureau of Investigation pursuant to a subpoena or court order, in connection with a judicial or administrative proceeding to enforce the provisions of this subchapter. Nothing in this section shall be construed to authorize or permit the withholding of information from the Congress.

(h) Reports to Congress

(1) On a semiannual basis, the Attorney General shall fully inform the Permanent Select Committee on Intelligence and the Committee on Banking, Finance and Urban Affairs of the House of Representatives, and the Select Committee on Intelligence and the Committee on Banking, Housing, and Urban Affairs of the Senate concerning all requests made pursuant to subsections (a), (b), and (c) of this section.

(2) In the case of the semiannual reports required to be submitted under paragraph (1) to the Permanent Select Committee on Intelligence of the House of Representatives and the Select Committee on Intelligence of the Senate, the submittal dates for such reports shall be as provided in section 415b of Title 50.

(i) Damages. Any agency or department of the United States obtaining or disclosing any consumer reports, records, or information contained therein in violation of this section is liable to the consumer to whom such consumer reports, records, or information relate in an amount equal to the sum of—

(1) $100, without regard to the volume of consumer reports, records, or information involved;

(2) any actual damages sustained by the consumer as a result of the disclosure;

(3) if the violation is found to have been willful or intentional, such punitive damages as a court may allow; and

(4) in the case of any successful action to enforce liability under this subsection, the costs of the action, together with reasonable attorney fees, as determined by the court.

(j) Disciplinary actions for violations. If a court determines that any agency or department of the United States has violated any provision of this section and the court finds that the circumstances surrounding the violation raise questions of whether or not an officer or employee of the agency or department acted willfully or intentionally with respect to the violation, the agency or department shall promptly initiate a proceeding to determine whether or not disciplinary action is warranted against the officer or employee who was responsible for the violation.

(k) Good-faith exception. Notwithstanding any other provision of this subchapter, any consumer reporting agency or agent or employee thereof making disclosure of consumer reports or identifying information pursuant to this subsection in good-faith reliance upon a certification of the Federal Bureau of Investigation pursuant to provisions of this section shall not be liable to any person for such disclosure under this subchapter, the constitution of any State, or any law or regulation of any State or any political subdivision of any State.

(l) Limitation of remedies. Notwithstanding any other provision of this subchapter, the remedies and sanctions set forth in this section shall be the only judicial remedies and sanctions for violation of this section.

(m) Injunctive relief. In addition to any other remedy contained in this section, injunctive relief shall be available to require compliance with the procedures of this section. In the event of any successful action under this subsection, costs together with reasonable attorney fees, as determined by the court, may be recovered.

15 U.S.C. § 1681v. Disclosures to Governmental agencies for counterterrorism purposes

(a) Disclosure. Notwithstanding section 1681b of this title or any other provision of this subchapter, a consumer reporting agency shall furnish a consumer report of a consumer and all other information in a consumer's file to a government agency authorized to conduct investigations of, or intelligence or counterintelligence activities or analysis related to, international terrorism when presented with a written certification by such government agency that such information is necessary for the agency's conduct or such investigation, activity or analysis.

(b) Form of certification. The certification described in subsection (a) shall be signed by a supervisory official designated by the head of a Federal agency or an officer of a Federal agency whose appointment to office is required to be made by the President, by and with the advice and consent of the Senate.

(c) Confidentiality. No consumer reporting agency, or officer, employee, or agent of such consumer reporting agency, shall disclose to any person, or specify in any consumer report, that a government agency has sought or obtained access to information under subsection (a).

(d) Rule of construction. Nothing in section 1681u of this title shall be construed to limit the authority of the Director of the Federal Bureau of Investigation under this section.

(e) Safe harbor. Notwithstanding any other provision of this subchapter, any consumer reporting agency or agent or employee thereof making disclosure of consumer reports or other information pursuant to this section in good-faith reliance upon a certification of a governmental agency pursuant to the provisions of this section shall not be liable to any person for such disclosure under this subchapter, the constitution of any State, or any law or regulation of any State or any political subdivision of any State.

Text of the Federal Credit Repair Organizations Act

15 U.S.C. § 1679. Findings and purposes

(a) Findings

The Congress makes the following findings:

(1) Consumers have a vital interest in establishing and maintaining their credit worthiness and credit standing in order to obtain and use credit. As a result, consumers who have experienced credit problems may seek assistance from credit repair organizations which offer to improve the credit standing of such consumers.

(2) Certain advertising and business practices of some companies engaged in the business of credit repair services have worked a financial hardship upon consumers, particularly those of limited economic means and who are inexperienced in credit matters.

(b) Purposes

The purposes of this subchapter are -

(1) to ensure that prospective buyers of the services of credit

repair organizations are provided with the information necessary

to make an informed decision regarding the purchase of such

services; and

(2) to protect the public from unfair or deceptive advertising

and business practices by credit repair organizations.

15 U.S.C. § 1679a. Definitions

For purposes of this subchapter, the following definitions apply:

(1) Consumer

The term "consumer" means an individual.

(2) Consumer credit transaction

The term "consumer credit transaction" means any transaction in which credit is offered or extended to an individual for personal, family, or household purposes.

(3) Credit repair organization

The term "credit repair organization" -

(A) means any person who uses any instrumentality of interstate commerce or the mails to sell, provide, or perform (or represent that such person can or will sell, provide, or perform) any service, in return for the payment of money or other valuable consideration, for the express or implied purpose of -

(i) improving any consumer's credit record, credit history, or credit rating; or

(ii) providing advice or assistance to any consumer with regard to any activity or service described in clause (i); and

(B) does not include -

(i) any nonprofit organization which is exempt from taxation under section 501(c)(3) of title 26;

(ii) any creditor (as defined in section 1602 of this title), with respect to any consumer, to the extent the creditor is assisting the consumer to restructure any debt owed by the consumer to the creditor; or

(iii) any depository institution (as that term is defined in section 1813 of title 12) or any Federal or State credit union (as those terms are defined in section 1752 of title 12), or any affiliate or subsidiary of such a depository institution or credit union.

(4) Credit

The term "credit" has the meaning given to such term in section 1602(e) of this title.

15 U.S.C. § 1679b. Prohibited practices

(a) In general

No person may -

(1) make any statement, or counsel or advise any consumer to make any statement, which is untrue or misleading (or which, upon the exercise of reasonable care, should be known by the credit repair organization, officer, employee, agent, or other person to be

untrue or misleading) with respect to any consumer's credit worthiness, credit standing, or credit capacity to -

(A) any consumer reporting agency (as defined in section 1681a(f) of this title); or

(B) any person -

    (i) who has extended credit to the consumer; or

    (ii) to whom the consumer has applied or is applying for an extension of credit;

(2) make any statement, or counsel or advise any consumer to make any statement, the intended effect of which is to alter the consumer's identification to prevent the display of the consumer's credit record, history, or rating for the purpose of concealing adverse information that is accurate and not obsolete to -

(A) any consumer reporting agency;

(B) any person -

    (i) who has extended credit to the consumer; or

    (ii) to whom the consumer has applied or is applying for an extension of credit;

(3) make or use any untrue or misleading representation of the services of the credit repair organization; or

(4) engage, directly or indirectly, in any act, practice, or course of business that constitutes or results in the commission of, or an attempt to commit, a fraud or deception on any person in connection with the offer or sale of the services of the credit repair organization.

(b) Payment in advance

No credit repair organization may charge or receive any money or other valuable consideration for the performance of any service which the credit repair organization has agreed to perform for any consumer before such service is fully performed.

15 U.S.C. § 1679c. Disclosures

(a) Disclosure required

Any credit repair organization shall provide any consumer with the following written statement before any contract or agreement between the consumer and the credit repair organization is executed:

"CONSUMER CREDIT FILE RIGHTS UNDER STATE AND FEDERAL LAW

"You have a right to dispute inaccurate information in your credit report by contacting the credit bureau directly. However, neither you nor any 'credit repair' company or credit repair organization has the right to have accurate, current, and verifiable information removed from your credit report. The credit bureau must remove accurate, negative information from your report only if it is over 7 years old. Bankruptcy information can be reported for 10 years.

"You have a right to obtain a copy of your credit report from a credit bureau. You may be charged a reasonable fee. There is no fee, however, if you have been turned down for credit, employment, insurance, or a rental dwelling because of information in your credit report within the preceding 60 days. The credit bureau must provide someone to help you interpret the information in your credit file. You are entitled to receive a free copy of your credit report if you are unemployed and intend to apply for employment in the next 60 days, if you are a recipient of public welfare assistance, or if you have reason to believe that there is inaccurate information in your credit report due to fraud.

"You have a right to sue a credit repair organization that violates the Credit Repair Organization Act. This law prohibits deceptive practices by credit repair organizations.

"You have the right to cancel your contract with any credit repair organization for any reason within 3 business days from the date you signed it.

"Credit bureaus are required to follow reasonable procedures to ensure that the information they report is accurate. However, mistakes may occur.

"You may, on your own, notify a credit bureau in writing that you dispute the accuracy of information in your credit file. The credit bureau must then reinvestigate and modify or remove inaccurate or incomplete information. The credit bureau may not charge any fee for this service. Any pertinent information and copies of all documents you have concerning an error should be given to the credit bureau.

"If the credit bureau's reinvestigation does not resolve the dispute to your satisfaction, you may send a brief statement to the credit bureau, to be kept in your file, explaining why you think the record is inaccurate. The credit bureau must include a summary of your statement about disputed information with any report it issues about you.

"The Federal Trade Commission regulates credit bureaus and credit repair organizations. For more information contact:

"THE PUBLIC REFERENCE BRANCH

"FEDERAL TRADE COMMISSION

"WASHINGTON, D.C. 20580."

(b) Separate statement requirement

The written statement required under this section shall be provided as a document which is separate from any written contract or other agreement between the credit repair organization and the consumer or any other written material provided to the consumer.

(c) Retention of compliance records

(1) In general

The credit repair organization shall maintain a copy of the statement signed by the consumer acknowledging receipt of the statement.

(2) Maintenance for 2 years

The copy of any consumer's statement shall be maintained in the organization's files for 2 years after the date on which the statement is signed by the consumer.

15 U.S.C. § 1679d. Credit repair organizations contracts

(a) Written contracts required

No services may be provided by any credit repair organization for any consumer -

(1) unless a written and dated contract (for the purchase of such services) which meets the requirements of subsection (b) of this section has been signed by the consumer; or

(2) before the end of the 3-business-day period beginning on the date the contract is signed.

(b) Terms and conditions of contract

No contract referred to in subsection (a) of this section meets the requirements of this subsection unless such contract includes (in writing) -

(1) the terms and conditions of payment, including the total amount of all payments to be made by the consumer to the credit repair organization or to any other person;

(2) a full and detailed description of the services to be performed by the credit repair organization for the consumer, including -

(A) all guarantees of performance; and

(B) an estimate of -

(i) the date by which the performance of the services (to be performed by the credit repair organization or any other person) will be complete; or

(ii) the length of the period necessary to perform such services;

(3) the credit repair organization's name and principal business address; and

(4) a conspicuous statement in bold face type, in immediate proximity to the space reserved for the consumer's signature on the contract, which reads as follows: "You may cancel this contract without penalty or obligation at any time before midnight of the 3rd business day after the date on which you signed the contract. See the attached notice of cancellation form for an explanation of this right."

15 U.S.C. § 1679e. Right to cancel contract

(a) In general

Any consumer may cancel any contract with any credit repair organization without penalty or obligation by notifying the credit repair organization of the consumer's intention to do so at any time before midnight of the 3rd business day which begins after the date on which the contract or agreement between the consumer and the credit repair organization is executed or would, but for this subsection, become enforceable against the parties.

(b) Cancellation form and other information

Each contract shall be accompanied by a form, in duplicate, which has the heading "Notice of Cancellation" and contains in boldface type the following statement:

"You may cancel this contract, without any penalty or obligation, at any time before midnight of the 3rd day which

begins after the date the contract is signed by you.

"To cancel this contract, mail or deliver a signed, dated copy of this cancellation notice, or any other written notice to (name of credit repair organization) at (address of credit repair organization) before midnight on (date).
"I hereby cancel this transaction,
(date)
(purchaser's signature)."

(c) Consumer copy of contract required

Any consumer who enters into any contract with any credit repair organization shall be given, by the organization -

(1) a copy of the completed contract and the disclosure

statement required under section 1679c of this title; and

(2) a copy of any other document the credit repair organization

requires the consumer to sign, at the time the contract or the other document is signed.

15 U.S.C. § 1679f. Noncompliance with this subchapter

(a) Consumer waivers invalid

Any waiver by any consumer of any protection provided by or any right of the consumer under this subchapter -

(1) shall be treated as void; and

(2) may not be enforced by any Federal or State court or any other person.

(b) Attempt to obtain waiver

Any attempt by any person to obtain a waiver from any consumer of any protection provided by or any right of the consumer under this subchapter shall be treated as a violation of this subchapter.

(c) Contracts not in compliance

Any contract for services which does not comply with the applicable provisions of this subchapter-

(1) shall be treated as void; and

(2) may not be enforced by any Federal or State court or any other person.

15 U.S.C. § 1679g. Civil liability

(a) Liability established

Any person who fails to comply with any provision of this subchapter with respect to any other person shall be liable to such person in an amount equal to the sum of the amounts determined under each of the following paragraphs:

(1) Actual damages

The greater of -

(A) the amount of any actual damage sustained by such person as a result of such failure; or

(B) any amount paid by the person to the credit repair organization.

(2) Punitive damages

(A) Individual actions

In the case of any action by an individual, such additional amount as the court may allow.

(B) Class actions

In the case of a class action, the sum of -

(i) the aggregate of the amount which the court may allow for each named plaintiff; and

(ii) the aggregate of the amount which the court may allow for each other class member, without regard to any minimum individual recovery.

(3) Attorneys' fees

In the case of any successful action to enforce any liability

under paragraph (1) or (2), the costs of the action, together

with reasonable attorneys' fees.

(b) Factors to be considered in awarding punitive damages

In determining the amount of any liability of any credit repair organization under subsection (a)(2) of this section, the court shall consider, among other relevant factors -

(1) the frequency and persistence of noncompliance by the

credit repair organization;

(2) the nature of the noncompliance;

(3) the extent to which such noncompliance was intentional; and

(4) in the case of any class action, the number of consumers adversely affected.

15 U.S.C. § 1679h. Administrative enforcement

(a) In general

Compliance with the requirements imposed under this subchapter with respect to credit repair organizations shall be enforced under the Federal Trade Commission Act (15 U.S.C. 41 et seq.) by the Federal Trade Commission.

(b) Violations of this subchapter treated as violations of Federal

Trade Commission Act

(1) In general

For the purpose of the exercise by the Federal Trade Commission of the Commission's functions and powers under the Federal Trade Commission Act (15 U.S.C. 41 et seq.), any violation of any requirement or prohibition imposed under this subchapter with

respect to credit repair organizations shall constitute an unfair or deceptive act or practice in commerce in violation of section 5(a) of the Federal Trade Commission Act (15 U.S.C. 45(a)).

(2) Enforcement authority under other law

All functions and powers of the Federal Trade Commission under the Federal Trade Commission Act shall be available to the Commission to enforce compliance with this subchapter by any person subject to enforcement by the Federal Trade Commission pursuant to this subsection, including the power to enforce the provisions of this subchapter in the same manner as if the violation had been a violation of any Federal Trade Commission trade regulation rule, without regard to whether the credit repair organization -

(A) is engaged in commerce; or

(B) meets any other jurisdictional tests in the Federal Trade Commission Act.

(c) State action for violations

(1) Authority of States

In addition to such other remedies as are provided under State law, whenever the chief law enforcement officer of a State, or an official or agency designated by a State, has reason to believe that any person has violated or is violating this subchapter, the State -

(A) may bring an action to enjoin such violation;

(B) may bring an action on behalf of its residents to recover damages for which the person is liable to such residents under section 1679g of this title as a result of the violation; and

(C) in the case of any successful action under subparagraph (A) or (B), shall be awarded the costs of the action and reasonable attorney fees as determined by the court.

(2) Rights of Commission

(A) Notice to Commission

The State shall serve prior written notice of any civil action under paragraph (1) upon the Federal Trade Commission and provide the Commission with a copy of its complaint, except in any case where such prior notice is not feasible, in which case the State shall serve such notice immediately upon instituting such action.

(B) Intervention

The Commission shall have the right -

(i) to intervene in any action referred to in subparagraph (A);

(ii) upon so intervening, to be heard on all matters arising in the action; and

(iii) to file petitions for appeal.

(3) Investigatory powers

For purposes of bringing any action under this subsection, nothing in this subsection shall prevent the chief law enforcement officer, or an official or agency designated by a State, from exercising the powers conferred on the chief law enforcement officer or such official by the laws of such State to conduct investigations or to administer oaths or affirmations or to compel the attendance of witnesses or the production of documentary and other evidence.

(4) Limitation

Whenever the Federal Trade Commission has instituted a civil action for violation of this subchapter, no State may, during the pendency of such action, bring an action under this section against any defendant named in the complaint of the Commission for any violation of this subchapter that is alleged in that complaint.

15 U.S.C. § 1679i. Statute of limitations

Any action to enforce any liability under this subchapter may be brought before the later of -

(1) the end of the 5-year period beginning on the date of the occurrence of the violation involved; or

(2) in any case in which any credit repair organization has materially and willfully misrepresented any information which -

(A) the credit repair organization is required, by any provision of this subchapter, to disclose to any consumer; and

(B) is material to the establishment of the credit repair organization's liability to the consumer under this subchapter, the end of the 5-year period beginning on the date of the discovery by the consumer of the misrepresentation.

15 U.S.C. § 1679j. Relation to State law

This subchapter shall not annul, alter, affect, or exempt any person subject to the provisions of this subchapter from complying with any law of any State except to the extent that such law is inconsistent with any provision of this subchapter, and then only to the extent of the inconsistency.

■

Forms and Letters

Outstanding Debts

Outstanding Debts	Monthly Payment	Amount Behind
Rent or mortgage (include second mortgage, home equity loans)		
Utilities and telephone		
Transportation expenses		
car loans		
maintenance payments		
auto insurance		
Child care		
Alimony or child support		
Education expenses		
student loans		
tuition expenses		
Personal and other loans		
bank loans		
loan consolidator		
Lawyers' or accountants' bills		

Outstanding Debts	Monthly Payment	Amount Behind
Medical (doctors' and hospital) bills		
Insurance		
homeowner's or renter's		
disability		
medical or dental		
life		
Credit and charge cards		
Department store charges		
Back taxes		
Federal		
State		
Other (such as property)		
Other unpaid bills		
TOTALS	$	$

Daily Expenditures for Week of _____

Sunday's Expenditures	Cost	Monday's Expenditures	Cost	Tuesday's Expenditures	Cost	Wednesday's Expenditures	Cost
Daily Total:		**Daily Total:**		**Daily Total:**		**Daily Total:**	

Thursday's Expenditures	Cost	Friday's Expenditures	Cost	Saturday's Expenditures	Cost	Other Expenditures	Cost
Daily Total:		**Daily Total:**		**Daily Total:**		**Weekly Total:**	

Monthly Income From All Sources

1 Source of Income	2 Amount of each payment	3 Period covered by each payment	4 Amount per month

A. Wages or Salary

    Job 1:

_____

    Gross pay, including overtime: $ _____   _____

    Subtract:

        Federal taxes   _____

        State taxes   _____

        Social Security (FICA)   _____

        Union dues   _____

        Insurance payments   _____

        Child support wage withholding   _____

        Other mandatory deductions (specify):

        _____ _____

Subtotal $ _____   _____   _____

    Job 2:

_____

    Gross pay, including overtime: $ _____   _____

    Subtract:

        Federal taxes   _____

        State taxes   _____

        Social Security (FICA)   _____

        Union dues   _____

        Insurance payments   _____

        Child support wage withholding   _____

        Other mandatory deductions (specify):

        _____ _____

Subtotal $ _____   _____   _____

    Job 3:

_____

    Gross pay, including overtime: $ _____   _____

    Subtract:

        Federal taxes   _____

        State taxes   _____

        Social Security (FICA)   _____

        Union dues   _____

        Insurance payments   _____

        Child support wage withholding   _____

        Other mandatory deductions (specify):

        _____ _____

Subtotal $ _____   _____   _____

Monthly Income From All Sources (cont'd)

1 Source of Income	2 Amount of each payment	3 Period covered by each payment	4 Amount per month

B. Self-Employment Income

Job 1:   Gross pay, including overtime: $ _____   _____

_____   Subtract:

        Federal taxes   _____

        State taxes   _____

        Self-employment taxes   _____

        Other mandatory deductions (specify):

        _____   _____

Subtotal $ _____   _____   _____

Job 2:   Gross pay, including overtime: $ _____   _____

_____   Subtract:

        Federal taxes   _____

        State taxes   _____

        Self-employment taxes   _____

        Other mandatory deductions (specify): _____

        _____   _____

Subtotal $ _____   _____   _____

C. Other Sources

Source	Amount of each payment	Period covered	Amount per month
Bonuses			
Dividends and interest			
Rent, lease or license income			
Royalties			
Note or trust income			
Alimony or child support you receive			
Pension or retirement income			
Social Security			
Other public assistance			
Other (specify):			

Total monthly income $ _____

_____

_____

_____

Attn: Customer Service

Date: _____

Name(s) on account: _____

Account number: _____

To Whom It May Concern:

I am writing to dispute the following charge that appears on my billing statement dated _____
_____, 20_____.

Merchant's name: _____

Amount in dispute: _____

I am disputing this amount for the following reason(s):

_____

_____

_____

_____

_____

_____

As required by law, I have tried in good faith to resolve this dispute with the merchant. [Describe your efforts. _____.]

Furthermore, I wish to point out that this purchase was for more than $50 and was made [cross out one:] in the state in which I live/within 100 miles of my home.

Please verify this dispute with the merchant and remove this item, and all late and interest charges attributed to this item, from my billing statement.

Sincerely,

_____
[your signature]

Name: _____

Address: _____

_____

Home phone: _____

_____

_____

_____

Attn: Customer Service

Date: _____

Name(s) on account: _____

Account number: _____

To Whom It May Concern:

I am writing to point out an error that appears on my billing statement dated _____,
20_____.

Merchant's name: _____

Amount in error: _____

The problem is as follows:

_____

_____

_____

_____

_____

_____

_____

_____

I understand that the law requires you to acknowledge receipt of this letter within 30 days unless you correct
this billing error before then. Furthermore, I understand that within two billing cycles (but in no event more
than 90 days), you must correct the error or explain why you believe the amount to be correct.

Sincerely,

_____
[your signature]

Name: _____

Address: _____

_____

Home phone: _____

_____

_____

_____

Attn: Customer Service

Date:_____

Name(s) on account:_____

Account number:_____

To Whom It May Concern:

On _____, 20_____, I received a copy of my credit report from
_____. It lists my payments to you as delinquent.

My past financial problems are behind me and I am now in a position to pay off this debt. I can pay a
lump sum amount of $_____ or I can pay installments in the amount of $_____
per month for _____ months if you will agree to either of the following:

☐ If I make a lump sum payment, you agree to remove the negative information from my credit file associated with the debt.

☐ If I agree to pay off the debt in installments, you agree to re-age my account—that is, make the current
month the first repayment month and show no late payments as long as I make the agreed upon
monthly payments.

If my offer is acceptable to you, please initial one of the above lines, sign the acceptance below and
return this letter to me in the enclosed envelope.

Sincerely,

_____
[your signature]

Name:_____

Address:_____

_____

Home phone:_____

Agreed to and accepted on this _____ day of _____, 20_____.

By:_____

Name (print):_____

Title:_____

_____

_____

_____

Attn: Customer Service

Date:_____

Name(s) on account:_____

Account number:_____

Date loan/account opened:_____

Total amount due:_____

Monthly payment amount:_____

To Whom It May Concern:

At the present, I cannot pay the monthly amount required under the agreement for the following reason(s):

_____

_____

_____

_____

_____

_____

I can pay $_____ per month right now and expect to resume making the full monthly payment when the following occurs:

_____

_____

_____

Please accept the reduced payments until then. If necessary, add the unpaid amount to the end of the loan or account period and extend it by a few months.

Thank you for your understanding and help. Please call or write within 20 days to let me know if this is acceptable.

Sincerely,

_____
[your signature]

Name:_____

Address:_____

_____

Home phone:_____

_____

_____

_____

Attn: Customer Service

Date:_____

Name(s) on account:_____

Account number:_____

Date loan/account opened:_____

Total amount due:_____

Monthly payment amount:_____

To Whom It May Concern:

At the present, I cannot pay the monthly amount required under the agreement for the following reason(s):

_____

_____

_____

_____

_____

_____

_____

_____

_____

I can pay you only $_____ per month for the indefinite future. Please accept the reduced payments. I promise to inform you immediately if my financial condition improves and I am able to resume making normal payments.

Thank you for your understanding and help. Please call or write within 20 days to let me know if this is acceptable.

Sincerely,

_____
[your signature]

Name:_____

Address:_____

_____

Home phone:_____

_____

_____

_____

Attn: Customer Service

Date:_____

Name(s) on account:_____

Account number:_____

Date loan/account opened:_____

Total amount due:_____

Monthly payment amount:_____

To Whom It May Concern:

At the present, I cannot pay the monthly amount required under the agreement for the following reason(s):

_____

_____

_____

_____

_____

_____

For now, I cannot make any payments. I expect to resume making the full monthly payment when the following occurs:

_____

_____

_____

If necessary, add the unpaid amount to the end of the loan or account period and extend it by a few months. Thank you for your understanding and help. Please call or write within 20 days if this is unacceptable.

Sincerely,

_____
[your signature]

Name:_____

Address:_____

_____

Home phone:_____

_____

_____

_____

Attn: Customer Service

Date:_____

Name(s) on account:_____

Account number:_____

Date loan/account opened:_____

Total amount due:_____

Monthly payment amount:_____

To Whom It May Concern:

At the present, I cannot pay the monthly amount required under the agreement for the following reason(s):

_____

_____

_____

_____

_____

_____

_____

_____

Due to my desperate financial situation, I cannot make any payments for the indefinite future. [Describe hardship. _____]

I promise to inform you immediately if my financial condition improves and I am able to resume making normal payments.

Thank you for your understanding and help. Please call or write within 20 days if this is unacceptable.

Sincerely,

_____
[your signature]

Name:_____

Address:_____

_____

Home phone:_____

_____

_____

_____

Attn: Customer Service

Date:_____

Name(s) on account:_____

Account number:_____

Date loan/account opened:_____

Total amount due:_____

Monthly payment amount:_____

To Whom It May Concern:

At the present, I cannot pay the monthly amount required under the agreement for the following reason(s):

_____

_____

_____

_____

_____

_____

_____

_____

_____

_____

_____

I would like the terms of the loan rewritten in order to reduce the amount of the monthly payments.

Thank you for your understanding and help. Please call me as soon as possible in order that we may discuss new loan terms.

Sincerely,

_____
[your signature]

Name:_____

Address:_____

_____

Home phone:_____

NOLO www.nolo.com

_____

_____

_____

Attn: Customer Service

Date: _____

Name(s) on account: _____

Account number: _____

Date loan/account opened: _____

Total amount due: _____

Monthly payment amount: _____

Collateral: _____

To Whom It May Concern:

I cannot pay the monthly amount required under my agreement with you. I invite you to come pick up the collateral, or to let me know where I can return it to you, if you can assure me in writing that the entire debt will be canceled when the property is returned, and that I will not be liable for any deficiency judgment.

Thank you for your attention to this matter. Please send me a confirmation within 20 days if this is acceptable.

Sincerely,

_____
[your signature]

Name: _____

Address: _____

_____

Home phone: _____

_____

_____

_____

Attn: Customer Service

Date:_____

Name(s) on account:_____

Account number:_____

To Whom It May Concern:

Enclosed is a check for $_____ to cover the balance of the account. Cashing this check constitutes payment in full.

Sincerely,

_____
[your signature]

Name:_____

Address:_____

_____

Home phone:_____

_____

_____

_____

Attn: Customer Service

Date:_____

Name(s) on account:_____

Account number:_____

To Whom It May Concern:

Regarding the above-referenced account, I dispute the amount you claim that I owe you for the following reason(s):

_____

_____

_____

_____

_____

_____

_____

_____

_____

_____

I believe that I owe you no more than $_____. It is obvious that there is a good faith dispute over the amount of this bill.

To satisfy this debt, I will send you a check for $_____ with a restrictive endorsement; if you cash that check, it will constitute an accord and satisfaction. In other words, you will receive from me a check that states "cashing this check constitutes payment in full." If you cash that check, it will take care of what I owe you.

Sincerely,

_____
[your signature]

Name:_____

Address:_____

_____

Home phone:_____

_____

_____

_____

Attn: Customer Service

Date:_____

Name(s) on account:_____

Account number:_____

To Whom It May Concern:

Between 15 days and 90 days have passed since I sent you a letter dated _____,
20_____ stating my intention to send you a check with a restrictive endorsement.

Enclosed is a check for $_____ to cover the balance of my account. This check is tendered
in accordance with my earlier letter. If you cash this check, you agree that my debt is satisfied in full.

Sincerely,

_____
[your signature]

Name:_____

Address:_____

_____

Home phone:_____

Enclosed: Check stating on front: "This check is tendered in accordance with my letter of
_____, 20_____. Cashing this check constitutes payment in full."

_____

_____

_____

Attn: Collections Department

Date: _____

Name(s) on account: _____

Account number: _____

To Whom It May Concern:

This letter is to advise you that I am not able to make payments on my account due to the following conditions:

_____

_____

_____

_____

_____

_____

I cannot work sufficient hours to meet my current expenses. My only sources of income are:

_____

_____

I am familiar with the law and know that I am "judgment proof." If I file for bankruptcy, I will claim all my property as exempt, and if you sue me and obtain a judgment, you could not collect any of my property to satisfy the judgment.

Please cease all collection activities you have taken or are considering taking. While I will provide you with reasonable financial or medical information, I must avoid stress. This includes high-pressure collection activity and lawsuits.

If my current situation improves and I am able to resume payments, I will notify you at once.

Thank you for your understanding and help.

Sincerely,

_____
[your signature]

Name: _____

Address: _____

_____

Home phone: _____

_____

_____

_____

Attn: Collections Department

Date:_____

Name(s) on account:_____

Account number:_____

To Whom It May Concern:

Please cease all collection activities you have taken or are considering taking against me. I am planning to file a petition in bankruptcy court in the coming months.

Sincerely,

_____
[your signature]

Name:_____

Address:_____

_____

Home phone:_____

_____

_____

_____

Date:_____

Name(s) on account:_____

Account number:_____

Creditor:_____

To _____:

I have been contacted several times by you regarding my past due account with the credit grantor referenced above. I do not, however, wish to discuss this matter with you. I would like to talk directly with the creditor's collections department.

Please contact the collections department of the credit grantor and indicate my desire to be in touch with them.

Thank you for your help.

Sincerely,

_____
[your signature]

Name:_____

Address:_____

_____

Home phone:_____

cc: Credit grantor, _____

_____

_____

_____

Date:_____

To _____ :

I am writing to dispute the following bill you are attempting to collect.

Name(s) on account:_____

Account number:_____

Creditor:_____

Amount in dispute:_____

I am disputing this bill for the following reason(s):

_____

_____

_____

_____

_____

_____

_____

_____

_____

Please return this bill to the creditor immediately and remove any "sent to collection agency" notation that may be in my credit file.

Thank you for your attention to this matter.

Sincerely,

_____
[your signature]

Name:_____

Address:_____

_____

Home phone:_____

cc: Credit grantor, _____

_____

_____

_____

Date:_____

Name(s) on account:_____

Account number:_____

Creditor:_____

To_____:

Since approximately _____, 20_____, I have received several phone calls and letters from you concerning my overdue account with the above-named creditor.

Accordingly, under 15 U.S.C. § 1692c, this is my formal notice to you to cease all further communications with me.

Sincerely,

_____
[your signature]

Name:_____

Address:_____

_____

Home phone:_____

_____

_____

_____

Date:_____

Name(s) on account:_____

Account number:_____

Date loan/debt incurred:_____

Original loan/debt amount:_____

Amount past due:_____

Re: Collection agency:_____

To Whom It May Concern:

I have been unable to pay the full amount of the loan/debt noted above for the following reason(s):

_____

_____

_____

Although I have an outstanding debt, I have the right to be treated by a collection agency with dignity and respect. The collection agency you hired (and noted above), however, has engaged in the following practices which violate the federal Fair Debt Collection Practices Act:

_____

_____

_____

I am willing to forego the legal remedies I have available, including a lawsuit in small claims court seeking punitive damages against you and the agency, in exchange for your written promise to permanently cease all efforts to collect this debt and remove all negative entries regarding this debt from my credit file. I expect to hear from you immediately.

Sincerely,

_____
[your signature]

Name:_____

Address:_____

_____

Home phone:_____

cc: Federal Trade Commission
     State Collection Agency Licensing Board
     Collection Agency:_____

_____

_____

_____

Date:_____

To Whom It May Concern:

Please send me a copy of my credit report.

Full name:_____

Date of birth:_____

Social Security number:_____

Spouse's name:_____

Telephone number:_____

Current address:_____

_____

Previous address:_____

_____

(Check one:)

☐ I was denied credit on _____ by _____

_____. Enclosed is a copy of the rejection letter.

☐ I hereby certify that I am unemployed and intend to apply for a job within the next 60 days.

☐ I hereby certify that I receive public assistance/welfare.

☐ I hereby certify that I believe there is erroneous information in my file due to fraud.

☐ I am requesting my annual complimentary credit report. Enclosed is a copy of a document identifying me by my name and address.

☐ I have not been denied credit within the preceding 60 days. Enclosed is a copy of a document identifying me by my name and address and payment in the amount of $_____.

Thank you for your attention to this matter.

Sincerely,

_____

[your signature]

_____

_____

_____

Date:_____

This is a request for you to reinvestigate the following items which appear on my credit report:

☐ The following personal information about me is incorrect:

Erroneous Information   _Correct Information_

_____

_____

_____

☐ The following accounts are not mine:

Creditor's Name   _Account Number_   _Explanation_

_____

_____

☐ The account status is incorrect for the following accounts:

Creditor's Name   _Account Number_   _Correct Status_

_____

_____

_____

☐ The following information is too old to be included in my report:

Creditor's Name   _Account Number_   _Date of Last Activity_

_____

_____

_____

☐ The following inquiries are older than two years:

Creditor's Name   _Date of Inquiry_

_____

_____

_____

☐ The following inquiries were not authorized:

Creditor's Name   _Date of Inquiry_   _Explanation_

_____

_____

_____

☐ The following accounts were closed by me and should say so:

Creditor's Name   Account Number

_____

_____

_____

☐ Other incorrect information:

Explanation

_____

_____

_____

I understand that you will check each item, above, with the credit grantor reporting the information, and remove any information the credit grantor cannot verify. I further understand that under 15 U.S.C. §1681i(a), you must complete your reinvestigation within 30 days of receipt of this letter. Thank you for your attention to this matter.

Sincerely,

_____
                    [your signature]

Name:_____

Address:_____

_____

Home phone:_____

Social Security number:_____

_____

_____

_____

Date:_____

To Whom It May Concern:

On _____, 20_____, I sent you a request to reinvestigate several items which were on my credit report. I have enclosed a photocopy of my original request. The federal Fair Credit Reporting Act requires that you complete your reinvestigation of my request within 30 days. It has been more than 30 days.

I assume that I have not received a reply because you have been unable to verify the information. Therefore, please remove the incorrect items from my credit report at once and send me and anyone who has requested a copy of my credit report within the previous six months or within the previous two years if requested for employment purposes a corrected credit report.

Thank you for your immediate attention to this matter. I have sent a copy of this letter to the Federal Trade Commission.

Sincerely,

_____
[your signature]

Name:_____

Address:_____

_____

Home phone:_____

Social Security number:_____

cc: Federal Trade Commission

_____

_____

_____

Date:_____

To Whom It May Concern:

On _____ , 20_____ , I received a copy of my credit report from

_____

credit bureau. Included in that report was the following incorrect information reported by you:

_____

_____

_____

I requested that the credit bureau remove that information from my file. The bureau has refused, however, informing me that your company claims the information is accurate as reported.

This is not true. The following is the correct information:

_____

_____

_____

_____

_____

I have enclosed copies of the following documentation supporting my claim that the information you reported is incorrect:

_____

_____

This negative mark is damaging my credit. Please contact Experian, Trans Union and Equifax immediately and remove this information from my credit file. I expect to receive confirmation from you within 20 days that you have directed the credit bureaus to remove this information.

Thank you for your immediate attention to this matter.

Sincerely,

_____
[your signature]

Name:_____

Address:_____

_____

Home phone:_____

Social Security number:_____

_____

_____

_____

Attn: Customer Service

Date:_____

Name(s) on account:_____

Account number:_____

To Whom It May Concern:

On _____, 20_____, I received a copy of my credit report from you.
It included erroneous information reported by _____.
I just received a letter from that creditor indicating that in fact, the information in my credit report is not
accurate and should not be in my credit file. I have enclosed a copy of the letter.

OR

On _____, 20_____, I met with _____
_____ from the above-named creditor. This person agreed
with me that the information in my credit report is not accurate and should not be in my credit file. You can
reach this person at (_____) _____.

This negative mark is damaging my credit. Please remove the information at once and issue me and anyone who has requested a copy of my credit report within the previous six months or within the previous two
years if requested for employment purposes a new credit report.

Sincerely,

_____
[your signature]

Name:_____

Address:_____

_____

Home phone:_____

Social Security number:_____

_____

_____

_____

Date: _____

Re (name): _____

Current address: _____

_____

Telephone number: _____

Date of birth: _____

Social Security number: _____

Spouse's name: _____

To Whom It May Concern:

I received a copy of my credit report from your company on _____ and found accounts missing. Please add the following account histories to my credit file. I have enclosed photocopies of my most recent account statement and photocopies of canceled checks showing my payment history.

Creditor's Name	Creditor's Billing Address	Account Number	Date Opened	Credit Limit or Amount of Loan	Outstanding Balance

Once you have processed this request, please send me an updated credit report. If there is a fee of any kind, please let me know the amount so that I can send you a check. If you are unable to add these accounts to my credit report, please send me an explanation.

Thank you for your prompt attention to this matter.

Sincerely,

_____

[your signature]

_____

_____

_____

Date: _____

Re (name): _____

Current address: _____

_____

Telephone number: _____

Date of birth: _____

Social Security number: _____

Spouse's name: _____

To Whom It May Concern:

I received a copy of my credit report from your company on _____ and found that important information was missing. Please add the following information to my credit file. I have enclosed photocopies of verifying documentation.

_____

_____

_____

_____

_____

_____

_____

_____

_____

Once you have processed this request, please send me an updated credit report. If there is a fee of any kind, please let me know the amount so that I can send you a check. If you are unable to add this information to my credit report, please send me an explanation.

Thank you for your prompt attention to this matter.

Sincerely,

_____

[your signature]

How to Use the Forms CD-ROM

The tear-out forms in Appendix 3 are included on a CD-ROM disk in the back of the book. This CD-ROM, which can be used with Windows computers, installs files that can be opened, printed and edited using a word processor or other software. It is NOT a stand-alone software program. Please read this Appendix and the README.TXT file included on the CD-ROM for instructions on using the forms CD.

Note to Mac users: This CD-ROM and its files should also work on a Macintosh and other operating systems. Please note, however, that Nolo cannot provide technical support for non-Windows users.

How to View the README File

If you do not know how to view the file README.TXT, insert the forms disk into your computer's CD-ROM drive and follow these instructions:

- Windows 9x, 200 and Me: (1) On your PC's desktop, double-click the My Computer icon; (2) double-click the icon for the CD-ROM drive into which the forms disk was inserted; (3) double-click the file README.TXT.
- Macintosh: (1) On your Mac desktop, double-click the icon for the CD-ROM that you inserted; (2) double-click on the file README.TXT.

While the README file is open, print it out by using the Print command in the File menu.

A. Installing the Form Files Onto Your Computer

Word processing forms that you can open, complete, print and save with your word processing program (see Section B, below) are contained on the CD-ROM. Before you can do anything with the files on the CD-ROM, you need to install them onto your hard disk. In accordance with U.S. copyright laws, remember that copies of the disk and its files are for your personal use only.

Insert the forms CD and do the following:

1. Windows 9x, 2000 and Me Users

Follow the instructions that appear on the screen. (If nothing happens when you insert the forms CD-ROM, then (1) double-click the My Computer icon; (2) double-click the icon for the CD-ROM drive into which the forms disk was inserted; and (3) double click the file WELCOME.EXE.)

By default, all the files are installed to the \Credit Repair Forms folder in the \Program Files folder of your computer. A folder called "Credit Repair Forms" is added to the "Programs" folder of the Start menu.

2. Macintosh Users

Step 1: If the "Credit Repair CD" window is not open, open it by double-clicking the "Credit Repair CD" icon.

Step 2: Select the "Credit Repair Forms" folder icon.

Step 3: Drag and drop the folder icon onto the icon of your hard disk.

B. Using the Word Processing Files to Create Documents

This section concerns the files for forms that can be opened and edited with your word processing program. All forms and their filenames are listed at the beginning of Appendix 3.

All word processing forms come in rich text format (these files have the extension .RTF).

For example, the form for the Form F-1: Outstanding Debts discussed in Chapter 1 is on the file F01.RTF. All forms, their file names and file formats are listed in Appendix 3.

RTF files can be read by most recent word processing programs including all versions of MS Word for Windows and Macintosh, WordPad for Windows, and recent versions of WordPerfect for Windows and Macintosh.

To use a form from the CD to create your documents you must: (1) open a file in your word processor or text editor; (2) edit the form by filling in the required information; (3) print it out; (4) rename and save your revised file.

The following are general instructions on how to do this. However, each word processor uses different commands to open, format, save and print documents. Please read your word processor's manual for specific instructions on performing these tasks.

Do not call Nolo's technical support if you have questions on how to use yoru word processor.

Step 1: Opening a File

There are three ways to open the word processing files included on the CD-ROM after you have installed them onto your computer.

- Windows users can open a file by selecting its "shortcut" as follows: (1) Click the Windows "Start" button; (2) open the "Programs" folder; (3) open the "Credit Repair Forms" subfolder; and (4) click on the shortcut to the form you want to work with.
- Both Windows and Macintosh users can open a file directly by double-clicking on it. Use My Computer or Windows Explorer (Windows 9x, 2000 and Me) or the Finder (Macintosh) to go to the folder you installed or copied the disk's files to. Then, double-click on the specific file you want to open.

Where Are the Files Installed?

Windows Users
- RTF files are installed by default to a folder named \Credit Repair Forms in the \Program Files folder of your computer.

Macintosh Users
- RTF files are located in the the "Credit Repair Forms" folder.

You can also open a file from within your word processor. To do this, you must first start your word processor. Then, go to the File menu and choose the Open command. This opens a dialog box where you will tell the program (1) the type of file you want to open (*.RTF); and (2) the location and name of the file (you will need to navigate through the directory tree to get to the folder on your hard disk where the CD's files have been installed). If these directions are unclear you will need to look through the manual for your word processing program—Nolo's technical support department will NOT be able to help you with the use of your word processing program.

Step 2: Editing Your Document

Fill in the appropriate information according to the instructions and sample agreements in the book. Underlines are used to indicate where you need to enter your information, frequently followed by instructions in brackets. *Be sure to delete the underlines and instructions from your edited document.* If you do not know how to use your word processor to edit a document, you will need to look through the manual for your word processing program— Nolo's technical support department will NOT be able to help you with the use of your word processing program.

Editing Forms That Have Optional or Alternative Text

Some of the forms have check boxes before text. The check boxes indicate:

- Optional text, which you choose whether to include or exclude
- Alternative text, where you select one alternative to include and exclude the other alternatives.

If you are using the tear-out forms in Appendix 3, you simply mark the appropriate box to make your choice.

If you are using the forms CD, however, we recommend that instead of marking the check boxes, you do the following:

Optional text

If you don't want to include optional text, just delete it from your document.

If you **do want** to include optional text, just leave it in your document.

In either case, delete the check box itself as well as the italicized instructions that the text is optional.

Alternative text

First delete all the alternatives that you do not want to include.

Then delete the remaining check boxes, as well as the italicized instructions that you need to select one of the alternatives provided.

Step 3: Printing Out the Document

Use your word processor's or text editor's "Print" command to print out your document. If you do not know how to use your word processor to print a document, you will need to look through the manual for your word processing program—Nolo's technical support department will *not* be able to help you with the use of your word processing program.

Step 4: Saving Your Document

After filling in the form, use the "Save As" command to save and rename the file. Because all the files are "read-only," you will not be able to use the "Save" command. This is for your protection. *If you save the file without renaming it, the underlines that indicate where you need to enter your information will be lost and you will not be able to create a new document with this file without recopying the original file from the CD-ROM.*

If you do not know how to use your word processor to save a document, you will need to look through the manual for your word processing program—Nolo's technical support department will *not* be able to help you with the use of your word processing program. ■

Index

CATALOG

...more from Nolo

	PRICE	CODE

BUSINESS

	PRICE	CODE
The CA Nonprofit Corporation Kit (Binder w/CD-ROM)	$59.95	CNP
Consultant & Independent Contractor Agreements (Book w/CD-ROM)	$29.95	CICA
The Corporate Minutes Book (Book w/CD-ROM)	$69.99	CORMI
The Employer's Legal Handbook	$39.99	EMPL
Everyday Employment Law	$29.99	ELBA
Drive a Modest Car & 16 Other Keys to Small Business Success	$24.99	DRIV
Form Your Own Limited Liability Company (Book w/CD-ROM)	$44.99	LIAB
Hiring Independent Contractors: The Employer's Legal Guide (Book w/CD-ROM)	$34.99	HICI
How to Create a Buy-Sell Agreement & Control the Destiny of your Small Business (Book w/Disk-PC)	$49.95	BSAG
How to Create a Noncompete Agreement	$44.95	NOCMP
How to Form a California Professional Corporation (Book w/CD-ROM)	$59.95	PROF
How to Form a Nonprofit Corporation (Book w/CD-ROM)—National Edition	$44.99	NNP
How to Form a Nonprofit Corporation in California (Book w/CD-ROM)	$44.99	NON
How to Form Your Own California Corporation (Binder w/CD-ROM)	$59.99	CACI
How to Form Your Own California Corporation (Book w/CD-ROM)	$34.99	CCOR
How to Get Your Business on the Web	$29.99	WEBS
How to Write a Business Plan	$34.99	SBS
The Independent Paralegal's Handbook	$29.95	PARA
Leasing Space for Your Small Business	$34.95	LESP
Legal Guide for Starting & Running a Small Business	$34.99	RUNS
Legal Forms for Starting & Running a Small Business (Book w/CD-ROM)	$29.95	RUNS2
Marketing Without Advertising	$24.00	MWAD
Music Law (Book w/CD-ROM)	$34.99	ML

Prices subject to change.

	PRICE	CODE
Nolo's Guide to Social Security Disability	$29.99	QSS
Nolo's Quick LLC	$24.99	LLCQ
Nondisclosure Agreements	$39.95	NAG
The Small Business Start-up Kit (Book w/CD-ROM)	$29.99	SMBU
The Small Business Start-up Kit for California (Book w/CD-ROM)	$34.99	OPEN
The Partnership Book: How to Write a Partnership Agreement (Book w/CD-ROM)	$39.99	PART
Sexual Harassment on the Job	$24.95	HARS
Starting & Running a Successful Newsletter or Magazine	$29.99	MAG
Tax Savvy for Small Business	$34.99	SAVVY
Working for Yourself: Law & Taxes for the Self-Employed	$39.99	WAGE
Your Crafts Business: A Legal Guide	$26.99	VART
Your Limited Liability Company: An Operating Manual (Book w/CD-ROM)	$49.99	LOP
Your Rights in the Workplace	$29.99	YRW

CONSUMER

	PRICE	CODE
How to Win Your Personal Injury Claim	$29.99	PICL
Nolo's Encyclopedia of Everyday Law	$29.99	EVL
Nolo's Guide to California Law	$24.95	CLAW
Trouble-Free Travel...And What to Do When Things Go Wrong	$14.95	TRAV

ESTATE PLANNING & PROBATE

	PRICE	CODE
8 Ways to Avoid Probate	$19.95	PRO8
9 Ways to Avoid Estate Taxes	$29.95	ESTX
Estate Planning Basics	$21.99	ESPN
How to Probate an Estate in California	$49.99	PAE
Make Your Own Living Trust (Book w/CD-ROM)	$39.99	LITR
Nolo's Law Form Kit: Wills	$24.95	KWL
Nolo's Simple Will Book (Book w/CD-ROM)	$34.99	SWIL

	PRICE	CODE

Plan Your Estate .... $44.99   NEST

Quick & Legal Will Book .... $15.99   QUIC

FAMILY MATTERS

Child Custody: Building Parenting Agreements That Work .... $29.95   CUST

The Complete IEP Guide .... $24.99   IEP

Divorce & Money: How to Make the Best Financial Decisions During Divorce .... $34.99   DIMO

Get a Life: You Don't Need a Million to Retire Well .... $24.99   LIFE

The Guardianship Book for California .... $39.99   GB

How to Adopt Your Stepchild in California (Book w/CD-ROM) .... $34.95   ADOP

A Legal Guide for Lesbian and Gay Couples .... $29.99   LG

Living Together: A Legal Guide (Book w/CD-ROM) .... $34.99   LTK

Using Divorce Mediation: Save Your Money & Your Sanity .... $29.95   UDMD

GOING TO COURT

Beat Your Ticket: Go To Court and Win! (National Edition) .... $19.99   BEYT

The Criminal Law Handbook: Know Your Rights, Survive the System .... $34.99   KYR

Everybody's Guide to Small Claims Court (National Edition) .... $26.99   NSCC

Everybody's Guide to Small Claims Court in California .... $26.99   CSCC

Fight Your Ticket ... and Win! (California Edition) .... $29.99   FYT

How to Change Your Name in California .... $34.95   NAME

How to Collect When You Win a Lawsuit (California Edition) .... $29.99   JUDG

How to Mediate Your Dispute .... $18.95   MEDI

How to Seal Your Juvenile & Criminal Records (California Edition) .... $34.95   CRIM

The Lawsuit Survival Guide .... $29.99   UNCL

Nolo's Deposition Handbook .... $29.99   DEP

Represent Yourself in Court: How to Prepare & Try a Winning Case .... $34.99   RYC

	PRICE	CODE
Bankruptcy: Is It the Right Solution to Your Debt Problems?	$19.99	BRS
Chapter 13 Bankruptcy: Repay Your Debts	$34.99	CH13
Creating Your Own Retirement Plan	$29.99	YROP
Credit Repair (Book w/CD-ROM)	$24.99	CREP
How to File for Chapter 7 Bankruptcy	$34.99	HFB
IRAs, 401(k)s & Other Retirement Plans: Taking Your Money Out	$34.99	RET
Money Troubles: Legal Strategies to Cope With Your Debts	$29.99	MT
Nolo's Law Form Kit: Personal Bankruptcy	$24.99	KBNK
Stand Up to the IRS	$24.99	SIRS
Surviving an IRS Tax Audit	$24.95	SAUD
Take Control of Your Student Loan Debt	$26.95	SLOAN

PATENTS AND COPYRIGHTS

	PRICE	CODE
The Copyright Handbook: How to Protect and Use Written Works (Book w/CD-ROM)	$39.99	COHA
Copyright Your Software	$34.95	CYS
Domain Names	$26.95	DOM
Getting Permission: How to License and Clear Copyrighted Materials Online and Off (Book w/CD-ROM)	$34.99	RIPER
How to Make Patent Drawings Yourself	$29.99	DRAW
The Inventor's Notebook	$24.99	INOT
Nolo's Patents for Beginners	$29.99	QPAT
License Your Invention (Book w/CD-ROM)	$39.99	LICE
Patent, Copyright & Trademark	$39.99	PCTM
Patent It Yourself	$49.99	PAT
Patent Searching Made Easy	$29.95	PATSE
The Public Domain	$34.95	PUBL
Web and Software Development: A Legal Guide (Book w/ CD-ROM)	$44.95	SFT
Trademark: Legal Care for Your Business and Product Name	$39.95	TRD

RESEARCH & REFERENCE

Legal Research: How to Find & Understand the Law .... $34.99   LRES

SENIORS

Choose the Right Long-Term Care: Home Care, Assisted Living & Nursing Homes .... $21.99   ELD

The Conservatorship Book for California .... $44.99   CNSV

Social Security, Medicare & Goverment Pensions .... $29.99   SOA

SOFTWARE

**Call or check our website at www.nolo.com
for special discounts on Software!**

LeaseWriter CD—Windows $129.95   LWD1

LLC Maker—Windows $89.95   LLP1

PatentPro Plus—Windows .... $399.99   PAPL

Personal RecordKeeper 5.0 CD—Windows $59.95   RKD5

Quicken Legal Business Pro 2004—Windows $79.95   SBQB4

Quicken WillMaker Plus 2004—Windows $79.95   WQP4

Special
Upgrade Offer

Save 35% on the latest edition of your Nolo book

Because laws and legal procedures change often, we update our books regularly. To help keep you up-to-date, we are extending this special upgrade offer. Cut out and mail the title portion of the cover of your old Nolo book and we'll give you **35% off** the retail price of the NEW EDITION of that book when you purchase directly from Nolo. This offer is to individuals only.

Call us today at 1-800-728-3555

Prices and offer subject to change without notice.

Order Form

Name

Address

City

State, Zip

Daytime Phone

E-mail

Item Code	Quantity	Item	Unit Price	Total Price

Method of payment

☐ Check   ☐ VISA   ☐ MasterCard

☐ Discover Card   ☐ American Express

Subtotal	
Add your local sales tax (California only)	
Shipping: RUSH $9, Basic $5 (See below)	
"I bought 3, ship it to me FREE!"(Ground shipping only)	
TOTAL	

Account Number

Expiration Date

Signature

Shipping and Handling

Rush Delivery—Only $9

We'll ship any order to any street address in the U.S. by UPS 2nd Day Air* for only $9!

* Order by noon Pacific Time and get your order in 2 business days. Orders placed after noon Pacific Time will arrive in 3 business days. P.O. boxes and S.F. Bay Area use basic shipping. Alaska and Hawaii use 2nd Day Air or Priority Mail.

Basic Shipping—$5

Use for P.O. Boxes, Northern California and Ground Service.

Allow 1-2 weeks for delivery. U.S. addresses only.

For faster service, use your credit card and our toll-free numbers

**Call our customer service group
Monday thru Friday 7am to 7pm PST**

Phone	1-800-728-3555
Fax	1-800-645-0895
Mail	**Nolo**
950 Parker St.
Berkeley, CA 94710

**Order 24 hours a day @
www.nolo.com**